CW00594949

THE RABBIT

GUIDE TO
BIRMINGHAM

The Rabbit Guide to Birmingham

www.rabbitguide.com

MANAGING EDITOR	David Clarke
CONCEPT EDITOR	Charles Smith
PRINCIPAL RESEARCHER	Yvonne Rush
CONTRIBUTORS	Charles Smith, Yvonne Rush
ADDITIONAL RESEARCH	Diane Broadfoot, Julie Burke, Ingrid Cattell, Caroline Clarke, Sue O'Callaghan
INDEXING	Michael Brinkman
ORIGINAL DESIGN	Arian Hashemi
PRINCIPAL DESIGNER	John Mackay
COVER DESIGN	Steve Bowgen
PUBLICITY DESIGN	Anthony O'Flaherty
SETTING	Jill Ince, Alison Shingler, Karen Stanley

MAPS
Marketing Birmingham and Ordnance Survey

PHOTOGRAPHY
John Mackay, Nick Rush, Tom Rush, Yvonne Rush, Charles Smith

CONTRIBUTED PHOTOGRAPHY
Many organisations and individuals have kindly supplied photographs and images. Other photographs have been obtained from the web sites of attractions and venues. In all instances, we acknowledge that the copyright in those images remains with the photographer and/or the organisation. Contributed photographs have been supplied by Arthur Smith/Rachel Bannister of Birmingham Walks, Asian Balti Restaurants Association, Aston Villa FC, Birmingham City Council, Birmingham Hippodrome, Brindleyplace, Botanical Gardens, Marketing Birmingham, Martin Brent Photography, National Trust, The National Forest Company/Lesley Hextall, David Wilkins ABIPP of First House Photography.

SPECIAL THANKS GO TO
Nicky Clarke and Andy Smith for being supportive of a whim as it was translated into reality and Angie Took who first said to Charles Smith: "What a great idea!"

Printed by Orphans Press
Leominster HR6 8JT

First published in Great Britain in 2004 by Polperro Heritage Press, Clifton-upon-Teme, Worcestershire WR6 6EN E-mail: polperro.press@virgin.net

©Rabbit Guides Ltd 2004

ISBN 0-9544233-3-X

HOW TO USE THIS GUIDE

The introductory section, **Welcome to Birmingham**, provides an overview of Birmingham's place in the world and its place in history.

Five quarters make a whole lot of city provides an overview of the city centre which is then divided into detailed descriptions of the five individual quarters. Each is colour coded corresponding with the main city centre map on the inside front cover. Enlarged quarter maps appear at the start of each quarter. Principal attractions/sites are numbered on the map and in the corresponding text.

Birmingham Beyond the centre is divided into four areas providing details of attractions and sites in each of those areas within the city boundaries.

Further Afield describes the principal attractions, sites and towns within the area covered by the regional map on pages 62/63.

The **If you like... section** is designed for those with special interests whilst the **Features** section provides additional background to some of the main attributes of Birmingham.

The **Gazetteer** provides all the essential information you need to know when visiting Birmingham.

Finally, **The Rabbit Guide to Birmingham** is editorially independent. We do not take advertising. All entries are unpaid and appear on their own merit.

Admission Prices:

Prices are based on the cost per adult and are categorised to provide an approximate comparison. Admission prices can be affected by the season, concessions and promotions. Family and group tickets offer savings which can sometimes be considerable. Always ask.

A	=	up to £3
B	=	£3 up to £6
C	=	£6 up to £10
D	=	£10 up to £20
E	=	£20 +

Accomodation prices:

Accommodation costs vary considerably according to the time of year and whether major conventions or exhibitions are being held. Many business hotels offer significant savings at weekends and in holiday periods – to the point where four star luxury can be enjoyed for similar prices to economy hotels. All prices are for a double room.

£	Less than £40
££	£40 - £60
£££	£61 - £85
££££	£86 + (rooms in 4 & 5* hotels are frequently £100 +)

Eating out prices:

Prices are based on the cost of an average two course meal per person without drinks to provide an approximate comparison.

£	Under £10 per head
££	Under £25 per head
£££	Over £25 per head

Compliments, comments and complaints

We would like to hear your views about how we can improve **The Rabbit Guide to Birmingham**. We would also be pleased to receive suggestions or corrections for inclusion in the next issue. Where corrections are verified, they will be included on our website under the appropriate page number.

Please send to:
The Rabbit Guide to Birmingham,
Polperro Heritage Press,
Clifton-upon-Teme,
Worcestershire WR6 6EN.
e-mail: birmingham@rabbitguide.com

CONTENTS

CONTENTS cont...

The Rotunda: loved or hated this building of the 1960s is still a frequent image of Birmingham.

Welcome to Birmingham

It might be called The Birmingham Challenge: travel to any part of the world and identify a product that proclaims the words "Made in Birmingham".

It is not too difficult!

In Hong Kong, those words can be found on its trams. In Australia, Sydney Harbour Bridge would not stand without Birmingham's engineering components. The city's tools, shovels and spades shaped the Indian sub-continent. And in the depths of the Atlantic are the remains of the Birmingham-made tunic buttons of the crew of SS *Titanic*.

It is not for nothing that Birmingham was once described as the "workshop of the world", "the city of a thousand trades" or "the toyshop of the world", for its products have been exported to just about every country in the globe.

Today, the city is less dependent on manufacturing but its output can still be found the world over. On California's highways you'll find the Jaguar S-Type - made in Birmingham, at Castle Bromwich where once Spitfires were made. On the streets of Tokyo, you'll find MG sports cars – made in Birmingham, at Longbridge. At the 2002 Football World Cup in Korea and Japan, it was Birmingham-made whistles that were used by the referees. And in distant countries, the first vehicle ever to be seen in remote parts is likely to be a Land Rover (manufactured just over Birmingham's border in neighbouring Solihull).

It is however, a source of some discontent to those commuting in the city that they do not have an underground railway system but are responsible for manufacturing the rolling stock used by London Underground.

Benetton at Bullring

It is a source of some frustration but even perverse pride that the city seems to miss out on every prize going: it failed in its bid to become European Capital of Culture 2008 (in spite of the city investing more in culture than all the other UK contenders combined); it was not successful in its endeavours to host the UK festival to celebrate the Millennium (in spite of it having developed Europe's busiest exhibition centre); and its bid to be the home of the national football stadium was foiled (despite it boasting a less costly scheme than rival London).

In spite of these disappointments – or maybe because of these disappointments – Birmingham is a city that instead gets on and does its own thing. It is, after all, the second largest city by population and employment in the world's fourth largest economy (and don't you forget it). It is home to no less than three universities including world-class institutions; to two football teams (Birmingham City and Aston Villa; three if you include West Bromwich Albion, a part of whose grounds fall within the Birmingham boundary). It has also witnessed the completion of Europe's largest city centre regeneration development with the infamous Bull Ring Shopping Centre being demolished, re-designed, re-built and re-branded Bullring so as to distinguish its 21st century glitz and glamour from its concrete 1960's predecessor.

It is a city of innovation (no less than 50% of all UK patents come from Birmingham) and a city whose wealth creation abilities has helped it attract nearly £10 billion worth of current and planned investment. It is the nation's melting pot which has reinvented itself as a meeting spot (home to some one million people of which 30% are of non-white ethnic origin and which attracts some 24 million visitors each year for conferences, exhibitions, conventions, shows, meetings and as tourists). It is a city where the service sector, including financial, professional and business support services, has taken over as the largest private sector employer.

It is also a city of contrasts. Within a mile or so of the glamour and "wear your wealth on your sleeve" of Broad Street in the city centre you will find one of Europe's most deprived municipal wards.

It is these facets that make Birmingham such an invigorating place to visit or spend a few hours. Yes, there are plenty of tourist attractions for young and old alike but there is also the gritty realism of a city where, as recently as the early 1970s, the majority of its workers were employed in manufacturing and where a good many of them had oil beneath their finger nails.

Not that you would think so now: Birmingham people (or Brummies as some prefer) seem almost startled at the way their city has changed: the elegant, peaceful and restored St Philip's Place; the car-free shopping streets; the refreshing light spray on a warm day as they walk through the fountains in Brindleyplace; the casual alfresco eating on the canal side; the formal grandeur of the Council House; the bustling streets of Europe's largest jewellery manufacturing area – or skipping the puddles on a wet winter's day darting from the warmth of one Irish pub to another.

If Brummies have a frustration, it's that too few people appreciate the city for what it is today. But take a look at Victoria Square on a summer's day, as office workers and shoppers dangle their feet in Europe's largest fountain, and you'll wonder what they have to be frustrated about.

Birmingham's place in the world

Birmingham is just about as far from the sea as it is possible to get in Britain. As the crow - or seagull - flies its nearest coastline is nearly 90 miles away. At the middle of the country (the actual centre of England is claimed to be Meriden, just 12 miles from the city centre), it owes much to its location at the heart of the country.

Most would regard Birmingham as a modern city and in truth it was not until the Industrial Revolution of the 18th century that its population expanded significantly.

Back in the 11th century, the hamlet that was to become Birmingham – its name derives from the Anglo Saxon settlement of Beorma's people - was recorded in the Domesday Book as having just nine peasant households and being worth a meagre 20 shillings. Eighty years later in 1166, Peter de Bermingham, head of the local manor, was granted a market charter from Henry II and a hundred years later still, Sir William de Bermingham, was granted permission to hold a four day fair over Whitsun.

The village – it could hardly be described as a town – developed as a market centre and by 1327, records showed craftsmen listed amongst its

England's centre: Meriden

taxpayers. By that time, it had a parish church and representatives at Parliament.

Nonetheless, there was still nothing at this stage to encourage anyone to think that the place would grow to become Britain's largest city outside London. It was, after all, smaller than neighbouring Coventry and Warwick and a cursory glance at the maps of the time show it is no more prominent than any other settlement.

However, the foundations for Birmingham's future prosperity and its place on the world-stage were being put in place. It initially met the needs of the agricultural communities of Warwickshire and Worcestershire and, as its reputation grew, so it became a town populated by blacksmiths (there were 69 forges by 1671), tanners and even those making jewellery and ornaments - the foundations of the city's Jewellery Quarter.

Descriptions from the 16th century reveal it to be a town "swarming with inhabitants, and echoing with the noise of anvils" manufacturing cutlery, scythes, swords and pikes – demand for the latter being fuelled by the Civil War (1642 –1646) when the city was responsible for many of the weapons made for the Roundheads and giving rise to its 'metal-bashing' reputation with which it has been associated ever since.

Big Brum: Victoria Square

Local historian Dr Carl Chinn – whose passion for Birmingham he is happy to share with anyone – says there is no logical reason as to why Birmingham rose to greatness and prominence. Clearly, it is not a major port; it does not have a significant river (visitors are hard-pressed to spot the diminutive and almost embarrassing rivers Rea and Cole) and neither does it sit at, say, the entrance to a mountain pass, mountains being hard to find in this area of England. Its reasons for being are less obvious but important nonetheless. It is south of the great coalfields of Staffordshire; a near neighbour of the Black Country to the north-west of the city with its abundance of raw materials and it had a supply of water – from that diminutive River Rea - and springs. Above all though, it emerged as a focal point for neighbouring towns and villages and its growing market status attracted people, locally and from further afield.

Its population expanded significantly from some 5,500 in 1666 to 23,000 in 1733. Most of this growth was due to immigration from the immediate surrounding areas with 90% from within 20 miles of Birmingham particularly the three counties of Warwickshire, Staffordshire and Worcestershire. This was the start of Birmingham's role as a melting pot – and a manufacturing centre.

New Street, Peace Day 1902

The Industrial Revolution, and Birmingham's contribution to that revolution, is fundamental to its growth. The town became the centre of Britain's canal network (and later, railway system and much later still, roads). It became home to the greatest thinkers of the modern world: James Watt, developer of the steam engine; Joseph Priestley who discovered oxygen; John Baskerville, founder of the world famous typeface and William Murdoch, inventor of gas lighting.

But it was not until 1889 that Birmingham became a city coinciding with visionary mayors such as Joseph Chamberlain (forefather of British Prime Minister Neville Chamberlain) and the construction of water works, a sewerage system, schools and libraries together with a new council house and law courts.

In 1888, to quote *'An Alphabetically Arranged Guide to the Industrial Resources of the Midland Metropolis'*, "upwards of 20,000,000 pens are sent out every week to the markets of the globe. Guns are made to the extent of 8,000, buttons 150,000,000, saddles nearly 1,500, copper or bronze coins 6,000,000, bedsteads 9,000, cut nails

500,000,000, spectacles 25,000 pairs, eight tons of papier mâché goods, gold and silver jewellery of every description about £20,000 worth..." The list goes on but you will get the drift. Birmingham was a productive place. Wandering around the streets of Birmingham still reveals some of the fine buildings that were erected at the time: the Council House (1834), The Birmingham Mint (1861) and The Midland Bank in Bennett's Hill (1830). Sadly, many more failed to survive the intensive bombing of World War Two and the equally damaging vision of 1950's and early 1960's planners who replaced many of Birmingham's buildings and bomb sites with a concrete-clad brave new world. In consequence, many

The Birmingham Mint

of the city's remaining older buildings are now, thankfully, under preservation orders whilst many of the well intentioned mistakes of the 1960s have been replaced by what, it is to be hoped, are longer-lasting city features. This rebuilding continues. The ringing of those 16th century anvils has been replaced by the power tools of construction.

Birmingham's place in history

Occupying pride of place in Centenary Square – built to commemorate the centenary of Birmingham being granted city status in 1889 – is a statue of three men, in long dress coats and poring over a series of plans. Their names are Matthew Boulton, James Watt and William Murdoch, all of whom played significant roles in the city's establishment as the "workshop of the world". They symbolise Birmingham's rise to prominence and dominance over its neighbours.

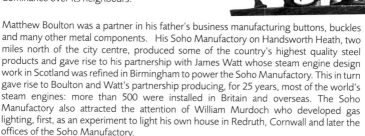

Matthew Boulton was a partner in his father's business manufacturing buttons, buckles and many other metal components. His Soho Manufactory on Handsworth Heath, two miles north of the city centre, produced some of the country's highest quality steel products and gave rise to his partnership with James Watt whose steam engine design work in Scotland was refined in Birmingham to power the Soho Manufactory. This in turn gave rise to Boulton and Watt's partnership producing, for 25 years, most of the world's steam engines: more than 500 were installed in Britain and overseas. The Soho Manufactory also attracted the attention of William Murdoch who developed gas lighting, first, as an experiment to light his own house in Redruth, Cornwall and later the offices of the Soho Manufactory.

These men's extraordinary vision and ability, using Birmingham as a focal point for their collaboration, are just three in a long list of individuals who put Birmingham on the world map and resulted in Birmingham exporting its products throughout the world.

There was Joseph Priestley, the discoverer of oxygen and minister of the New Meeting House in 1780, a Presbyterian place of worship known for liberal and radical thinking.

Then there was Dr William Withering, who discovered how digitalis could be used in the treatment of heart disease. Extracted from the foxglove, it remains in use today as a component of the drug digoxin. Then there was John Baskerville, originally an inscriber of gravestones before establishing himself as a japanner – manufacturing goods protected by a black and very glossy hard varnish. It was he who advanced printing – and hence helped the transfer of knowledge – as well as developing a new type font, Baskerville, which has become a classic (but which found no English buyer; it was bought four years after his death in 1775 by a Parisian literary society and was used initially to print an edition of the works of Voltaire).

It was one of Baskerville's former apprentices, Henry Clay, who patented the making of papier-mâché. The technique, now used by children the world over in their arts and crafts classes, involves pasting numerous layers of paper which are then moulded, dried and finished. The board could be cut, planed or turned, and was used to manufacture all manner of goods ranging from tea trays to tables and even door panels for coaches. Finished in oil and varnish – japanned - they were the equivalent of today's moulded plastics and compressed boards.

Industrialist John Taylor created a process for plating goods with thin layers of gold leaf and the gilding of metal buttons (Birmingham was the undisputed button capital of the world; you'd be hard pressed to fasten any item of clothing without a product of the city).

And so the list goes on with one of the common denominators in this hothouse of invention and creation being the Birmingham Lunar Society. Their meetings, held each month at full moon (it is said to enable its members to return home safely by the light of the moon, although for a group of inventors this story seems somewhat

When the borough of Birmingham was incorporated in 1888, it adopted the armorial bearings of the de Bermingham family as its seal. When in 1889 it was granted city status it gained the right to add figures to the shield. The female figure represents art; the male figure representing industry.

incredible) brought inventors and philosophers alike together to share views and exchange ideas. (The Lunar Society room in Soho House, which includes the original table around which these great minds sat, remains.)

Right Hon. Joseph Chamberlain

However, it was not only inventors and philosophers that gathered in Birmingham - but also politicians.

Joseph Chamberlain, a Londoner by birth, arrived in 1854 from London to help in the screw making factory of his uncle, J S Nettlefold, but went on to become town councillor, mayor of Birmingham and later still, Member of Parliament (his son Neville followed in his footsteps becoming Prime Minister in 1937 prior to the Second World War). It is Joseph Chamberlain who can rightly be credited with improving the lot of those living in the city.

In those days, one in five children died before being old enough to walk and it was he that spearheaded the town's municipal development: a medical officer was appointed, the Drainage Board established to safely dispose of sewerage and refuse, slums were demolished and the grand vision for the present day city centre was established. Parks provided breathing space, schools and educational institutions were built.

It had taken Birmingham some 700 years for it to develop significantly from a small muddy settlement to a heaving and vibrant town but its contribution in the next 200 years to the world was enormous.

Arguably, its production skills made Birmingham the world's manufacturing capital of the 19th century.

Reflections: 9 Colmore Row

Five Quarters make a whole lot of City

Birmingham's very own chocolate manufacturer, Cadbury's, used to boast in its advertising that it squeezed a glass and a half of milk into each bar of Cadbury's dairy milk chocolate.

This concept of squeezing in more content than seems physically possible, is also true of Birmingham city centre which is divided into not four quarters to a make a whole but five.

Leaving aside the fact that the idea of dividing the city centre into five quarters was not undertaken by any great mathematician or that the concept is relatively new (few local people can name or identify the five quarters), and that the names of each quarter do not have universal acceptance, it is, nonetheless, a useful device for visitors to Birmingham.

Confused? You need not be.

Thomas Attwood MP reclining, Chamberlain Square

The **Central Quarter** is the very heart of the city: including the civic centres, principal museums (but you may wish to travel further afield to see some of Birmingham's other great treasures), the business district and most – but certainly not all – of its shops and stores. It also boasts some fine buildings, some less fine buildings, plenty of bars, cafes and eating places plus the city's principal train stations: New Street and Snow Hill.

Eastside is Birmingham's newest baby. From the Central Quarter, it is best approached through the city's new, bold and bright Bullring (Shopping Centre) which lies on the cusp of the two quarters. Eastside has been designated Birmingham's new learning district. It already houses Millennium Point, with its bang up-to-date museum, 3D Theatre and a host of other attractions, and also includes Aston University and a few notable buildings such as the recently restored Moor Street Station and Curzon Street Station which, just to confuse, is no longer a station at all.

Walking around Eastside is not as pleasant as some of the other quarters - road works, construction work and the general melee of an area that is shortly to be transformed, are not easy bedfellows with pedestrians but stand in the centre, perhaps near Millennium Point looking towards the Central Quarter, and just imagine that in ten years time or so, you will be surrounded by parkland which incorporates what every Birmingham citizen hopes will be some stunning new buildings. OK, you do need a lot of imagination at the moment but there again, this city was founded on imagination and if the enthusiasm of the city fathers is anything to go by, that vision will become a reality.

There are 29 other Birminghams in the universe including one on the moon (crater No. 357). The earthly ones are to be found in Australia (1), Canada (2), Ireland (3), USA (22). Birmingham has six partner towns and cities: Chicago, Frankfurt, Johannesburg, Milan, Leipzig and Lyons.

Moving to the west, you come across **The Chinese Quarter**. In truth, this area could just as easily be called The Irish Quarter or even the Entertainment Quarter (although that would put it into dispute with neighbouring Convention Quarter of which more later). So for the time being, we will call it The Chinese Quarter but do not expect to see the enormous and marked China Towns of, say, London or even Manchester. Instead, what you will find is a hotchpotch of cultures and attractions – ranging from the doughnut-shaped Arcadian Centre, which boasts a number of Chinese restaurants and shops as well as more mainstream eating houses and entertainment, the magnificent refurbished Hippodrome Theatre which successfully combines old and new, Birmingham's famous markets – quite possibly the very reason for Birmingham's origination as a major town – including wholesale (get up early if you want to see what's going on there) and the vast indoor and outdoor markets adjoining the Bullring. Then there's a proliferation of side streets which house the Irish pubs, at their best and busiest on St

Patrick's night (March 17th), but fascinating to see and drink in at any time of the year.

Moving further west still we come to the **Convention Quarter** or as it might also be called, Westside. This houses those great monuments to the 20th and 21st century: The International Convention Centre (ICC), Symphony Hall (within the ICC itself) and the neighbouring National Indoor Arena (NIA). It is also home to the canal side setting of Brindleyplace, Broad Street (once retail dominated but now largely, but not exclusively, given over to hotels, restaurants, offices and nightlife), Mailbox (with its designer shops and eating places and proving that you can turn a sow's ear into a silk purse) and, on the very edge of the city centre, Five Ways with yet more entertainment facilities as well as the splendid, although rather out on a limb, Marriott Hotel.

Continuing the journey round, and you arrive in the area that might well be described as being unspoilt by progress: **The Jewellery Quarter**. This is the closest that Birmingham ever gets to portraying itself as it used to be: a hotchpotch of workshops, small manufacturers and cheek by jowl side streets which are home to thousands of jewellery workers. Not as many as in its heyday but

Many films & TV productions feature Birmingham Scenes including *Doctors, All About Me, NCS Manhunt, Brum, Dalziel & Pascoe, Large, Nasty Neighbours, Felicia's Journey, Brassed Off, Clockwise, Take Me High* and many more...

St Paul's, Jewellery Quarter

nonetheless it is still Europe's largest concentration of jewellery manufacturers who sell not only to the trade but also to the public (sometimes at prices that are considerably less than the high street offering). It also includes a few oases particularly in the form of old churches and churchyards. Plus, as you might expect in a city that has built itself on creativity and ingenuity, a few art establishments also.

The Jewellery Quarter, Central Birmingham and Eastside all lay claim to parts of what has been known as the city's Gun Quarter. Lying close to St. Chad's Cathedral, the Gun Quarter is still a manufacturing area of traditional and sporting guns. Birmingham has long been a centre for the mass productions of weapons – even back to the time of the Civil War when it made swords for the Roundheads. BSA (Birmingham Small Arms) had a factory in Small Heath and there was Kynoch's in Witton; both were major, large-scale suppliers of armaments and munitions during both the First and Second World Wars.

Symphony Hall from Centenary Square

The Walking City

Birmingham city centre is, on the whole, easily walked. This is perhaps just as well, given the fact there is no underground transport system or that its Metro is not particularly extensive or even helpful to the leisure or business visitor. True, at night when it is wet and windy, you may prefer to resort to the privacy of your own taxi or the mugginess of one of the many buses that travel, seemingly confusingly, around the city streets (but see 'Gazetteer' for an explanation). But in the main, it is at its best when walked – especially when you consider that from one extreme of the city centre to the other it is less than three miles, that most city centre sights are within a radius of two miles and that the city fathers have done much to bury or remove the barrier of what was once the inner ring road (now no longer named as such but often referred to as Birmingham's concrete collar) which threatened the city centre's expansion.

Brindleyplace, Convention Quarter

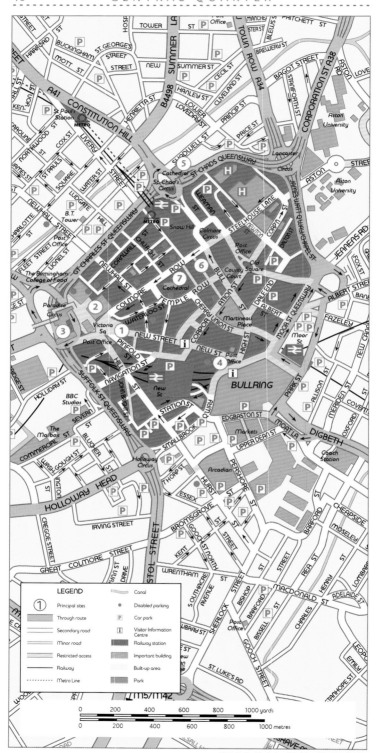

The Central Quarter

The Central Quarter is that area of the city that was once contained within the inner ring road or "concrete collar" as it became known. It radiates in an arc from the city's civic heart of the Council House and Victoria Square and encompasses the Central Library, Museum and Art Gallery and the shopping areas of New Street and Corporation Street which adjoins High Street, Dale End and Bull Street. It also includes the city's foremost business district with its main artery of Colmore Row and the city's old and new Law Courts.

It is a quarter of contrasts – from busy, sharp suited business people flitting from one building to the next to complete yet another business deal (Birmingham's professional/financial sector is the largest outside London, employing an estimated 100,000) - to traditional Brummies as they go about their shopping in streets that have resounded to the footsteps of their forefathers.

It also combines specialist privately owned shops, particularly dominant in various arcades together with all the usual high street retailers you would want or even need to find. It is here you will find the city centre High Street (previously King's High Street and before that Old London Road which served as the starting point for coach journeys to the capital).

The Council House

Much of the Central Quarter results from Mayor Joseph Chamberlain's grandiose 19th century vision. He initiated the slum clearances that preceded the construction of Colmore Row as it is now (it has also been known as Haymarket and Mount Pleasant amongst others) and Corporation Street. His dream of fine, new, boulevard-style streets was influenced by Haussmann's work in Paris.

He saw the new Corporation Street and surrounding streets as a grand commercial area full of thriving enterprise and wealth. He would be satisfied to see his vision is still fulfilled, despite the city having been largely re-built, in part because of the destruction wrought on it during the Second World War, when Birmingham was heavily targeted owing to its industrial might. The night of August 25, 1940 saw the first air raid with the old market hall taking a direct hit. It was completely destroyed and 25 people died. In October of the same year, the Council House, Town Hall and Art Gallery were all damaged. However, the heaviest bombardment was on November 19, 1940, when 350 Luftwaffe bombers attacked for a whole night.

The destruction of the market area was significant – it was a catalyst for change. No time was wasted; plans to re-develop the Bull Ring and build an inner ring road were drawn up in 1940 by Henry Manzoni. Twenty years later, work on the 'concrete collar' began. It was a decision later town planners would regret and a barrier they would endeavour to remove: not completely but sufficient to give the Central Quarter easy access to the rest of the city centre.

Chamberlain Fountain: Chamberlain Square

Victoria Square①
New Street

A wonderfully spacious square complete with fountain, surrounded by some fine, 19th century buildings like the Council House, the Town Hall and the Old Post Office. The people of Birmingham like to think of it as their very own Spanish Steps. Dominating the square is

The River, known affectionately as The Floozie in the Jacuzzi, designed by Rory Coonan. The two mythical beasts sitting sedately either side of the steps are by Dhruva Mistry. The words around the pool's edge are by poet, playwright and critic T.S. Eliot.

"And the pool was filled with water and out of sunlight and the lotus rose, quietly, quietly, the surface glittered out of heart of light, and they were behind us, reflected in the pool. Then a cloud passed, and the pool was empty."

> Victoria Square hosts one of the largest fountains in Europe - known as 'The River' but nicknamed ' the Floozie in the Jacuzzi' it has a flow of 3,000 gallons per minute.

The Council House
Victoria Square (1874-9)

This glorious, Renaissance-style building, designed by H. R. Yeoville-Thomason includes a projecting arch above the portico with a mosaic by Salviati and a sculpture above showing Britannia with the manufacturers of Birmingham. The foundation stone was laid by Joseph Chamberlain.

Directly opposite is the city's former **Head Post Office**, another decorative, Renaissance-style building from 1890, designed by Sir Henry Tanner. It is reminiscent of a French chateau with lantern shaped domes and a round, domed tower. It escaped demolition thanks to the support of the Victorian Society.
(Not open to the public)

The Town Hall
Victoria Square

A Grade I listed building based on the Temple of Castor and Pollux in the Forum, Rome, the Town Hall was opened in 1834 but it wasn't completed until some time later. One of the architects was Joseph Hansom, the inventor of the Hansom cab. Inside, it seats 4,000 and resounds with the hallmarks of a Georgian Assembly Room. The decorative ceiling is by Sir

Charles Allom. It was refitted in 1927. The organ was played by Felix Mendelssohn back in 1846. Birmingham Town Hall doubled for the Royal Albert Hall in the film, *Brassed Off*. The people of Birmingham have been pretty brassed off too with the inordinate time it has spent empty. Now it is being completely refurbished and it is hoped will reopen sometime soon. For the time being, visitors have to content themselves with the view from the outside.

The statue of **Queen Victoria** in Victoria Square is by Thomas Brock, RA. She once stood with her consort, Prince Albert but is now alone.

A little further down is the very modern **The Iron Man** by Anthony Gormley (1993), a 20ft (6.1m) high sculpture made from cast iron and nickel. It was cast at Firth Rixon Castings in nearby Willenhall. He stands rather ignominiously on the ground, not on a plinth, and the sculpture's position - tilting slightly back and to one side - is by design, not accident.

Chamberlain Square

Chamberlain Square is often bustling; on sunny days people congregate on the steps in front of Central Library and the square is often used as a forum for music. The square itself is in memory of the former MP and Mayor of Birmingham, Joseph Chamberlain with the Chamberlain Memorial Fountain taking pride of place in the centre. It was designed by John Henry Chamberlain - who was not related to his work of art. The fountain was restored and new pools added in 1978.

A life-like bronze statue of **Thomas Attwood** by Siobhan Copinger (1992) sits on the steps behind the Town Hall with a book in one hand and a pen in the other. On the top step is a sheaf of his papers. He was a banker and Birmingham's first MP. He founded the Birmingham Political Union which pressed for parliamentary reform.

Birmingham Museum & Art Gallery [2]

Chamberlain Square:
Tel: (0121) 303 2834

Birmingham Museum and Art Gallery is easily identified by its clock tower, sometimes referred to as 'Big Brum'. It was opened by the Prince of Wales, the future King Edward VII in 1885. It is home to the largest Pre-Raphaelite art collection in the world as well as collections of silver, sculpture, ceramics and ancient and social history. Sir Jacob Epstein's magnificent bronze Lucifer is in the gift shop. Afternoon tea in the Edwardian tea room is a lovely interlude. The adjacent Gas Hall Gallery formerly the place where gas bills were paid, has a constantly changing programme of exhibitions.

Open Mon-Thurs & Sat 10am-5pm; Fri 10.30am- 5pm; Sun 12.30pm-5pm.
Admission
Museum: free (voluntary contributions welcome).
Gas Hall: admission varies.

The nearby **Waterhall** (where water bills were once paid) focuses solely on modern art.

Birmingham Central Library [3]

Paradise Circus:
Tel: (0121) 303 4229

Europe's largest library is also the city's busiest building – it lends eight million books a year. Up to an hour's free internet access is available although there may be a wait for a computer. The library has an outstanding archive collection. Visitors should call in advance to apply for a reader's ticket and order specific materials. The library was opened in 1973. It is not universally liked. Prince Charles described it as "a place where (it looks as if) books are incinerated, not kept! ...an ill-mannered essay in concrete 'brutalism' intended to shock (which it certainly does). An insult to the grand civic

Birmingham's Central Library loans over 8 million books each year.
The Central Library is home to the world's largest Shakespeare works folio.

buildings amongst which it squats". Doubtless he would be pleased to learn its life is now short. There are grand plans to build a new central library in Eastside. Designs by Richard Rogers Partnership have already been approved in principle.

Open: Daily 9am – 8pm except Saturday 9am - 5pm; Sunday closed.
Admission: Free. Birmingham City Archives, Reference Library
Tel: (0121) 303 4217
www.birmingham.gov.uk

The nearby and inaptly named Paradise Forum (it takes its name from **Paradise Circus** but is only approaching paradise if you like fast food outlets and tacky architectural features) includes the entrance to the home of The Birmingham Conservatoire which includes the **Shakespeare Memorial Room**. A Victorian room designed by Chamberlain to hold the Shakespeare library it includes inlaid wood, carvings and decorative glass.

Open: By appointment and on City Discovery Days.
Admission: Free.

Outside Central Library are the **statues of Watt and Priestley**. Joseph Priestley was a Birmingham minister and the man who discovered oxygen whilst James Watt was instrumental in the development of the steam engine.

Tales of terracotta

Wandering around Birmingham, you will find that many of the older buildings are constructed in a distinctive red brick – terracotta. Moulded clay bricks, available predominantly in red but also in a yellow/brown buff colour, were well suited to Birmingham's industrial environment resisting corrosion and retaining intricate detail not achievable by carving. Production of terracotta bricks was concentrated in the surrounding towns although many of the facades came from North Wales where clay was more plentiful and a by-product of mining. Two of the finest terracotta buildings are Moseley Road Baths and Library (page 56) and also the Victoria Law Courts (page 22), a great example of how terracotta could be used with exuberance (although one suspects that those being sentenced were less exuberant).

Close to Victoria Square are **122 & 124 Colmore Row**. These two buildings, designed by Prof. W. R. Lethaby and C. L. Ball and built in 1900, are significant, identified as Birmingham's first examples of 'modern' architecture.

The Exchange, 19 Newhall Street, is another of Birmingham's fine, Victorian terracotta buildings with a very ornate porch and decorative gate. It was Birmingham's original telephone exchange. Look up above street level to see the beautiful decorated gables and filigree work and its pepperpot and Jacobean-style chimneys.
(Not open to the public).

Around the corner from The Exchange is **The Birmingham Institute of Art and Design**, 9 Margaret Street. Another Chamberlain and Martin building (see also the Ikon page 41) and Grade II listed, it is impressive and imposing, decorated with mosaics and stone carvings. The two asymmetrical gables ensure the top floor studios benefit from constant natural light. It includes buttressing and three gabled arches on its Edmund Street side. The Institute was founded in 1854 by an Act of Parliament for the "diffusion and advancement of science, literature and art amongst all classes of persons resident in Birmingham and the Midland counties." One of the Institute's early presidents was the novelist, Charles Dickens.

Open: Mon – Fri 9am – 5pm.
Tours by appointment.
Admission: Free.

If you are walking up or down **Temple Street**, look at No.8, Birmingham Law Society. The tiny entrance conceals an interesting staircase which leads up to the Society's library – originally a temperence hall and theatre. Today in need of restoration, it is home to the only law lending library in England.

Just off New Street is Bennetts at **8 Bennett's Hill**. Built in 1869 for most of its life it has been a bank before becoming a bar. A corner entrance through an impressive, high domed porch between two Doric columns, leads to the banking hall, much as it was with more Doric columns supporting the decorated ceiling.

Open: During licensing hours.

In close proximity is the Bennett's Hill branch of what started as The Birmingham Banking Company (the initials can still be seen over the entrance) before becoming part of the **Midland Bank** in 1914. This building was designed by Thomas Rickman and was constructed in 1830.

Staying with banks, New Street boasts what must

be one of the grandest bookshops in the world. **Waterstones** was originally the headquarters of the Midland Bank, constructed in 1869 and with a wonderful feeling of space. It includes a magnificent central staircase, balconies, stained glass ceiling and a coffee shop at the rear.

Open: Normal shopping hours.

Grosvenor House
New Street/Bennett's Hill

An entertaining example of what has been called 'adventurous architecture'. Grosvenor House (a listed building) was built for petroleum giant, Shell-Mex & BP by Cotton, Ballard & Blow back in 1953. The side facing New Street has an undulating feel, which contrasts with the triangular windows facing Bennett's Hill.

The Burlington Arcade/Piccadilly Arcade
Off New Street

Running parallel to each other, The Piccadilly Arcade is the most authentic with an intriguing ceiling, whilst the recently restructured Burlington Arcade leads to the stylish Burlington Hotel. Originally the Midland Hotel, it still retains many

of its fine Victorian features (as well as having its own well). Steps down take you towards the less than attractive Stephenson Street.

Pallasades
Above New Street Station

This typical 1970/80's shopping centre (but tweaked a bit since with some success) sits atop New Street Station and includes a number of eating places as well as a number of high street names and the occasional specialist independent retailer.

New Street Station

Back in 1846, the building of New Street station first meant clearing seven acres of slum housing and demolishing three churches, a graveyard and a synagogue. The area was one of the town's poorest neighbourhoods and the heart of the Jewish community at the time. It was the golden age of steam and New Street was to be the main LMS Railway Station in Birmingham. In 1880, it was expanded to double its original size with its massive iron and glass roof said at the time to be the largest single span roof in the world at 370yds (338m) long x 70 yards (64m) wide x 27 (25m) yards high. The original station cost £500,000 to build and was known briefly as Birmingham Grand Central. George and Robert Stephenson were the engineers for the building of the London to Birmingham railway during the 1830s.

Today's New Street Station is far from welcoming, its

subterranean platforms and cramped facilities are an embarrassment to the city fathers who have fought, for many years, for its replacement. Originally designed to handle 640 trains a day, it now copes with an average of 1,400 a day. On an average day, a train leaves the station every 58 seconds. The station welcomes, if that is the right word, 130,000 people to its platforms every day. And just to prove its unpopularity, New Street Station was voted the second worst eyesore in Britain by *Country Life* readers. (The first? Wind Farms!).

Odeon
New Street

The first of the world-famous cinema chain was opened in Birmingham by Oscar Deutsch on Birchfield Road on the borders of Perry Barr and Kingstanding in 1930. It could seat 1,820 people and there was room for a 17 piece orchestra. Tickets cost from 6d to 1/3d (equivalent to between 2p and 6p in today's currency). The cinema on New Street, bears little resemblance to the city centre picture palace in its heyday when the organ, complete with organist, would rise through the stage floor between performances. For many years it was the pop concert venue in Birmingham. Odeon is an acronym of Oscar Deutsch Entertains Our Nation.

The Rotunda ④
New Street

One of Birmingham's most recognisable buildings, a major city landmark in a prominent position at the end of one of the city's main streets. A 265ft (81m) circular tower, it was built in 1964 and designed by architect James A. Roberts. Roberts had initially wanted the building to be twice as high and glazed throughout but this was not to be because of insufficient foundations and restrictive planning regulations. Rumour has it that the building is capable of rotating but rumours are not to be believed! It is the only building from the 1960s' Bull Ring development to be integrated into the redevelopment of the area and is likely to become an apartment building.

High Street

Containing yet more multiple retailers and the entrance to **The Pavilions Central** which boasts a food court at upper level but is dominated by high street names. Nearby **Martineau Place** is more of a backwater but pleasant for all that. Giant sails give it protection from the weather and the cafes provide a welcome spot for a sit-down – in or out.

93 Bull Street is where one of the best known brand names developed. An early Cadbury shop was to be found here.

The statue in **Old Square** of Birmingham-born comedian, Tony Hancock is by Bruce Williams. It was unveiled in 1996 by Sir Harry Secombe and includes the inscription "I do not think I met a man as modest or humble".

Corporation Street

This is Birmingham's longest city centre street. It was integral to Joseph Chamberlain's grand plans for the city. He instigated a slum clearance programme in order for work to begin on it in 1878.

At its far end, you'll find the Law Courts. The distinctive, red terracotta **Victoria Law Courts** were designed by Sir Aston Webb and Ingress Bell with Queen Victoria laying the foundation

stone. Arts and crafts-style gates are flanked by octagonal turrets. Inside is a large stained glass window by Walter Lonsdale, depicting scenes from Birmingham's history.

Open: Mon – Fri 9am – 4pm.

Opposite is yet another of Birmingham's magnificent, ornate, terracotta buildings, the **Methodist Central Hall**. Designed by Ewan & James A Harper it took four years to construct opening in 1903.

Birmingham Children's Hospital
Steelhouse Lane

There has been a hospital on this site since 1779. The present building dates back to 1897 when it had only 340 beds and was opened by Princess Christian, daughter of Queen Victoria. Most recently, it has become home to the Diana, Princess of Wales Children's Hospital (more often called Birmingham Children's Hospital), a world renowned institution which has undertaken much pioneering work, not only for those living in Birmingham but from throughout the UK (and occasionally, worldwide).

St. Chad's Cathedral ⑤
St Chad's Circus
Tel: (0121) 230 6208.

St. Chad's Roman Catholic cathedral was the first Catholic Cathedral to be built in Britain since the Reformation. St. Chad was the first Bishop of Mercia. A superbly commanding neo-gothic design with 19th century stained glass it includes a 15th century statue of the Virgin Mary -

Pavillions central

a gift from the cathedral's designer, A. W. N. Pugin. The cathedral contains the largest new manual organ in the UK.

Open: Daily 8am - 8pm.

The Kennedy Memorial
St Chad's Circus

The construction of the inner ring road provided great opportunities for murals and this is arguably the finest. Designed by Kenneth Budd and constructed in 1976, the 180' mural pays tribute to President John F. Kennedy's international-

ism. It is accessible only through pedestrian underpasses. The question facing planners is what will become of it when this section of the ring road is redeveloped.

Snow Hill Station
Colmore Row

The present day Snow Hill Station is not even a shadow of the original which opened in 1852, taking all the Great Western Railway routes through the city. Today it is barely recognisable as a station but provides an alternative, and prettier, route to London. It also includes the Metro station to the Jewellery Quarter and Wolverhampton.

The Great Western Arcade ⑥
Colmore Row

This, the first of several attractive, covered shopping arcades in the city,

opened in 1875. Constructed over the tunnel containing the railway that gave it its name, it once boasted 42 shops at ground floor level and 42 offices overhead. The fine balcony remains and replicas of the original lighting have been installed since it was badly damaged in World War II.

Birmingham Cathedral (St. Philip's) ⑦
St Philip's Place
Tel: (0121) 236 4333

A wonderful, English Baroque design by Thomas Archer who visited Rome for inspiration. It features a concave tower topped by a fine cupola. St Philip's became the cathedral for the new diocese of Birmingham in 1905 although it was consecrated as a church back in 1715. It is a small cathedral but full of warmth and light. The colours in the four, massive, stained glass windows, without mullions or transoms, by Edward Burne-Jones are electrifying. The weather vane that tops the tower includes a boar's head from the Gough-Calthorpe family crest (these being major benefactors of the city). The cathedral suffered some fire damage as a result of incendiary bombs during 1940.

Open Daily weekdays 7am – 7pm and weekends 9am – 5pm

St Philip's Place

St Philip's Place is surrounded by some particularly fine buildings from both the 18th and 19th centuries as well as the more recent day (the Bank

of England was once located in the building that is now home to The Bank of Scotland and also home to England's largest barristers' chambers). The square itself, much used by local office workers during the summer months, has recently been totally restored. Although looking the part, the railings surrounding the Cathedral are recreations of the originals removed in the early 1940s to be made into armaments.

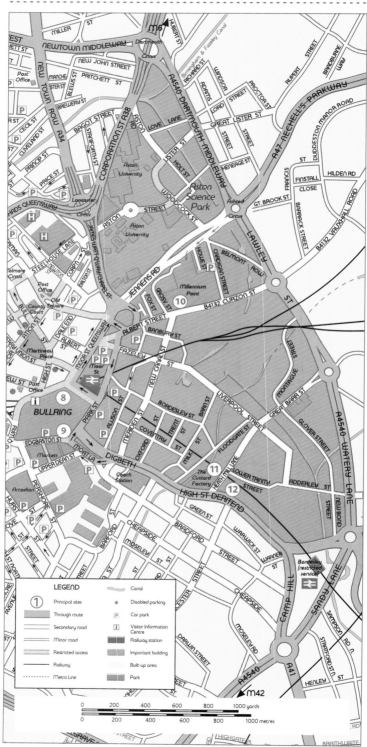

© Marketing Birmingham/Birmingham City Council, 2004

Eastside

Eastside, a name not coined until the late 1990s, is a planner's dream, and, for parts of it, a walker's nightmare. However, it does contain some of Birmingham's must-see buildings including, at its centre, Millennium Point, where technology and entertainment are combined, Aston University which neighbours Aston Science Park (home to developing technology-related businesses) and, on its western fringe, nestling between the Central and Chinese quarters, the Bullring and the Bull Ring markets.

The picture and description in ten years time is likely to be significantly different: this is Birmingham's project for the next decade. At £6 billion, the development of Eastside will be the most ambitious regeneration scheme and the largest project of its type in Europe. The new quarter is to be based around the themes of learning, technology and heritage and will include a new city park – the first to be developed in any European city this century – surrounding Millennium Point which in itself will form the centrepiece of a network of streets, piazzas and spectacular buildings.

Admiral Nelson by Sir Richard Westmacott

Until then though, visitors will inevitably concentrate on the main existing features: the ultra new Bullring, Millennium Point, historic sites such as Curzon Street Station and the youthful and vibrant Custard Factory which is home to hundreds of artists and creative types and acts as a cultural oasis.

In spite of the city's present day plans, this area is the city's historic heart. This was where the great markets were held (and where they remain) and Digbeth, bordering Eastside and the Chinese quarter, with St Martin's Church acting as its focal point, is the city's original manufacturing heart.

> Birmingham is home to Bird's Custard invented by Alfred Bird in the 1840s.

This area was once blessed with natural springs and streams. Digbeth's original mill was used for grinding corn and later the area became known for its manufacture of sword blades for the Parliamentary troops during the English Civil War. This didn't go down too well with Prince Rupert's royalist forces; they attacked the town in the little known Battle of Birmingham in 1643. The mill was later rebuilt by Sampson Lloyd II – whose son was the founder of Lloyds Bank.

Curzon Street Station

Stairways to shopping heaven, inside Selfridges

The Bullring ⑧

The new £500 million Bullring development is helping to bring life and vitality to the the Eastside quarter. With 140 stores on three main shopping levels and a vast markets area it's a retail mecca. There has been a market at the Bull Ring since 1154 when a royal charter was awarded to the Lord of the Manor, Peter de Bermingham. Back then, Thursday was market day but now every day but Sunday is market day attracting more than 30 million projected visitors a year. The old Market Hall Clock, with four, life-size

past the city does well to forget. A long lost view of St Martin's Church has been restored and the sloping site – it falls close on 50ft (15m) - has been used to imaginative effect. Completely pedestrianised, it includes both interior and exterior squares. It also includes

The new 185,000 sq ft (17,186 sqm) **Selfridges** store is a triumph of design with an exterior that before it was even opened attracted international attention. It was designed by Amanda Levete and Jan Kaplicky of Future Systems and has been described by architectural commentators as space fungus and a curvaceous caterpillar. Locals were quick to christen it 'The Armadillo' because of its 15,000, circular, shiny aluminium discs.

Built at a cost of £60 million, including the interior, the eminent architect Sir Richard Rogers has described it as a "brilliant, optimistic, elegant enclosure, which is why I make regular detours to see it because it lifts my spirits". Whilst it is not quite on a par with Frank Gehry's Guggenheim museum in

Why is it called the Bull Ring?

Back in the early 1500s, John Cooper – who is believed to have lived at The Dogg Tavern in Spiceal Street (although whether it was known as such in those days is not clear), donated the first recreation ground to the town. As a result, a licence was granted for bull-baiting in an area near to St Martin's – which became known as the Bull Ring.

Spiceal Street disappeared – but has since been reinstated as part of the new Bullring development.

automatons ringing the bell every 15 minutes, was destroyed in 1940. There has been talk of producing a replica as the drawings by the original manufacturers, William Potts & Sons, have been preserved.

Bullring's northern edge is built above both the roadway and railway tunnels with the buildings supported on four, gigantic, steel trusses. In addition to famous department stores, such as Selfridges and Debenhams, it includes French Connection, Kookai, Mikey and Flannels and Europe's biggest Benetton shop.

The new Bullring is significantly different to the old, a part of Birmingham's

some notable features: Laurence Broderick's Bronze Bull is a twice lifesize (7'2" [2.2m] high x 14'3" [4.4m] long, 6.5 tonnes) sculpture of a Hereford bull, turning.

Skyplane connects New Street and High Street through Bullring. The glass ceiling seems to float above the buildings. The construction allows up to 100mm of movement to account for wind sway and heat expansion.

Bilbao (and it did cost significantly less) it nonetheless is a startling vision of what Birmingham is trying hard to be: recognised and admired.

The first of Debenhams' '2010' flagship stores' main entrance is through a triple height glazed entrance. It features a curved central atrium and a glass walled scenic lift. It was designed by architect Bernerd Englehas.

St. Martin in the Bull Ring ⑨

A vibrant public space with areas for performance arts, sculptures and water features, this new square was designed by landscape architect, Gross Max. It incorporates three, 16ft (5m) - high coloured glass cubes with water detail.

Parliament in London. His high Gothic design for St Martins cost £32,000 to build in the early 1880s. The use of local, red sandstone has posed a problem over the centuries – by the late 17th century, the church built on the site in around 1290 had to be encased in three layers of red brick to prevent dam

aging erosion. Inside, is the oldest monument in Birmingham, an effigy of Sir William de Bermingham dated 1325. The church has a stained glass window by Edward Burne-Jones and William Morris. The most recent restoration of St Martin was completed mid - 2003 and cost in the region of £5.5 million. It has the only full-time market's chaplainin the country and the world's only change ringing peal of 16 bells.

> St. Martin welcomes around 82,000 visitors a year.

On April 10, 1941, the Bishop of Birmingham ordered the immediate removal and storage of St. Martin's famous Burne-Jones stained glass window. That night, a bomb destroyed all the other windows in the church.

The iron cross on the steeple is a replica of the 8ft (2.5m) original, which crashed onto the roof of the church's north aisle, rolled off and embedded itself in the ground during the 1996 Easter service.

St. Martin in the Bull Ring

The Bull Ring
Tel: (0121) 643 5428

St. Martin, a Grade II listed building, is Birmingham's oldest church. Evidence suggests there was a place of worship here as far back as the 12th century. The tower and spire date from 1781. The architect of the current church, Alfred Chatwin, was a Birmingham man, a Gothic specialist who also worked on the Houses of

Millennium Point

Moor Street Station

The £9 million refurbishment of this Grade II listed, Edwardian station is now completed although not all of its platforms are in immediate use. It was originally opened in 1909 by

St Martin

Great Western Railways to relieve the congestion at Snow Hill and experienced its heyday in the 1930s. With the new Bullring and Selfridges on its doorstep, heady days could soon return.

Millennium Point [10]

Curzon Street

Millennium Point is a fusion of technology and entertainment. It's the size of six, international football pitches, cost £114 million and houses the University of the First Age, The Technology Innovation Centre, Birmingham's new museum of science and discovery, Thinktank, and the Midlands' first 3D Theatre.

Thinktank: The Birmingham Museum of Science & Discovery

Millennium Point
Tel: (0121) 202 2222.
www.thinktank.ac

One of the biggest museums outside London with ten themed galleries over four floors, this interactive science museum has more than 200 hands-on exhibits. Thinkback features the world's oldest working steam engine, planes and a record-breaking car. In Thinknow see whether you can solve a street crime or perform a virtual hip operation. Thinkhere traces Birmingham's history from Domesday to now and Thinkahead is a vision of the future – visitors can explore the cutting edge of science and technology. Lots of fun for children and adults of all ages.

Open: Daily 10am – 5pm.
Last admission 4pm.
Admission: C.
How to get there: 15 min. walk from New Street, Moor Street and Snow Hill stations. There is a fee-paying car park on site.

University of the First Age
Millennium Point

The UFA is designed to take visitors on a quest for knowledge focusing on how the brain works and how it can be stimulated and developed.

The Technology Innovation Centre (TIC)
Millennium Point

A resource open to companies and individuals for the development of technological understanding and skills.

The Hub

Millennium Point

Social centrepoint with some cafes. Free access.

Close to Millennium Point is the site of the new **Central Library** scheduled for opening in 2007. The new Library of Birmingham will be the 10th largest in the world and a new home for the Birmingham Conservatoire. It has been described as Britain's answer to Paris's Pompidou Centre. The proposed 985ft (300m) long, four storey, glass-fronted, elliptical building with rooftop park will incorporate 40,000 sq ft (3,716 sqm)of floor space. Designer: Richard Rogers Partnership.

Eastside is the proposed setting for **The Needle**, another landmark reminiscent of Paris, and incorporating an £18 million media hub.

Gun Barrel Proof House

Banbury Street/ Andover Street

A grade II listed building within the Warwick Bar Conservation Area and backing onto the Digbeth Branch Canal. Built in 1813, it is one of only two proof houses in the country.

Curzon Street Station

Curzon Street

A Grade I listed building, designed by Philip

Hardwick and built in 1838, this was the original Birmingham to London railway terminus and incorporates a cantilevered stone staircase. It is soon to be home to the Royal College of Organists. Undergoing a £7.2m makeover, the building will be adjacent to a new recital hall. Once completed, parts will be open to the public with education rooms, talks, demonstrations and concerts. (Not open to the public yet).

On Lancaster Circus is the **Central Fire Station**, built in the 1930s, with **Aston University** behind it. Formerly the College of Advanced Technology, Aston was granted university status in 1966.

The Custard Factory ⑰

Gibb Street

Bird's Custard is, as any Anglophile knows, the sauce eaten with so many traditional puddings. It was created in the 1840s by pharmacist Alfred Bird for his wife, Elizabeth. Elizabeth who couldn't eat anything containing eggs or yeast; cornflower-based custard was an egg-free alternative. Guests who were inadvertently served the sauce with dessert at a dinner

party loved it and custard went into mass production.

The Custard Factory is now a thriving community of arts and media professionals. The centre's GreenHouse building features colourful steel balconies giving it a Le Courbusier feel. Shops and bars are chic – Über interior accessories, Gogo Lounge, 20.24.26 for clothes and machines for boarders and bikers, Inspired for designer jewellery and glass and The Medicine Bar.

At the beginning of the complex is the UK's largest living sculpture, Green Man by Tawny Gray.

On a wall facing the main road, opposite the old Bird's Custard Factory is a plaque to the martyr, John Rogers, who was born in Deritend c.1505. He was burned at the stake on February 4, 1555 for assisting in the translation of the Bible into English. He was the first martyr of what became known as the Marian persecution.

Deritend Free Library

Gibb Street

Back in the 1860s, Deritend Free Library, designed by Victorian architect John Henry Chamberlain, was visited daily by nearly 600 people. Back in those days more than a fifth of its 2,113 members had no occupation and it held 4,441 books (with 2,495 being literature and fiction and only 43 for children). Since its closure in 1941, it has performed different roles: as a bakery, metal workshop and martial arts studio. Now all that has changed with its £500,000 renovation by Custard Factory owner Bennie Gray with support from the city council and English Heritage. The old library is now a venue for the arts, conventions and exhibitions.

Close to the Custard Factory are rock group **UB40's recording studios** - founded in 1980. Redevelopment of the site will create a five acre media village with recording and rehearsal studios and a new, live music venue as part of a Media and Performing Arts campus for **South Birmingham College**. The plans also include a mix of commer cial, retail and residential properties.

The Old Crown Inn ⑫

High Street, Deritend
Tel: (0121) 248 1368

Interesting because it is one of the few half-timbered buildings in this industrial city, this restored timber-framed inn dates from 1368. With its carved gables with interlaced arcading, wattle and daub infill, the original ground floor comprised a large room and smaller rooms at either end. Today it has an à la carte restaurant, bars and eight bedrooms.

Open: during licensing hours.

The Anchor Inn

Bradford Street
Tel: (0121) 622 4516

A red terracotta building c.1760, the corner entrance to the public bar and large leaded stained glass windows are typical of this era. Having inn sta-

> Digbeth resident, blacksmith John Roberts, died c.1792 aged 103. He had married three times and fathered 28 children.

tus allowed The Anchor to stay open as long as there was a bed empty for a visitor to the city.

Open: licensing hours.

Stratford House

Camp Hill

A rare example in the city of traditional, timber-framed Elizabethan tudor manor house with towering chimneys. Built in C1601, it was restored in 1954 but is tucked away behind the Stratford Road. (Not open to the public).

Paragon Hotel

145 Alcester Street, Digbeth
Tel: (0121) 672 0627

An impressive, Grade II listed building, which has recently been carefully restored.

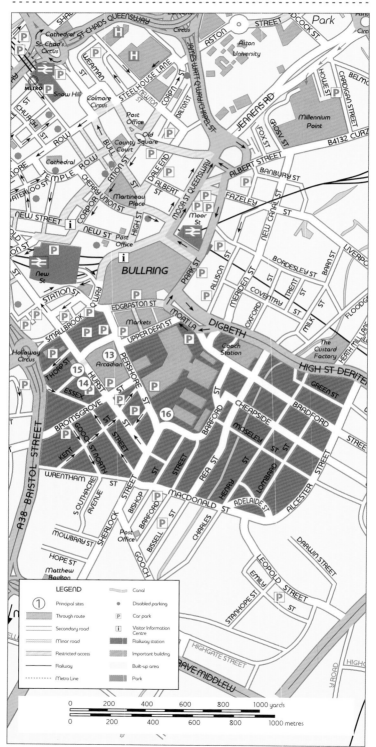

© Marketing Birmingham/Birmingham City Council, 2004

The Chinese Quarter

In spite of being the smallest, there is no other quarter in the city that has such incredible cultural diversity. Its particularly cosmopolitan and colourful atmosphere is home to Chinese, Irish, Italian and Jewish businesses. There's a sprinkling of gay bars, lots of straight bars and establishments offering more adult entertainment. It is also home to Birmingham Hippodrome Theatre and the acclaimed Birmingham Royal Ballet.

The area, once wet and swampy in medieval times, became home to the growing community of immigrant Jews. By the early 19th century, the migrants that settled here tended to be Italians –

so much so that the area around Deritend became known as 'Little Italy'. In 1915, between 600 and 700 Italians were living in the area.

The community's growing prosperity caused many to move to more affluent Aston before World War II resulted in mass internment on the Isle of Man. Little Italy then disappeared and the area became depressed.

In the late 1950s, the first Chinese restaurant opened in Holloway Head. It was the start of the area's renaissance. Large Chinese restaurants, like the Slow Boat and Heaven Bridge, opened in the early 60s. Each catered for several hundred diners and in 1969, Mr Wing Yip and his brother, Sammy, opened their

first specialist Chinese grocery store. The entrepreneur arrived in the UK with only £10 in his pocket and embarked on creating an influential business empire.

The first Chinese community centre was in Hurst Street – the centre doubled as a bean curd and bean sprout factory. In the late 70s and early 80s the Happy Gathering restaurant (lost as part of the Arcadian redevelopment) attracted increasing numbers of diners.

Although the Chinese community accounts for less than one per cent of the city's current population, its influence is significant. The area is now synonymous with all things Oriental including noodle bars, Cantonese, Malaysian and Japanese restaurants. Specialist bakers, a casino, Eastern fast food bars and practitioners in Chinese herbal medicines can all be found here.

The Chinese New Year celebrations (February) are easily comparable with those in London. The fireworks, dragon processions and street entertainment show the quarter at its most lively, vivid and enthusiastic best.

In March though, it is time for the Irish community – and thousands of would-be Irish - to celebrate St. Patrick's Day (March 17th). The area becomes the focus of the celebrations with the St. Patrick's Day Parade (normally on the Sunday nearest the day itself) extending throughout the day.

There is a further cosmopolitan feel to the doughnut-shaped Arcadian Centre which opened in the early 1990s and gave the area a further 'lift' and focus. The influx of bars, nightclubs and a comedy venue has introduced life and vigour along with new visitors. On a warm summer weekend evening especially, the Arcadian becomes one huge party.

The Arcadian Centre ⑬

Hurst Street
www.thearcadian.co.uk

In the heart of Chinatown, the Arcadian Centre is a buzzing entertainment complex with restaurants, bars, cinema, comedy club, hotel, shops and open-air piazza plus a dedicated Chinese shopping street.

Back-to-back houses ⑭

Court 15, Inge Street/Hurst Street   Tel: (0121) 753 7757 www.nationaltrust.org.uk

This 19th century courtyard of 11 back-to-back houses, has been restored by the Birmingham Conservation Trust and the National Trust. The houses show how working people have lived over the past 160 years.

Thousands of houses like these were built, literally back-to-back, around a courtyard, for the rapidly increasing, multi-cultural working population of Britain's expanding industrial towns. Court 15 Inge Street is of immense historical importance as it is the city's only remaining example of such a common housing type. Thousands were demolished as part of slum clearance programmes.

The story of Court 15 is told through the lives of the people who lived and worked there. Visitors move through four different time periods, from 1840 to 1977. The design of each interior reflects the varied lives, cultures, religions and occupations of the families who lived there. During much of the 19th century, Court 15 was occupied by artisans engaged in various small trades, some of whom worked from home. They included button-makers, glass-workers, woodworkers, leatherworkers, tailors and craftsmen in the jewellery and small metal trades. By 1900, the lower floors of the terrace on Hurst Street had been converted to retail shops: a cycle maker, hairdresser, ticket-writer, fruiterer and furniture dealer. Most of the buildings around Court 15 continued to be occupied wholly or partly as homes until 1966 – when they were condemned as being unfit for habitation.

Open: daily except Mondays from July 24, 2004 except December 25,26 and January 1.
Admission: B

The Hippodrome ⑮

Hurst Street
Tel: (0870) 730 1234
www.hippodrometheatre.co.uk

The Hippodrome first opened its doors in 1899 and is the city's oldest existing theatre. The Queen and Prince Philip attended the final Royal Variety Show of the last millennium at the Hippodrome – the first staged outside London. The home of Birmingham Royal Ballet and the

DanceXchange (0121 689 3174) the theatre was refurbished to incorporate a new and sparkling entrance which includes several bars and Leith's Restaurant. The theatre itself retains the elegance of the past. The season often includes productions by major opera companies. Traditional Christmas pantomimes are real spectacles. Theatre-goers can treat themselves to a pre-

theatre meal in the Hippodrome Restaurant returning to the table in the interval for desserts and coffee.

The Pagoda

Smallbrook Ringway

A gift to Birmingham from one of the most prominent members of Birmingham's Chinese community, Wing Yip. The Pagoda was created in China and stands at one of the gateways to the Chinese quarter. Back in the 1970s there was a statue in Smallbrook Queensway of Hebe, a bronze figure by Robert Thomas. It was stolen in 2001 but recovered soon after. Hebe is now in the Birmingham Museum and Art Gallery.

Wholesale Markets ⑯

Pershore Street

Reckoned to be about the largest wholesale markets in Britain, this massive site is largely invisible to the public gaze although the foodstuffs from all over the world appear on everyone's tables. It includes Birmingham Flower Market: a sensory delight that assaults with colours and fragrances. (You have to be up early as the market opens at 4am when it is too dark to appreciate the full, floral glory except in mid-summer.)

Open: Mon - Fri 4am - 11.15am. Sat 4am - 9.15am (no vehicles permitted).

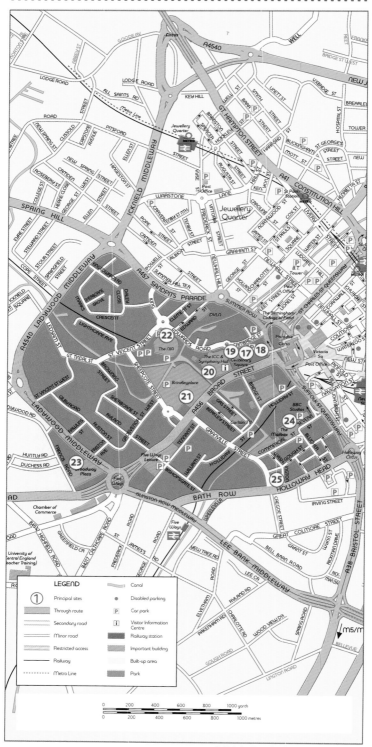

The Convention Quarter

Broad Street is neither particularly broad, nor very long but it is the main artery in an area that attracts millions of visitors each year – whether for the conventions, the peace of the canals or the buzz of the area's nightlife. As its name implies, the Convention Quarter is home to the International Convention Centre (ICC) but it also includes the stylish Mailbox retail and leisure development, Brindleyplace, a host of clubs, pubs, cafe bars and cinemas (not to mention two theatres) and the tranquillity of the Peace Garden.

Up until the 1770s, the area around Broad Street was considered to be the 'back of beyond'. It was the construction of a canal by James Brindley from Birmingham to Wolverhampton, some 14 miles distant, that changed all that. For his achievement, which resulted in halving the distribution costs of coal from the Black Country to Birmingham, he has had a pub dedicated to him and a plaque erected behind the ICC. More symbolically, his is the name that graces Birmingham's regeneration jewel: Brindleyplace. Once Europe's largest urban regeneration project (you get used to these claims in Birmingham; it is a city that does not believe in doing things by halves and it is never happier than when it is trumpeting that a scheme is Britain's or Europe's biggest or best), Brindleyplace is remarkable: successfully combining a diverse range of building styles. It is difficult to appreciate when wandering around, that hardly any of it is more than ten years old (with the exception of those buildings preserved within the development). Its variety of architectural styles has resulted in a community where it is possible to work, live, eat, drink and be entertained.

The exterior of the neighbouring ICC is not though, in the same architectural league. This is a great shame since it not only houses what is arguably one of the world's greatest (there we go again) symphony halls, but a remarkable complex of state-of-the-art meeting facilities catering from small gatherings to a thousand plus. This is the place where the G8 world leaders came together in 1998, NATO convened in 2000, business organisation CBI meets almost annually and that has seen numerous product launches.

Although the ICC was only opened (by HM the Queen) in 1991, it stands on the site of Britain's first purpose built exhibition centre: Bingley Hall. It was here in 1888 that William Gladstone, whilst taking a rest from his four terms as Liberal Prime Minister, addressed the largest indoor gathering Britain had ever known. Even more were to hear him later as his address was the first political speech recorded on an Edison phonograph.

The hall, erected in 1850 and capable of accommodating 20,000 people, remained in use until the 1980s. It had something reminiscent of a railway station about it – not surprising since its iron columns were intended for London's original Euston station. The area also played a part in the Great Exhibition of 1851 in London. It is said that when Prince Albert visited Bingley House, which preceded Bingley Hall and was the home of the chairman of Lloyds Bank, the concept of a great exhibition was hatched. Birmingham played a further role in that event: for the one million square feet (92,900sqm) of glass required to build Crystal Palace, the exhibition's centre piece in Hyde Park, came from the city. (Crystal Palace also included a crystal glass fountain by F.C. Osler of Broad Street, which was the centrepiece of the Palace's nave.)

The Convention Quarter also includes Centenary Square, even better when viewed from a height, the National Indoor Arena, home to international sporting events, and a number of excellent galleries. Oh, and right at its western fringe, the city's latest entertainment offering, Broadway Plaza which, just to prove versatility, was originally Birmingham Children's Hospital.

Centenary Square [17]

Centenary Square was given its name in 1989 to commemorate the 100th anniversary of Birmingham being granted city status. It was completed in 1991. The square was designed by artists Tess Jaray and Tom Lomax with the City Council architects. More than half a million individual bricks were used to create the wide, open space that fronts the ICC and Birmingham Repertory Theatre. The square is made up of an elaborate and complex

statue, designed and created by Raymond Mason and still appearing in many postcard views of Birmingham, occupied a prominent position until it was the subject of an arson attack on Maundy Thursday, 2003. The attack was not rendered by any of its many critics but attributed to youngsters on Easter holiday. Centenary Square also includes some fine works of art, both old and new. Amongst these, four sculptures in bronze by Albert Toft, surround the Hall of Memory.

enterprise. The flow of the water represents the passing of time.

Take a close look too at the monument to industrialist-cum-typographer John Baskerville. Between the Hall of Memory and Baskerville House, close to his home at Easy Hill, it represents the Baskerville type spelling out the name of his first book, Virgil.

Birmingham's Centenary Square is made up of over 500,000 individual hand laid bricks.

design, best appreciated from high up such as from the internal balconies of the Symphony Hall. Tess Jaray, designed the square as a total concept "as a painting must be. Every aspect, each element, must function in its own right, for its own purpose but still be a part of the whole," she said.

A highly visible element is however, no more. The controversial Forward

An appealing water sculpture, The Spirit of Enterprise created in 1981 by Tom Lomax, celebrates the roles of commerce, industry and

John Baskerville is not a man who has rested easily. On his death in January 1775, he was buried, as he requested, in a vertical position in his garden at Easy Hill (but why you might well ask). In the 1820s Easy Hill was required for canal construction, and his body uncovered. Found to be in reasonable condition, it was exhibited to the public until a bookseller put a stop to it by transferring the body secretly to the vaults of Christchurch in New Street. But peace was still not to be. Christchurch was demolished in 1899 – and the body of the mobile Baskerville taken to the catacombs of Warstone Lane cemetery in the Jewellery Quarter. It remains there to this day.

Flame of Hope

Centenary Square

Between Baskerville House and the Repertory Theatre is The Flame of Hope, a revolving blue globe with a flame above it. It was first lit to mark the passing of the Millennium and was saved by a local businessman from being extinguished.

The Hall of Memory [18]

Centenary Square

The adjacent domed, octagonal building is the Hall of Memory (1923/4). Built from Portland stone, it is carved on the inside by William Bloye. A memorial to those who died in the 1st and 2nd World Wars, it houses a book of remembrance.

Open: Mon – Sat 10am – 4pm.
Admission Free

Baskerville House

Centenary Square

Baskerville House was built in 1939 and named after John Baskerville. Originally local government offices the building is destined to be commercial office space.

Former Municipal Bank and Masonic Hall

Broad Street

Opposite the Hall of Memory can be seen the former Masonic Hall which later became the head office of Birmingham Municipal Bank.

Birmingham Repertory Theatre (The Rep) [19]

Centenary Square
Tel: (0121) 236 4455
www.birmingham-rep.co.uk

Next to the ICC and at the heart of Centenary Square, Birmingham Rep was designed by Graham Winteringham and built in 1971. It flaunts a lot of the features that epitomised design at the time – a functional appearance, large windows and little noticeable decoration. The auditorium seats 900. The theatre is respected for the calibre of its productions, its innovative approach to drama and making theatre accessible to all.

The International Convention Centre (ICC) [20]

Centenary Square
Tel: (0121) 200 2000
(See pages 126 and 127)

If there has been one building in Birmingham responsible for the city centre's regeneration, it is the International Convention Centre (ICC) which incorporates Symphony Hall.

Opened by HM The Queen in 1991 it remains one of the foremost convention centres in the world. Its somewhat dull exterior fails to do justice to its interior. A covered mall – open to the public – connects Centenary Square with the canal-side development of Brindleyplace.

In addition to Symphony Hall, it includes conference rooms accommodating just a handful up to a 1500 seat auditorium providing simultaneous translation into twelve languages, communication facilities as well as full theatrical staging. It also includes one of the largest fly towers in Europe.

Smaller auditoriums are built to the same specification.

It is here that world leaders, of virtually all political persuasions, have met.

It also includes some interesting items of public art.

The entrance from Centenary Square is bedecked with Birdlife, a neon sculpture, providing a canopy at the front entrance. Ron Haselden devised it as an abstract tree making its way through an aviary. Computer controlled, the sculpture is designed to simulate the migration of birds.

Within the ICC, can be seen a large abstract stained glass panel by Alexander Beleschenko. Created in 1991, it contains more than 50,000 pieces of hand cut and shaped coloured glass, contained within two further sheets of toughened glass.

You will also find a chromium-plated and bronze sculpture which marks, appropriately in this building, the history of building techniques. Construction: An Allegory, was completed in 1992 and designed by Vincent Woropay.

There is also a four storey mural, somewhat obviously entitled Symphony Hall Mural, by Deanna Petherbridge, on the wall of Symphony Hall.

The Convention is a wooden sculpture near to Symphony Hall by Richard Perry.

Outside, on the approach to Brindleyplace, two bronze constructions are entitled The Battle of the Gods and Giants by Coventry-born artist Roderick Tye.

Symphony Hall [20]

ICC, Broad Street.
Box Office Tel: 0870 730 0196
www.symphonyhall.co.uk

Standing on the site of the Old Birmingham Music Hall (1856) where Charles Dickens read 'A Christmas Carol' in 1861 and which changed its name to The Prince of Wales Theatre in 1863, Symphony Hall is regarded by many experts as the finest concert hall in the world.

If you visit during the day, and the concert hall is not in use, you may well be able to have a sneak peek. Just standing gives some sense of the acoustics.

Enormous baffles enable Symphony Hall to be tuned, as a musical instrument.

Incredibly, Symphony Hall was constructed immediately above a mainline railway tunnel.

In order to avoid vibration and noise intrusion, the entire auditorium and a significant part of the ICC, effectively floats on rubber bearings. Not only do these provide completely effective sound insulation but Symphony Hall can also settle several centimetres when its 2,200 seats are occupied. Jacks below the hall enable the bearings to be replaced as necessary.

Noise from nearby Broad Street or indeed the Mall has been prevented by inserting a continuous buffer of plastic and rubber between the concert hall and the outside walls.

Brindleyplace [21]

Brindleyplace, has imbued Birmingham with new life, energy and direction. It attracts some 3 million visitors a year. Just looking at the architecture is inspiring with curves and angles, glass and brick –

Symphony Hall and the ICC directly connects with the neighbouring Hyatt Hotel, constructed at the same time. Take a close look at the bridge between the two for much to the embarrassment of those involved, when the bridge was lifted into position one Sunday morning, it was found to be too short. Or rather, more accurately, the hotel had been constructed just a few feet further away from Broad Street than had originally been intended. Rumour has it that nobody told the bridge manufacturers. You can see the join – well disguised though it is – at the Hyatt Hotel end.

Number Three has more than a hint of Moorishness to it and the new blends effortlessly with all the old canal-side buildings.

There are lawns, a fountain display, modern street art and black arches along with a peaceful, Pagoda-style retreat.

In 1995, Brindleyplace became the first UK winner of the International Excellence on the Waterfront Award, ranking it alongside New York, Sydney, Amsterdam and Boston.

Just a few paces away is the peace and tranquillity of Oozells Square. A gently moving stream quietly traverses this Oriental-style square with its benches designed for reflection. Brindleyplace is also home to one of the city's newest works of art: the Future statue. Representing the vision of Birmingham's young professional community, it was commissioned by Birmingham Future. (see page 128)

Ikon Gallery [21]

1 Oozells Square.
Tel (0121) 248 0708. www.ikon-gallery.co.uk

In a wonderful, neo-gothic school building, the Ikon is internationally renowned for the best in contemporary art. Talks, tours, events, bookshop, cafe.

Open: Tues – Sun 11am – 6pm. Closed Mondays exc. Bank Holidays.
Admission Free.

National Sea Life Centre [21]

The Water's Edge
Tel: (0121) 633 4700

Designed by Sir Norman Foster, it is one of the largest inland aquaria in Europe where it's possible to experience life beneath the oceans and seas in all its glory. Just what you'd expect in land-locked Birmingham. Feeding demonstrations, talks and presentations both entertain and educate. The 'discovery trail' is a hit with younger visitors.

Open: Daily 10am – 6pm (last admission 5pm) **Admission: C**

The National Indoor Arena (NIA) ㉒

King Edwards Road
Tel: (0121) 644 6011

The NIA is one of the world's leading athletics and entertainments venues. In March 2003 it was the venue for the largest indoor single sport event staged in the UK, the IAAF World Indoor Championships in Athletics. Over 500 athletes from 140 countries competed. The NIA has seating for 8,000 people.

Open: varies according to events
Admission: varies according to events

Broad Street

It's a lot brasher and louder along modern day Broad Street and up to Five Ways. The new Broad Street is dedicated to entertainment with hotels, places to eat, clubs, bars, a casino and a 12 screen cinema. There are Continental-style cafes with terraces and if you want to view or buy modern art, there are a number of galleries.

Lee Longlands

Broad Street

The first shop was opened by Robert Lee and George Longland in 1902. It attracted wealthy and influential customers from nearby Edgbaston. The current store was opened in 1931. It is made from brick clad with Portland stone. Architect Hurley Robinson submitted plans for a 5th floor but the building has only four, the fifth was curtailed due to World War II.

The Brasshouse

Broad Street
Tel: (0121) 633 3383

The building housed the city's brass factory. In 1781, the price for imported brass was deemed exorbitant and making it seemed the sensible option. Brass production ceased in the mid 19th century. It's now a pub.

Open: Licensing hours.

Reflex (The Crown)

Broad Street
Tel: (0121) 643 0444

Originally The Crown, this 18th century hostelry, opened to ensure travellers on the journey from Birmingham to Five Ways didn't experience deprivation. Water troughs were outside for the horses. It was sold to William Butler who had seen the potential of the location. Five hundred feet below, there was a natural spring, enough to provide him with the 30,000 gallons (113,500Lt) of water a day he needed for the brewery he built on land behind the inn. Now renamed Reflex, it still boasts the original clock tower below which can be seen the old name.

Gas Street Basin

Gas Street

Not the most romantic sounding place until you realise that Gas Street, off busy Broad Street, was the first street in Birmingham to boast gas lighting. The nearby canal basin was, and still is to a large degree, the hub of the canal network. It can be reached from the tow path by Brindleyplace and also from a side entrance in Gas Street itself. Victorian property stands next to 20th and 21st century architecture whilst colourful narrow boats, most privately owned and some providing city centre living, create a picturesque scene.

Broadway Plaza ㉓

Ladywood Middleway
www.broadway-plaza.com

You have to have a pretty good imagination to realise that this latest leisure offering was once, in part, Birmingham Children's Hospital. It features multi-screen cinema, bowling, health and fitness club, restaurants, cafes and you can live there too.

Joseph Sturge statue

Five Ways, Edgbaston

Situated at the front of The Marriott Hotel, Joseph Sturge was a fervent supporter of the anti-slavery movement.

The Mailbox [24]

Suffolk Street Queensway, Royal Mail Street
Tel (0121) 643 4080

Who would think that a Royal Mail postal sorting office would end up as a chic and upmarket shopping venue (with stylish bars, restaurants and cafes too)? Whether you love or hate its architecture, you have to admit that the developers have tried and succeeded in converting a utilitarian building into a remarkable and stunning structure. It is the largest single collection of stand-alone designer stores outside London, like Hugo Boss, Harvey Nichols, Emporio Armani, Jaeger and lots of others too, it also includes a range of eating and drinking places, many of which overlook the canal. Being open at the top it can be chilly on a winter's evening. But don't let that put you off. Even if you don't spend a penny (and you probably will) it's worth a visit. You can also take a look into BBC studios as it's home to BBC Midlands – and the production of the world's longest running radio soap The Archers.

St. Thomas' Peace Garden [25]

Bath Row

St. Thomas' church cost £14,000 to build back in 1829. One evening in December, 1940, the church was hit by a bomb – only the tower remained with the clock stopped at 7.25pm - the time of destruction. The idea of a peace memorial came from local students Dawn Blake, Donna Reynolds and Emma Spence. They worked on the project with artist, Anurhada Patel. St. Thomas' Peace Garden is a place of serenity and tranquillity.

Open: daily from dawn to dusk.
Admission: Free.

Birmingham Hebrew Congregation

Singer's Hill, Ellis Street
Tel: (0121) 643 0884

Built in 1856, this is the oldest Jewish congregation in the city and a Grade II listed building. It is one of the few synagogues in Britain that is recognised as having architectural importance. Interestingly, it was designed by a young gentile, a Scotsman, H. Yeoville Thomason (1826-1901) who favoured Italianate styling. Later in his career he was to design part of the Council House (1874 – 1884). The builder was Samuel Biggs of Bradford Street. There are two projecting wings to form a courtyard in the front and seven long bays with balconies behind. The initial number of seats was increased by 226 in 1937. Inside there are large, ornate chandeliers. Visitors should phone in advance for an appointment. There are civic services in the summer with prayers and readings in English. Men should cover their heads upon entering.

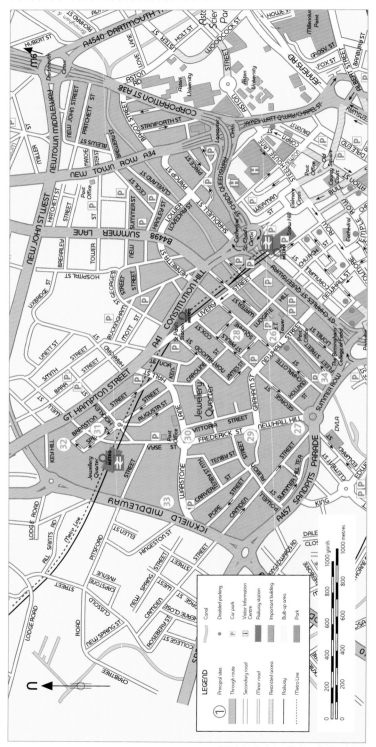

© Marketing Birmingham/Birmingham City Council, 2004

The Jewellery Quarter

Birmingham's Jewellery Quarter is Europe's largest concentration of businesses involved in the jewellery trade – more than 500 at the latest count. It is a fascinating reminder of Birmingham's past and an important part of the present day. Half of all the jewellery made in the UK is created in the quarter that is also home to the world's largest Assay Office in Newhall Street. Dating from 1773 it still hallmarks between 40,000 and 70,000 items of precious metal every day.

The entire quarter has been designated a Conservation Area and includes Birmingham's only remaining Georgian square – St Paul's.

Precious metals have been worked in this area since the 14th century. In the 17th century, local artisans produced trinket boxes called 'Brummagen toys' and in the early 20th century, 30,000 people were employed in the jewellery trade. Many of the buildings are Victorian – built by wealthy gold and silverware manufacturers. More modest houses were occupied by artisans and as the area grew, so the gardens of the larger houses were taken over by workshops. As you walk around consider that many of those working in the quarter also lived there

and that some never left there. It was, to all intent, an enclosed community.

Today, the situation is different. True some live and work there but many more commute as do other city workers. And whilst employment in the quarter is considerably less than 100 years ago, the area in daytime is still a hive of activity; a bustling side of the city that, because of its architecture, alleyways, shops and workshops, can seem a million miles from the extravagances of Victoria Square and the excesses of Broad Street.

Tips for jewellery buyers:

- The JQA sign on a jeweller's door indicates membership of the Jewellery Quarter Association.
- The law requires gold and silver to be hallmarked (the exception is light pieces such as earrings).
- Ask the quality of carat if buying gold.
- Have the quoted weight of any diamonds written on your receipt and, if a gem, the size, colour and shape.

Whilst the Jewellery Quarter is a manufacturing centre, it is also an important retail outlet. There are some establishments that are strictly trade only but most welcome the public and the prices can be less than you'll find in high street outlets.

Next time you watch the changing of the guard at Buckingham Palace, just remember that much of the ceremonial wear is produced in Birmingham's Jewellery Quarter by Firmin & Sons - one of Britain's oldest companies

Most jewellery shops are located in the Vyse Street, Frederick Street and Warstone Lane area. Many individual artists and designers work on-site in the area between Warstone Lane and Vyse Street known as the 'Golden Triangle'.

J. Hudson & Co (Acme Whistles) in Barr Street is the world's largest whistle makers producing over 4 million whistles per year. It still produces whistles on the original equipment used to produce those for SS *Titanic*. The world's first police whistle was made by J. Hudson & Co.

Pavement Trails

Two Pavement Trails, developed by Groundwork Birmingham, provide visitors with an opportunity to take a closer look at some of the Quarter's 'secrets'.

The Finding Trail [26]

Designed by jeweller, Laura Potter, this trail reflects both the historic and contemporary aspects of the area. Thirty stainless steel plaques, based on a design to represent a hallmark tag found in jewellery, contain both information and a touch of humour. Each contains a glass cat's eye – a reflective device – to represent a gemstone set in jewellery. The trail starts at Newhall Street, past the Assay Office, passing close to the Royal Birmingham Society of Artists gallery, along Graham Street returning past the Ramgarhia Sikh Temple and the old Elkington Building where electroplating was invented.

The Charm Bracelet Trail [27]

Artist partnership Renn and Thacker created this trail – which celebrates the area's rich and sometimes unusual history. Taking the form of a giant bronze charm, each set in the pavement, the trail starts at the junction of Sandpits Parade and Newhall Hill and past the Argent Centre in Frederick Street, which once contained a giant Turkish Bath. The Victoria Works once produced 75% of the world's pen nibs, whilst the School of Jewellery, opened in 1890, is still going strong. The trail ends at the Chamberlain Clock.

Birmingham Assay Office [26]

Newhall Street

Established in 1773 this is the world's busiest Assay Office, stamping up to 70,000 pieces of precious metal a day. The Jewellery Quarter wasn't its original location; the city's first

assay office was in The Kings Head Inn in New Street.

The BT Tower

Lionel Street

Standing 498ft (153m) tall behind the Birmingham and Fazeley Canal, The BT Tower is a prominent city

> The anchor is the Birmingham assay mark. When Matthew Boulton was in London, he and his associates from Sheffield would meet in the Crown & Anchor Tavern on The Strand. The symbols for the assay offices in Sheffield and Birmingham became a crown and anchor, respectively.

landmark whose design reflects practical purpose over architectural aesthetics. Now boasting a fresh colour scheme of light pastels and vibrant shades, so as to highlight its corners and balconies, it is illuminated at night. Painting the tower involves more than a simple trip to the DIY store: its latest spruce-up took a team of 18 working for ten weeks and applying more than 2,000 gallons of paint. Most recently it has become Birmingham's weather barometer with the tower being red, amber or green - according to local weather.

In the 19th century Birmingham was the centre of the world's pen trade. The operative part of manufacture was exclusively managed by women who each made more than 18,000 nibs a day and all for a salary of 35p per week!

St Paul's Church 28

St. Pauls Square

Set within Birmingham's last remaining Georgian Square is St Paul's Church. A beautifully restrained church in architectural terms it was designed by Robert Eykyn and inspired by the designs for St. Martin's in the Field in London. The body of the church was built in 1777-9 with the belfry and spire added in 1823. The east window shows Francis Eginton's the 'Conversion of St. Paul'. Those who had pews here include Matthew Boulton, James Watt and the poet Washington Irving.

Open: Monday to Friday noon – 2.30pm.

Royal Birmingham Society of Artists

4 Brook Street
Tel: (0121) 236 4353
www.rbsa.org.uk

One of the oldest art societies in the UK, it was given royal status by Queen Victoria in 1868. The RBSA in St Paul's Square, is the home of several Midland art societies with regular exhibitions of not only members' works but also contemporary exhibitions.

Open: Monday – Wednesday & Friday 10.30am – 5.30pm. Thursday 10am – 7pm, Saturday 10.30am – 5pm.
Admission: Free.

St Paul's Gallery

94 Northwood Street
Tel: (0121) 236 5800

Formerly a carpentry works, this large warehouse-style space is now the largest commercial, contemporary gallery outside London, featuring rising stars in the art world.

Open: Tuesday – Saturday 10am – 6pm. Private views by appointment.
Admission Free.

The Argent Centre 29

Frederick Street

This beautiful example of Lombardic Renaissance style architecture includes two Italianate towers, multi-coloured brickwork and Florentine tracery around the windows. Hollow bricks with wrought iron ties were used to increase the load bearing capacity of the upper floors. It was built in 1863 for gold pen and pencil maker, W. E. Wiley who also used recycled steam to operate a Turkish baths.

The Pen Room 29

Unit 3, The Argent Centre, 60 Frederick Street, Hockley.
Tel (0121) 236 9834.
www.bptha.xoasis.com.

Birmingham helped spread literacy worldwide as world's the centre of pen manufacture for over a century. Demonstrations and displays and classes

in calligraphy, braille and grapho-analysis.

Open: Monday – Saturday 11am – 4pm, Sunday 1pm – 4pm.
Admission: Free.

The Prince of Wales' gates

(gates to the Business Centre) Spencer Street

The permanently opened gates were designed by Michael Johnson and are made from stainless steel, cast brass and glass representing base materials growing into fine jewels. The gates won 1st Prize in the 1992 Birmingham Design Awards.

Whilst in the area take a look at the Plantagenet Buildings, Spencer Street - Italianate-style houses and workshops c.1871.

The Pelican Works, 44-45 Great Hampton Street was previously an electro-plating factory from around 1868. The pelican's still there.

Celluloid was invented by Elkington, a company from Birmingham's Jewellery Quarter

The Chamberlain Clock ㉚
Warstone/Vyse Street

At the heart of the Jewellery Quarter, the clock was originally powered by clockwork and hand-wound but when adapted to run on electricity didn't chime for some time. Intended as a memorial to Joseph Chamberlain in recognition of his services to South Africa it was erected in 1903 and unveiled by his wife in 1904. It fell into disrepair and was restored in 1989, complete with new chiming bell.

Diagonally opposite the clock, Rose Villa Tavern (1919-20) was built in commemoration of Joseph Chamberlain's visit to South Africa in 1903.

Take a peek through the window of 7 Warstone Lane (c.1855) and you might well see a jeweller working.

The grave of John Baskerville is in Warstone Lane Cemetery. Next to the cemetery is the War Stone, a glacial boulder that's a reminder of the last Ice Age.

Spring Hill Library
Icknield Street

Just over the Jewellery Quarter boundary, you will find this Gothic style, red brick and terracotta library designed by architects Martin & Chamberlain.

The Museum of the Jewellery Quarter ㉛
75 – 79 Vyse Street.
Tel: (0121) 554 3598.
www.bmag.org.uk

You can step back in time at this remarkable time capsule of a museum, once a jewellery workshop little changed since 1914, which closed in 1980. It remained undisturbed: the tools left on the benches, the personal belongings collecting dust. The Smith and Pepper works (specialities: bamboo, Nellie Stewart and slave bangles) is now a working museum. The museum provides a fascinating insight into jewellery making from the Middle Ages to the present

Guided tours (around 1hr) include a visit to a jewellery factory with demonstrations and meeting jewellers at work. Tea room, shop selling contemporary Birmingham-made jewellery, exhibitions and events programme.

Open: Easter to end - October, Tues - Sun: 11.30am - 4pm, Saturday: 11am – 4pm. Closed Monday except Bank Holidays
Admission: A

Key Hill Cemetery ㉜

Dating from 1836, this was Birmingham's first cemetery. Joseph Chamberlain is buried here.

In nearby Vyse Street, at number 94, there is a workshop and house from 1860 and, towards the junction with Warstone Lane, a beautifully preserved public urinal, unveiled in 1883. History does not include details of how it was opened but its cast iron panels are believed to have been produced in Glasgow. At 27-29 Warstone Lane there are two decorative, small fac-

tories built between 1860 and 1875.

Birmingham Mint [33]

Icknield Street

The oldest continuously working mint in the world

may or may not be working, as – believe it or not – financial pressures have hit it. Its origins go back to 1794 and were the inspiration of die sinker Ralph Heaton whose descendants created a company which manufactured coins, and machinery which enabled others to make coins. The factory was purpose built in 1860 and since then has minted coins for countries world-wide and to commemorate events and people with medals and tokens.

> Washington Irving's classic *Rip Van Winkle* was written during his stay in the Jewellery Quarter in 1818.

Newman Brothers

13 - 15 Fleet Street

There is no longer a death knell ringing in the last rites on this coffin furniture works – after its purchase by regional development agency Advantage West Midlands and its appearance on the BBC *Restoration* series.

This near-perfectly preserved workshop is planned as a visitor centre illustrating its former use. Amongst others whose coffins have borne its manufactured output are Sir Winston Churchill and Princess Diana.

Birmingham College of Food, Tourism & Creative Studies

Summer Row
Tel: (0121) 604 1010 (restaurant reservations)

Approached through an impressive entrance built in 1997, this is the centre of Birmingham's culinary and hospitality arts. There are three training restaurants open to the public - The Cap & Gown Tavern, The Brasserie and The Atrium – offering fine food for very little outlay. You just have to be aware that the chefs and the waiting staff are students, that sittings are normally a term-time affair and advance booking is advisable.

> In 1780, Samuel Harrison produced one of the first handmade pens for Joseph Priestley, the man who discovered oxygen.

Summerrow [34]

Summer Row

One the edge of the quarter, New York-style Summerrow opened in winter 2002. Sympathetic restoration incorporates the facade of the original buildings with a new roof made from the existing Victorian tiles. The original brickwork was cleaned and repaired. Eating, drinking and delis give the area a New York feel.

Red Palace

Constitution Hill

This proud, terracotta and red brick building was built in 1896 and is a memorial to Lord Roberts of Kandhar – a former commander-in-chief of the British Empire who finally becme commander-in-chief of the British Army (1901-1904). It spent some time as a dye making factory.

Birmingham North-West

Highlights: Soho House, Handsworth Old Town Hall and the beach under Spaghetti Junction (don't make a special trip; you will be disappointed).

Birmingham North-East

Highlights: Aston Hall, nearby Aston Villa (see page 111), Castle Bromwich Hall Gardens, the wildlife of Sutton Park and the nightlife of Star City.

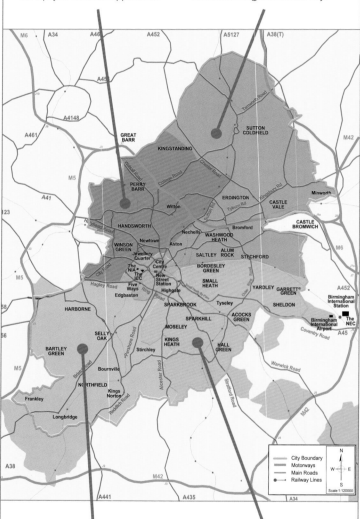

Birmingham South-West

Highlights: Cannon Hill Park, Birmingham Botanical Gardens, Barber Institute of Fine Arts, Bournville, Cadbury World and the Lickey Hills Country Park.

Birmingham South-East

Highlights: Moseley Road Baths, Highbury, JRR Tolkien (Moseley Bog and Sarehole Mill), Blakesley Hall and a ride on the Shakespeare Express.

Birmingham: Beyond the Centre

If it were possible to stand on the top of Perrotts Folly in Edgbaston, to the south-west of the city centre (which provided inspiration for author JRR Tolkien), it is likely that your overriding impression would be the amount of greenery.

It is said that there is at least one tree for every man, woman and child living in the city. Some even claim Birmingham has more trees than Paris (but which sad soul counted them?).

Seeing so much greenery is a useful reminder that Birmingham was once located in the forest and that it today incorporates some long established villages, each one once set in clearings in the woodland, many with their own fine manor houses, churches and village greens.

As Birmingham's industrial might increased so the 19th century saw industrial busi-nesses setting up within the city centre which inevitably resulted in society's more affluent members moving to the suburbs – initially Acocks Green and Moseley and then beyond the then city boundaries to Hagley, Solihull, Knowle and Royal Sutton Coldfield.

With the development of suburban transport, not only people but also factories spread further afield. British car manufacturing, which started in Birmingham in 1895, forever transformed areas such as Longbridge where, in 1905, Herbert Austin set up his own car plant on a two and a half acre site. Today, the name is synonymous with British motor manufacturing and is home to MG Rover.

Bournville is synonymous with chocolate with the Cadbury family establishing a sub-urb based on a humanist's vision.

Kings Norton has a lovely village green. There are two botanical gardens in Edgbaston which in itself is distinctive because of its fine Victorian and Edwardian buildings – and its lack of factories (the land-owning Calthorpe family refused permission for their construction).

In Wylde Green there is a working watermill and in Handsworth the beautifully restored Soho House. In Hall Green can be found Sarehole Mill, a further inspiration for Tolkien's fantasy masterpieces.

For most visitors though, the difficulty is one of logis-tics. One attraction tends to be some distance from the next. If time is limited, the best bet is to concentrate on the area that has the most elements that appeal.

A walk around Edgbaston, perhaps taking in neigh-bouring Harborne and the Botanical Gardens, provides a pleasant excursion as does a stroll in Bournville, including the heady choco-holic delights of Cadbury's World. Or you could com-bine culture with sport by visiting the Jacobean-built Aston Hall with a look at neighbouring Aston Villa Football Club.

Bournville village green

South-West

Edgbaston

A leafy suburb with many fine buildings and numerous attractions. Originally called Celboldstone in the Domesday Book, it's today one of Birmingham's finest addresses. A walk along its Georgian and Victorian side roads is recommended.

Cannon Hill Park

Edgbaston Road, Edgbaston

Cannon Hill Park was the result of a gift from a generous landowner. In 1873 Louisa Anne Ryland gave 57 acres (23ha) of land at Cannon Hill Fields to Birmingham of which 35 acres (14ha) were landscaped into a botanic garden. Two large and several smaller lakes were created. One of the larger pools was for bathing with the other for boating. Ducks, geese and swans were introduced. The project cost £80,000. On a warm Sunday in summer you can meet the people of Birmingham in Cannon Hill Park. There are boating lakes, playgrounds, tennis courts, conservation areas, a cycle route, a bandstand, lots of Canada Geese and an intriguing replica of the reservoirs of the Elan

Valley in Wales, which supplies Birmingham with its water. The park's adjacent to Birmingham Nature Centre and opposite Edgbaston Cricket Ground.

Open Park all year.
Visitor Centre Summer (daily) 10am – 7pm. Winter (weekends only) 10am – 4.30pm.
Admission Free.
How to get there: B4217 (off A441). 2 miles from city centre. Bus: 35 & 45 from city centre.

The Golden Lion

Cannon Hill Park

A half-timbered, Elizabethan house moved from its original site in Deritend to the park in 1911. It is said to be where martyr John Rogers, editor of the first English Bible, taught. No access.

Statue of Sir Robert Peel

(outside) **Police Training College, Pershore Road, Edgbaston**

One of the first works of art by a Birmingham artist (Peter Hollins) and the first bronze statue to be cast in one piece. The over lifesize statue of former prime minister and father of the modern police force, Sir Robert Peel, was unveiled in 1855. It originally stood at the junction of Colmore Row and Congreve Street. In 1871 it was moved to New Street where on

November 11, 1926, it was struck by a lorry.

Birmingham Nature Centre

Pershore Road, Edgbaston
Tel: (0121) 472 7775
www.birmingham.gov.uk/parks

Over 130 species of wildlife – mainly British and European – living in as natural an environment as possible. Wonderful for small children. Cafe. Gift shop.

Open End March to end October, daily 10am – 5pm. November to March, Sat & Sun only 10am – 4pm (Last admission 1 hour before closing).
Admission Child: Free (but must be accompanied by an adult). Adult **A**. Free parking. How to get there: On A441, 2 miles south of city centre. Bus: 45 & 47 from city centre. Disabled access: Most of the site is wheelchair accessible.

Birmingham Botanical Gardens

Westbourne Road, Edgbaston
Tel (0121) 454 1860.
www.birminghambotanicalgardens.org.uk

Home to the National Bonsai Collection and tropical, desert and Mediterranean glasshouses. Adventure play area, a Discovery Garden for children with cafe bar. Exotic birds in indoor and outdoor aviaries. Relax to the sound of music from the bandstand on Sunday afternoons during the summer. This 15 acre (6ha) oasis of calm amidst the frenetic activity of the city has to be on the list of best places to unwind.

Open Daily 9am – 8pm (or dusk if earlier).
Admission Under 5s Free. Weekdays, Adult **B**. How to get there: Buses 10, 21, 22, 23, 29 & 103. Disabled access.

University of Birmingham Botanic Garden at Winterbourne

58 Edgbaston Park Road, Edgbaston
Tel: (0121) 414 5590.
www.botanic.bham.ac.uk

A six-acre (2.4ha) Edwardian garden, home to over 3,000 plants from all parts of the world. There are woodland walks and herb, bog and rock gardens. Many of the garden's original features remain including a 'crinkle crankle' wall.

Open Weekdays only, 11am – 4pm but telephone to confirm as the gardens are closed on bank holidays and at Easter & Christmas.
Admission A.
How to get there Buses 61, 62, 63. Disabled access.

The Oratory

141 Hagley Road, Edgbaston
Tel: (0121) 454 0496
www.birmingham-oratory.org.uk

Baroque style church built in 1907-10 as a memorial to Cardinal Newman, founder of the English Oratory. Classical dome, exterior cloisters, impressive interior.

Open: by arrangement.

University of Birmingham

Off Edgbaston Park Road, Edgbaston
www.bham.co.uk

Mason's College, Chamberlain Tower – a campanile nicknamed Old Joe – and the Great Hall were built 1900-9 and designed by Sir Aston Webb and Ingress Bell. The university is one of England's leading research-based universities with a highly regarded medical school. Vitamin C was discovered at Birmingham and Elgar was its first professor of music. (see page 129)

Barber Institute of Fine Arts

The University of Birmingham, Edgbaston
Tel: (0121) 414 7333.
www.barber.org.uk

One of Europe's finest small galleries, the Barber Institute has been compared with the Frick Collection in New York. Founded in 1932 by Lady Barber in memory of her husband, Sir William Barber, the building was completed in 1938 and contains works by Rubens, Van Dyck and Poussin. Murillo's Marriage at Cana (c1672) is considered one of the Institute's chief glories. British artists include Gainsborough, Reynolds and Turner. French Impressionists are represented by Monet, Degas, Renoir, and Van Gogh.

Open Mon – Sat 10am – 5pm. Sun 12noon – 5pm.
Admission Free.
How to get there: 3 miles SW of city centre, at the East Gate of the University, off Edgbaston Park Road. Bus: 61, 62, 63 from city centre. Train New Street Station, Birmingham to University. Wheelchair access and lift to the galleries.

The constituency of Birmingham Edgbaston is the only seat to have been held continuously by a female Member of Parliament for 50 years. Dame Edith Pitt was elected in 1953, succeeded by Dame Jill Knight in 1966 and then by Gisela Stewart in 1997.

Selly Manor

Maple Road, Bournville
Tel: (0121) 472 0199
www.bvt.org.uk/sellymanor

Dating from the 14th century, Selly Manor is one of Birmingham's oldest buildings. It was saved from demolition and moved here by George Cadbury and contains Cadbury family furniture. The house has links to witches and witch-hunts.

Open: Tues – Fri 10am – 5pm, Sat & Sun (April – Sept) 2pm – 5pm. Bank Hols 2pm – 5pm.
Admission: A
How to get there: by train from New Street to Bournville. Buses 61, 62 & 63 from city centre; change to 11 in Selly Oak.

Lapworth Museum

Birmingham University, Edgbaston
Tel: (0121) 414 7294

One for geologists – a collection of minerals, rocks and fossils including a dinosaur's footprint.

Open: Mon – Fri 9am – 5pm, Sat and Sun 2pm – 5pm.
Admission: Free.
How to get there: On the University campus.

Bournville Carillon

Bournville

The Carillon is a musical instrument – albeit a large one – and rare in the UK. The 48 bell

Bournville Carillon was installed in 1906 by George Cadbury. It requires an energetic playing technique.

Demonstrations can be seen by visitors on Saturdays (exc Jan) at noon and 3pm. Special events throughout the year. Tradition dictates that each carillon recital concludes with the hymn tune 'St Clements'.

Bournville Visitor Centre

Village Green, Bournville

Visits to the carillon can be booked in at the Visitor Centre – also known as The Rest House. The Rest House dates from 1914 and was given to George Cadbury and his wife on the occasion of their Silver Wedding anniversary by the company's employees.

The Serbian Orthodox Church of the Holy Prince Lazar

131 Cob Lane, Bournville
Tel: (0121) 486 1220

Tucked away amidst the trees, behind the Bristol Road, The Serbian Orthodox Church was designed in the mid 1960s by renowned Serbian architect, Dr Dragomir Tadic. It is in the traditional style of the Morova School of the mid 14th century.

Cadbury World

Linden Road, Bournville
Tel: (0121) 451 4180.
www.cadburyworld.co.uk

A must for chocoholics. A great family day out dedicated to the delights of Cadbury's chocolate with lots of tasting opportunities.

Open: Daily March-October; limited at other times. See website for details.
Admission: C
How to get there: Off A38, on A4040 1m S of Selly Oak. Bus from city centre 11A, 11C, 35 or 85 to Bournville. We strongly recommend pre-booking tickets for this attraction as it is incredibly popular.

King's Norton Church, School and Saracen's Head

King's Norton Village
Tel: (0121) 458 3289

The church of St Nicholas dates from the 13th century and the tower from the 15th century. The upper storey of the grammar school is thought to be 15th century with the lower built in the 16th century. It was probably initially a house although records show it was a school in 1549 and it is thought it may once have been on stilts. The Saracen's Head is a striking example of 15th century architecture although there are suggestions of an inn being on the site back in the 11th century. The manor was a portion of the dower of Queen Henrietta Maria, wife of Charles I. The Queen's Room is so named because she stayed at the inn on July 10, 1643 en route to Oxford.

St Laurence Church

Rectory Road, Northfield
Tel: (0121) 475 1518

The chancel of this 13th century church in a secluded location is considered a perfect example of early English architecture. The chancel screen was carved by Thomas Stock in 1881. The north aisle was added in the 19th century.

Weoley Castle Ruins

Alwold Road, Weoley Castle
Tel: (0121) 303 4698

Once the medieval manor of Northfield, now picturesque ruins and an archaeological museum.

Open: Pending major repairs the ruins are open in 'Archaeology Week' and 'Heritage Open Weekend'.

Bell's Farm

Bell's Close, Druids Heath
Tel: (0121) 433 3532

Grade II listed, timber-framed house that has changed little since the 16th and 17th centuries. There was a home here 300 years before then. Primarily an education centre which specialises in training in traditional crafts – weaving, stone-making, calligraphy etc. Opposite the 50 bus terminus off Bell's Lane.

Lickey Hills Country Park

**The Visitor Centre,
Warren Lane, Rednal**
Tel: (0121) 447 7106
www.birmingham.gov.org

A haven for wildlife with strong conservation emphasis, 524 acres (212ha) of woodland and heathland can be explored independently or via guided walks. The bluebells in late spring are beautiful. 18 hole golf course, tennis courts, bowling and putting greens. Tea room. Adventure playground.

Open all year.
Visitor Centre (summer) daily 10am – 7pm (winter) daily 10am – 4.30pm.
Admission: Free.
How to get there: Off A38, 10 miles from city centre. Bus 62 from city to Rednal. Train to Barnt Green Station. (About 1 mile walk to the Visitor Centre from both bus terminal and train station).

South-East

Central Mosque

Belgrave Road,
Tel: (0121) 440 5355

A traditional-style mosque and one of the largest in Europe, holding 200 people. Planning began in 1961 and although the mosque was opened in 1980, it wasn't until 1982 that the impressive central dome was finally placed upon the minaret.

Open: By appointment.

Moseley Road Baths

Moseley Road, Moseley
Tel: (0121) 464 0150

The baths and library became part of Birmingham when Moseley village became a part of the city in 1907. Two figures support the entrance. Signs still show the separate Men's and Women's entrances. Wonderful atmosphere if somewhat jaded now.

Open: Variable but generally 7am-8pm weekdays; Sat: 9am-4.30pm; Sun: 8am-12.30pm.
Admission: A.

St Agatha's Church

Stratford Road, Sparkbrook.
Tel: (0121) 449 2790

A Grade 1 listed building, this neo-Gothic church was completed in 1901, features a wonderful tower and a beautiful interior including an 18th century font.

Open: during service times.

West Midlands Police Museum

Sparkhill Police Station, 639 Stratford Road
Tel: (0121) 626 7181

Displays of police memorabilia from 1839 onwards within a former magistrates' court. Mainly aimed at education groups.

Open: Ring for details.
Admission: B.
How to get there: Bus 2 from city centre to Court Road. On A34, 3 miles from city centre.

Highbury

Tel: (0121) 449 6549

Joseph Chamberlain's former home, Highbury is a lovely brick mansion set in a large garden. Now owned by Birmingham

City Council it is used for entertainment and conferences.

Open: Varied

Kings Heath Park

Vicarage Road, King's Heath
Tel: (0121) 444 2848.
www.birmingham.gov.uk/parks

Fantastic displays of colour. Home to the BBC *Gardeners' World* gardens. Courses and activities available.

Open: All year round.
Admission Free.
How to get there: Off B4122 4m S of city centre.

Birmingham has more parks than any other UK city.

Moseley Bog

Yardley Wood Road, Moseley
Tel: (Moseley Bog Conservation Group) (0121) 777 6570

A local nature reserve, Moseley Bog is delightfully incongruous in the heart of a multi-cultural city suburb. This Bronze Age site was once inhabited, proved by the two ancient 'burnt mounds', heat-shattered stones which were once used for cooking. It has an eerie, ethereal charm. It is easy to see how the lively imagination of a young boy like J.R.R. Tolkien could conjure magical creatures out of the shadows.

Open: Varied.

Moseley Old Dovecote and Icehouse

Alcester Road, Moseley
Entrance by Moseley Hall Hospital
Tel: (0121) 449 2133

An 18th century dovecote that is still in use.

Sarehole Mill

Cole Bank Road, Hall Green
Tel: (0121) 777 6612
www.bmag.org.uk

A working watermill and a childhood haunt of novelist J.R.R. Tolkien. It features in the fantasy stories of *The Lord of the Rings* author. The mill dates from 1542 and used to be for grinding corn. It was converted for metal working in 1775 by Matthew Boulton.

Open April – Oct. Tues – Fri 1pm – 4pm. Sat & Sun 12pm – 4pm. Closed Mondays exc. Bank Holidays (times as weekends).
Admission Free.
How to get there B4146 3m SE of city centre. Bus: 11.

Blakesley Hall

Blakesley Road, Yardley
Tel (0121) 464 2193
www.bmag.org.uk

£2 million was spent in 2002 restoring Blakesley Hall, one of the few remaining timber-framed buildings in Birmingham to its Tudor glory. Visitor centre and tea room.

Open April – October, Tues – Fri 1pm – 4pm, Sat & Sun 12pm – 4pm. Closed Mon (except Bank Holidays).
Admission Free
How to get there: A45 to Yardley, A4040. Bus 96, 97, 11.

The Shakespeare Express

670 Warwick Road, Tyseley
Tel: (0121) 707 4696.
www.vintagetrains.co.uk

Billed as 'England's fastest regular steam train', the Shakespeare Express runs from Birmingham to Stratford-upon-Avon through scenic countryside. A relaxing way to travel, it enables you to also view Shakespeare's Stratford before returning to Birmingham.

Open: Sundays July-October (phone for other times)
Pickup: Birmingham Snow Hill/Tyseley; return from Stratford.
Fare: D

The Sleeping Iron Giant Bordesley Green

Heartlands

This giant head lying on its side can be found close to Birmingham City football ground. It was commissioned to mark the Heartlands boundary. The artist is Ondre Nowakaski.

Birmingham has 6 million trees.

North-West

Soho House

Soho Avenue, Handsworth
Tel: (0121) 554 9122.
www.bmag.org.uk

The former home of industrialist Matthew Boulton. Soho House was a favourite meeting place of the Lunar Society, which comprised some of the greatest minds of the generation including James Watt, Erasmus Darwin and Joseph Priestley. It is said that it got its name after Boulton heard a hunting cry on the heath. Now restored to its original 18th century glory with wonderful Adam fireplaces.

Open Tues – Sat 10am – 5pm. Sun 12pm – 5pm. Closed Mondays exc. Bank Holidays and Oct - April.
Admission to house **A**.
How to get there: Off A41 (Soho Road), 2 miles from the city centre. Bus: 74, 78, 79. Metro: To Benson Road (there is a steep climb to the house).

Handsworth Old Town Hall

College Road/Slack Lane, Handsworth
Tel: (0121) 554 1179.

Built in 1460, this is one of the finest examples of early 'cruck' timber frame construction.

Admission: Free
Open: First Tuesday, every month 6.30pm-8.30pm.

William Murdock who worked for Boulton & Watt in Handsworth invented gas lighting and his cottage was the first to be lit by gas back in 1798.

Spaghetti Junction

Don't, whatever you do, walk out to take a look, unless you are a motorway junction fanatic, but it would be wrong to exclude this landmark which was the UK's first free-flow traffic interchange that had neither traffic lights nor roundabouts. An amazing engineering feat, Gravelly Hill Interchange, to give it its proper name, includes 2.5 miles (4Km) of slip roads and spans two rivers, three canals and a railway line. It is in the Guinness Book of World Records as the most complex interchange on the British road system. A group of performance

Spaghetti Junction is elevated for 3.5 miles (5.6Km), it is supported by 559 columns and covers a site of 30 acres. To cover every road on the junction adhering to the *Highway Code* would involve a 73 mile trip.

artists stage occasional events here on ground underneath the motorway. In 1972, around 40,000 cars per day used Spaghetti Junction; today it is more than 140,000. It took four years to complete, cost £10.8 million and carries around five million tonnes of freight every week. Since 1972, an estimated 1.25 billion vehicles have passed through. Oh, and there is a beach overlooking the canal.

North-East

Aston Hall

Trinity Road, Aston
Tel: (0121) 327 0062.
www.bmag.org.uk

An impressive Jacobean mansion built 1618 – 35 by Sir Thomas Holte. There is a main section with two projecting wings and an enclosed courtyard. Highlights inside include a cantilevered staircase, impressive fireplaces and 17th century plasterwork. The Christmas 'candlelight' tours are fun with period music and atmospheric lighting.

Open April-October, Tuesday to Sunday 11.30am-4pm. (Closed Mondays except Bank Holidays).
Admission Free
How to get there: 3m N city centre, off J6, M6 on B4137. Bus 65, 104, 7, 11, 653.

Aston Manor Road Transport Museum

208-216 Witton Lane, Aston
Tel: (0121) 322 2298.
www.amrtm.org

A museum of restored commercial vehicles including lorries, trams, buses and vans.

Open: Weekends & Bank Holiday Mondays
Admission; A
How to get there: Bus 11, 7, opposite Aston Villa.

Aston Parish Church

(St Peter & St Paul's), Aston Hall Road
Tel: (0121) 327 3880
www.astonparishchurch.org.uk

Cathedral sized, Gothic church with Tudor tower.

Admission: Free.
How to get there: Train to Aston or Witton stations. Bus (from the city centre) 65, 104, 7, 653 or Outer Circle, No.11.

Castle Bromwich Hall Gardens

Chester Road, Castle Bromwich
Tel: (0121) 749 4100.
www.cbhgt.swinternet.co.uk

A hidden gem. Lovely 18th century walled gardens with holly maze and parterre.

Open: April – October, Tues – Thurs 1.30pm – 4.30pm. Sat, Sun & Bank Holidays 2pm – 6pm.
Admission: B
How to get there: Off B4114, 1m from J5, M6. Bus 59A, 590, 92, 693.

New Hall Mill

Off Wylde Green Road, Sutton Coldfield
Tel: (0121) 355 3268
www.newhallmill.org.uk

A restored grade II listed working watermill. Flour produced from locally grown wheat on open days.

Miller's Garden. Tea room.
Open: May – Sept, 2nd Sunday in the month, 10am – 4pm.
Admission: Free

Sutton Park – National Nature Reserve

Park Road, Sutton Coldfield
Tel: (0121) 355 6370
www.birmingham.gov.uk/parks

Sutton Park is Europe's largest urban nature

reserve. It's also the largest of Birmingham's many open spaces with 2,400 acres of woodlands, wetlands, heaths and seven lakes. Wild Exmoor ponies roam free, children's playground, 18 hole golf course, cafes, restaurants and Visitor Centre.

Open all year round. Visitor centre April – Sept. 10am – 7pm. Oct – March 10am – 4.30pm.
Admission Free.
Parking: Pay & Display charge from Easter – Sept. (Sun & BHs) £1. Free disabled parking. Disabled access and toilets.
How to get there: 6m north of the city. Bus 107. Train to Sutton Coldfield railway station (approx. 10 min walk to park).

Star City

Off Lichfied Road; Junction 6, M6
Tel: 08708 446600
www.starcitym6j6.com

Easily visible from the motorway, with its fluorescent lighting and brash colours, this all-year-round venue features restaurants, bowling alley, entertainment centre, casino and the largest multiplex cinema in the UK.

Open all year round.

Further Afield

Birmingham is at the heart of the West Midlands region which includes some of the country's most visited tourist attractions.

Royal Shakespeare Theatre

The area is one of enormous variety, from the hills of the Malverns, which so inspired composer Edward Elgar, to the industry of the Black Country and Wolverhampton, to the tourist magnets of Stratford-upon-Avon and Warwick.

This variety is one of the attractions of the area. It is not dramatic but includes scenes that are quintessentially English: a fine castle in Warwick, boating on the Avon, glass blowing in Stourbridge and acre after acre of gently undulating farmland to the east.

The area's abundance of natural resources was instrumental in creating its prosperity coupled with the industriousness of its people along with their entrepreneurial attitude and adaptability.

The handing down of skills from generation to generation has provided the region with an important sense of continuity.

Black Country Living Museum

The Black Country Living Museum in Dudley and the Iron Gorge Museums give a remarkable insight into how the UK's industrial heartland led not only Britain but the world into a new age. The skills of glass-making, leather-working, brewing, carpet manufacture, to name but a few, are all still highly visible.

But it's not all about industry. Some 80% of the West Midlands' land area is classed as rural and the region has 11 National Nature Reserves.

There are some beautiful stately homes – Packwood House and Baddesley Clinton in Warwickshire, Lord Lichfield's seat at Shugborough and Wightwick Manor, an arts and crafts house in Wolverhampton. There's the excavated Roman town at Wall outside Lichfield and the magnificent castles of Warwick and Kenilworth. The cathedrals of Lichfield, Coventry, Worcester and Hereford are all remarkable for their architecture, memorials, history and atmosphere.

Stratford-upon-Avon is best known as the birthplace of William Shakespeare. Indeed, without the Bard the town would be no more significant than many other river crossings and market towns. A 45 minutes drive or train ride (from either Birmingham Snow Hill or Moor Street stations) it includes attractive riverside walks, large park, a brass rubbing centre and a butterfly farm, too. It's also home to the Royal Shakespeare Company and Royal Shakespeare Theatre plus, of course, Shakespeare's birthplace. Sadly, it's also home to the less attractive aspects of tourism: the place can be heaving at summer weekends and at holidays and a smell of fish and chips and burger bars can pervade the air.

The region offers much by way of open spaces, a new National Forest to the north-east of Birmingham is being created transforming what was once a mix of industrial mining and agricultural land; Cannock Chase offers excellent walking country whilst the Cotswolds, to the south of the area, contains sleepy villages, the smell of log burning fires and the warmth of some fine country pubs.

There's the beautiful Biddulph Grange Gardens in Stoke-on-Trent, Walsall Arboretum, the fine landscapes of country homes such as Coughton and the county towns of Warwick, Hereford and Evesham.

We have split the region into four. It is impossible to list all the attractions of the area but these should give you a flavour of a region that is so close to the commercial might of Birmingham but so often, feels hundreds of miles away.

National Forest: New Lount nature reserve

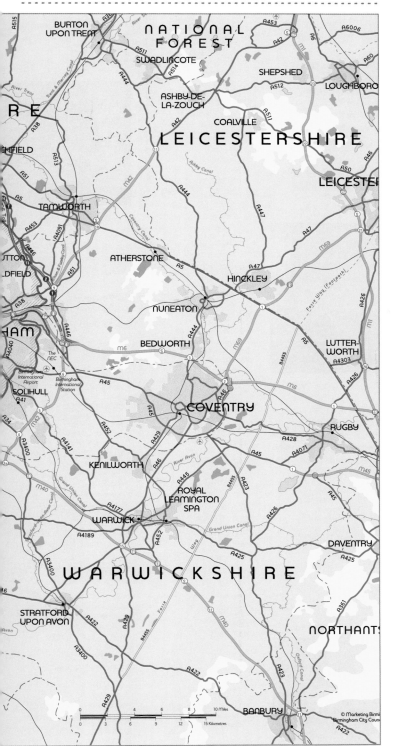

North-west of Birmingham:

(Black Country, Walsall, Wolverhampton, western Staffordshire and Shropshire)

The New Art Gallery, Walsall

Gallery Square, Walsall
Tel: (01922) 654400
www.artatwalsall.org.uk

Works by Manet, Epstein, Van Gogh, Picasso and Modigliani are featured in this striking new £21 million gallery. Children's discovery gallery, exhibitions, cafe, shop and rooftop restaurant.

Open: Tues-Sat 10am-5pm, Sun 12pm-5pm. Closed Mondays (exc. Bank Holidays).
Admission: Free.
How to get there: Walsall Town Centre. Train: To Walsall Station from Birmingham New Street followed by 10 min walk.

Walsall Leather Museum

Littleton Street, Walsall
Tel (01922) 721153
www.walsall.gov.com (follow links)

SPRATT'S MOTORING GOGGLES

With the rise of the motor car, Walsall saddlery firms had to adapt to a changing world or disappear. Some diversified into products they believed would be well suited to the new motoring generation.

Walsall is the heart of England's leather industry producing everything from wallets to saddles. Current customers include top high street retailers and international show-jumpers. The museum is in a former leathergoods factory dating from 1891.

Open: Tues – Sat 10am – 5pm (Nov – March 10am – 4pm), Sun 12pm – 4pm. (Apr – Oct 10am – 5pm) Open BH Mondays.
Admission: Free.
How to get there: 5 mins walk from Walsall Town Centre and bus and train stations.

Walsall Arboretum

Walsall
Tel: (01922) 653183 (bookings)
www.walsall-lights.com

Walsall Arboretum boasts more than 80 acres (32ha) of parks, lakes and gardens. Since 1951 the arboretum has been illuminated every September-November; now, over 25,000 lights create a magical, ethereal atmosphere to rival the displays of Blackpool. A busy, popular event attracting entire families.

Open: Sept – Oct. (dates vary).
Admission: Varied according to whether tickets bought in advance or on the door.
How to get there: Car: follow AA signposts. J/A461 (Lichfield St) & A 4148 (Broadway North). Park & Ride. Disabled parking opp. cash gate entrance. Train: To Walsall Station from Birmingham New Street followed by 10 min walk.

Wightwick Manor

Wightwick Bank, Wolverhampton
Tel: (01902) 761108

A rare example of a house built and furnished under the influence of the Arts and Crafts Movement. Original William Morris wallpaper and fabrics, Pre-Raphaelite paintings, Kempe glass and attractive gardens.

Open: March to December, Thursday and Saturday and Bank Holiday weekends, 2.30pm-5.30pm. Gardens 11am-6pm on Wednesday, Thursday; 1pm-5.30pm Saturday and Bank Holidays.
Admission: B
How to get there: Train: Wolverhampton; bus to the Mermaid Inn, then walk 100yds.

Wolverhampton Art Gallery

Lichfield Street, Wolverhampton
Tel: (01902) 552055
www.wolverhampton.org.uk

Said to hold one of the finest collections of contemporary art in the Midlands including Pop Art by Andy Warhol.

Open: Mon – Sat 10am- 5pm.
Admission: Free.
How to get there: city centre.

Black Country Living Museum

Tipton Road, Dudley
Tel: (0121) 557 9643
www.bclm.co.uk

You can wallow in nostalgia and stand in awe of industrial revolution working practices at this recreation of a Black Country village. Complete with bakers, ironmongers and pub, the Black Country of old's all brought vividly to life by costumed guides. Try the street games - hula-hoop or walk on stilts, admire the skill of the chain maker, 'leg' down the canal, experience the claustrophobia of being down a mine and the strict regime of a day in a Victorian school. A full day out for adults and children.

Open: March – Oct, daily 10am – 5pm. Nov – Feb, Wed – Sun 10am – 4pm.
Admission: C
How to get there: On A4037, Tipton Road. 3 miles from J2/M5. Train: Birmingham New Street to Tipton Station.

Crooked House Pub

Coppice Mill, Himley, Nr Dudley
Tel: (01384) 238 583

The pub where you can see a marble rolling uphill – before you've even had a drink! The optical illusions are due to the subsidence as a result of mining. Its real name is The Glynne Arms but it's known locally as the Crooked House for obvious reasons!

Open: during licensing hours.

Dudley Zoo & Castle

2 The Broadway Dudley
Tel: (01384) 215313
www.dudleyzoo.org.uk

First mentioned in the Domesday Book, Dudley Castle was once the feudal stronghold of the Earls of Dudley. It was partly demolished in the English Civil War. The price of the breathtaking views over the Black Country is difficulty for visitors with mobility problems although wheelchairs can be used.

Open: Winter daily 10am – 3pm. Summer daily 10am – 4pm.
Admission: C.
How to get there: On A461 (Castle Hill), 3m from J2/M5. Dudley bus station is 2 minutes walk.

Dudley Museum & Art Gallery

St James's Road, Dudley
Tel: (01384) 815575
www.dudley.gov.uk

Within walking distance of the town centre, there is a permanent display in the Geological gallery and changing exhibitions.

Open: Mon-Sat 10am – 4pm (contact direct for closure days).
Admission: free.
How to get there: Railway Station at Dudley Port then No. 7 bus to Dudley Bus Station (short walk).

Himley Hall & Park

Himley, Dudley
Tel: (01902) 326665
www.dudley.gov.uk

This 18th century, Grade II listed building is set in Capability Brown landscaped grounds. It was the home of the Earl of Dudley and used as a royal honeymoon retreat in the 1930s. During the WW2, the south wing of the hall became a Red Cross hospital.

Open: April – Sept 2 – 5pm daily except Mon.
Admission: free.
How to get there: B4176 Dudley to Himley Road where it joins the A449. Train: Dudley or Wolverhampton main railway stations.

Broadfield House Glass Museum

Compton drive, Kingswinford
Tel: (01384) 812745
www.dudley.gov.uk

Renowned collection of British glass from the 17th century with emphasis on the local glass industry.

Open: Tues – Sun 10am – 4pm.
Admission: Free.
How to get there: Train: B'ham New Street to Wolverhampton, bus to Kingswinford.

The Black Country

It is said that Queen Victoria asked for the blinds of her railway carriage to be closed whilst passing through the Black Country. Evidently the site of factories, iron workings and coal extraction offended her eyes. Whether true or not, the story is a reminder of how The Black Country got its name – and what it was once like. Far from being a vast sprawl of urban hinterland, The Black Country – which stretches in an arc to the north-west of Birmingham and includes Walsall, Sandwell (including West Bromwich), Dudley, Stourbridge and Wolverhampton, is, in fact, a number of tightly knit communities. Each of these developed their own specialisms: Walsall for the leather industry, Stourbridge for glass, Willenhall for locks, and so on.

Royal Air Force Museum

Cosford, Shifnal
Tel: (01902) 376 200.
www.rafmuseum.org

See a Spitfire, Hurricane, Vulcan and British Airways' airliner collection along with missiles and aero-engines at RAF Cosford. Call for details of the annual Air Show.

Open: Daily 10am – 6pm (closed Dec 24 and Jan 1).
Admission: Free.
How to get there: A41, 1 mile south of J3/M54.

Dudmaston Hall

Quatt, Nr Bridgnorth
Tel: (01746) 780 866.

A late 17th century house with old masters and more contemporary works of art. The gardens are particularly pretty. Lake and woodland walks. Special events including theatre productions.

Open: Sun, Tues and Wed 2pm – 5pm. Mon gardens only noon – 6pm.
Admission: B.
How to get there: A442 Nr Bridgnorth.

Weston Park

Weston-under-Lizard, Nr. Shifnal, Shropshire
Tel: (01952) 852 100
www.weston-park.com

Ancestral seat of the Earls of Bradford, the house gave novelist PG Wodehouse his inspiration for Blandings Castle. Parkland designed by Capability Brown.

Open: Easter – June Sat & Sun, July – August daily.
Admission: A.
How to get there: A5, 3 miles from J3/M54, 8 miles from J12/M6.

Ironbridge Gorge Museums

Ironbridge, Telford, Shropshire
Tel: (01952) 432 166
www.ironbridge.org.uk

Designated a World Heritage site, this was once the heart of the Industrial Revolution. There are ten museums and monuments including the amazing Iron Bridge, cast in 1779 by Abraham Darby III, a Victorian town (change your money for tokens to spend in the shops) and a tar tunnel (you'll need to wear a hard hat for this underground tour). Shops, restaurants and cafes

Open: Daily 10am – 5pm (some museums close Nov – March). Closed Dec 24 – 26 & Jan 1.
Admission: D (The Passport ticket covers all museums and is cheaper than buying individual tickets.)
How to get there: Close to J4/M54, 40 miles from Birmingham. Train: Telford Central railway station is 4 miles.

Enginuity

Ironbridge
Tel: Tickets (0800) 590 258

The UK's first design and technology attraction cost £7 million. It opened in 2002 in a 150 year old, Grade II listed building. Hands-on and interactive, it aims to inspire and stimulate young minds, encouraging them to be the engineers and designers of the future. Come and levitate thanks to a hi-tech magnetic carpet.

Open: Daily 10-5pm
Admission: B
How to get there: Junction 4 from M54; signs to Ironbridge.

Wenlock Priory

The Bullring, Much Wenlock.
Tel: (01952) 727 466
www.english-heritage.org.uk

A free audio tour gives an insight into this once prosperous, Cluniac monastery with the

remains of an early 13th century church and Norman chapter house. Lovely gardens with topiary and rare lavatorium. Very atmospheric.

Open: April – Oct daily 10am – 6pm, Nov – March Wed – Sun 10am – 4pm. (Closed 24 – 26 Dec and 1pm – 2pm during winter).
Admission: B.
How to get there: Much Wenlock centre, in The Bullring, behind the Church.

Wroxeter Roman City

Wroxeter.
Tel: (01743) 761 330

Get an insight into what life would have been like in the fourth largest city in Roman Britain around 2,000 years ago. The site includes the remains of a large bath-house.

Open: April–Oct daily 10am – 6pm (or dusk if earlier). Nov–March daily 10am – 4pm, 1pm–2pm during Winter (closed 24–26 Dec and 1st Jan).
Admission: B.
How to get there: Wroxeter, 5 miles E of Shrewsbury on B4380 to Iron Bridge.

Attingham Park

Shrewsbury
Tel: (01743) 708 162
www.nationaltrust.org.uk

An elegant, 18th century mansion set in landscaped grounds with river walks and deer park.

Open: House 21 March – 2 Nov 1pm – 4.30pm except Wed; Deer Park March – Oct 9am – 8pm, Nov – Feb 9am – 5pm.
Admission: B.
How to get there: 5m SE of Shrewsbury on N side of B4350 in Attingham village.

Stokesay Castle

Stokesay, Nr Craven Arms
Tel: (01588) 676000
www.english-heritage.org.uk

A beautifully preserved, fortified 13th century manor house. The house and gardens are little changed from 1291. Moat walk, audio tours, and tea room.

Open: April – Sep daily 10am – 6pm. Oct daily 10am – 5pm, Nov – Mar Wed – Sun 10am – 4pm. Closed 1pm – 2pm during the winter. (Closed Dec 25, 26, Jan 1).
Admission: B.
How to get there: Ludlow Road, Craven Arms (A49). Nearest train station, Craven Arms 1m.

Secret Hills The Shropshire Hills Discovery Centre

Craven Arms
Tel: (01588) 676 040 www.shropshire-cc.gov.uk/discover.nsf

The grass-roofed building is a gateway into the Shropshire Hills bringing nature and archaeology to life with simulated hot air balloon rides and a giant mammoth.

Open: Daily from 10am; last admission 4.30pm April-November, 3.30pm November-March
Admission: B
How to get there: Off A49 between Craven Arms and Ludlow.

Shugborough

Milford, Nr Stafford
Tel: (01889) 881 388
www.shugborough.org.uk

Home of Lord Lichfield. Lovely parkland. Events include falconry displays and craft fairs.

Open: March – Sept 11am – 5pm. Closed Mon.
Admission: A.
How to get there: Signposted from J13 of M6.

North-East of Birmingham:

(eastern Staffordshire, Leicestershire and north Warwickshire)

Roman City of Wall

Watling Street, Wall, Nr Lichfield
Tel: (01543) 480 768

Originally the Roman staging post of Letocetum on Watling Street, the road linking Kent with North Wales. Foundations of an inn and a bath-house. Museum of artefacts. Audio tour.

Open: April 1 – Oct 31 daily 10am – 6pm. Closed 1pm - 2pm
Admission: A.
How to get there: Off A5 at Wall, near Lichfield. Train: Nearest station Shenstone (1.5 miles).

Samuel Johnson Birthplace Museum

Breadmarket Street, Lichfield
Tel (01543) 264 972
www.lichfield.gov.uk/sjmuseum

The house in which he was a born is a museum to one of Britain's greatest writers and thinkers.

Open: April – Sept 10.30am – 4.30pm, Oct – Jan, March noon – 4.30pm.
Admission: A.
How to get there:Lichfield city centre

Lichfield Cathedral

The Close, Lichfield
Tel: (01543) 306 240
www.lichfield-cathedral.org

The only English medieval cathedral with three spires. Fascinating history and treasures from the 8th century onwards. The Cathedral Close is thought to be one of the finest in the country.

Open: daily 7.30am – 6.30pm.
Admission: B
How to get there: Lichfield city centre

Tamworth Castle

The Holloway, Ladybank, Tamworth
Tel: (01827) 709 626
www.tamworth.gov.uk

A Norman castle reputedly haunted. Dungeons, a chance to take brass rubbings, quizzes and clothes to try on.

Open: Tues– Sun noon - 4.30pm.
Admission: B.
How to get there: Tamworth town centre.

Polesworth Abbey & St Editha Church

Polesworth
Tel: (01827) 892 340
www.polesworthabbey.co.uk

Now in ruins, the abbey was founded by Editha, Princess of Mercia in the 9th century. The abbey church later became the Parish Church of St Editha. The nave dates from the 12th century.

Open: Abbey church open daily 8.30am for morning prayer and 6pm evening prayer
Admission: Free
How to get there: Near M42, J10

Pooley Fields Heritage Centre

Pooley Lane, Polesworth
Tel: (01827) 897 438 www.warwickshire.gov.uk/countryside

Heritage centre, nature reserve, and children's play area on a former colliery site utilising wind and solar generated electricity. Its tea room overlooks the Coventry canal.

Open: Easter – Sept Thurs – Mon 10am – 6pm, Oct – Easter Sat and Sun 10am – 4pm.
Admission: free.
How to get there: Off B5000 Tamworth to Atherstone Road. Polesworth Train: 5 minutes walk from station.

Hoar Park Craft Centre

Nr Ansley
Tel: (024) 7639 4433.
www.hoar-park.co.uk

This 17th century farm building has been converted into a craft and antiques village, set in 143 acres (58ha). There is a children's farm and garden centre.

Open: Tues - Sun 10am – 5pm (open Bank Holiday Mondays).
Admission: free but charge for farm.
How to get there: On B4114 between Nuneaton & Coleshill

The National Forest

Leicestershire, Staffordshire, Derbyshire
Tel: (01283) 551 211
www.nationalforest.org

Don't expect endless vistas of woodland and dappled glades – for The National Forest is, at least at present, a forest in the making.

It is a vast undertaking: transforming 200 square miles (518sqKm) spanning three counties into mixed forestry, agricultural land and local communities.

The remarkable aspect of this place is that it is happening at all: with the support of government (and all three main political parties), it is enabling landowners to make alternative uses of land, encouraging entrepreneurs to take advantage of the new-found tourists and local people to appreciate the landscape of the past - and the future.

Far from taking a passive role, visitors to The National Forest are encouraged to plant and adopt trees and become involved in what is the country's future heritage in the making. There are walks aplenty, cycle trails

and attractions ranging from a ski toboggan run at Swadlincote to a time-warp stately home at Calke Abbey. Then there's the hands-on Conkers: a visitor centre dedicated to all things timber where it is possible to have fun and learn indoors and out.

Open: All year round.
How to get there: Well signed from M42/M1/A38

Conkers

Moira, Swadlincote, Derbyshire
Tel: (01283) 216 633
www.visitconkers.com

A hands-on (and they encourage visitors to touch) discovery centre with woodland fun and facts for all the family. Different zones enable visitors to understand the life and energy of forests

whilst shops specialise in wooden crafts and even wattle fencing.

Open: daily 10am - 5pm (Last admission 4pm).
Admission: B
How to get there: M42/J11; near junction of A444/B5003

National Memorial Arboretum

Croxall Road, Alrewas, Burton upon Trent
Tel: (01283) 792 333 www. nationalmemorialarboretum.co.uk

Created as a tribute to the people of the 20th century with various specific gardens.

Open: daily 10am - 5pm or dusk if earlier. Phone for Winter opening times.
Admission: Free.
How to get there: Signposted from A38 & A513.

Bass Museum

Horninglow Street, Burton-upon-Trent
Tel: (0845) 600 0598
www.bass-museum.com

History of beer and brewing with England's oldest Micro-brewery and Coors' famous Shire horse team. Back a few generations, the brewery draymen who worked with the horses were also the town's firemen.

Open: daily 10am – 5pm.
Admission: B.
How to get there: A4564/A38.

South-West of Birmingham:

(Worcestershire, Herefordshire)

The Red House Glass Cone

Wordsley, Stourbridge
Tel: (01384) 812750
www.redhousecone.co.uk

The Red House Glass Cone is in the heart of Stourbridge's Glass Quarter – which, for 400 years, has produced some of the world's finest cut glass. Built around 1790, the Cone was used for the manufacture of glass until 1936 and is now one of only four left in the UK. The site has remained virtually unaltered and

provides a fascinating insight into the history and tradition of glassmaking.

Open: April-October: 10am- 5pm; November -March (closed 25/26 December & 1 January): 10 am- 4pm
Admission: A
How to get there: 10 miles from M5 Junction 2 or Junction 4. Near Stourbridge town centre A491. Rail stations at Wolverhampton and Stourbridge Town, bus route 256

Broadfield House Glass Museum

Compton drive, Kingswinford
Tel: (01384) 812745
www.dudley.gov.uk

Renowned collection of British glass from the 17th century with emphasis on the local glass industry.

Open: Tues – Sun 10am – 4pm.
Admission: Free.
How to get there: Train: B'ham New Street to Wolverhampton, bus to Kingswinford.

Birmingham and Midland Museum of Transport

Chapel Lane, Wythall
Tel: (01564) 826 471
www.bammot.org.uk

Commercial vehicles, fire engines, battery electric milk floats, buses and coaches.

Open: Sat and Sun Easter – last Sun in Oct.
Admission: B
How to get there: Off A435 between the Maypole and Becketts Farm.

Forge Mill Needle Museum & Bordesley Abbey Visitor Centre

Needle Mill Lane, Riverside, Redditch
Tel: (01527) 62509
www.redditchbc.gov.uk

At the heart of the country's needle making industry, an insight into what life was like,

complete with working water wheel, machinery, audio visual display. Archaeological museum.

Open: Feb – Easter & Oct – Nov: Mon-Thurs 11am – 4pm, Sun 2pm – 5pm; Easter to Sept Mon – Fri 11am – 4.30pm, Sat and Sun 2pm – 5pm.
Admission: B.
How to get there: J2 of M42, off A441 on North side of Redditch.

Arrow Valley Country Park

Batten's Drive, Redditch
Tel: (01527) 464 000

Brand new lakeside visitor centre set in 900 acres (364ha) of parkland. Events and activities, cafe, shop, play area, picnic places.

Open: Daily 10am - 4pm (Nov - March); 10am - 5pm (March - Oct).
Admission: free.
How to get there: Off Coventry Highway.

Hagley Hall

Hagley, Worcestershire
Tel: (01562) 882 408
www.hagleyhall.info

This fine Palladian house was built by Lord Lyttleton between 1754 and 1760. It boasts exquisite Italian rococo plasterwork and a collection of furniture and paintings. An Ionic temple, rotunda and fake gothic ruins can be found in the grounds.

Open: 2pm-5pm.
Admission: B
How to get there: Off J3/M5.

Severn Valley Railway

The Railway Station, Bewdley
Tel: (01299) 403 816
www.svr.co.uk

Relive the glory days of steam engines with a day out on the Severn Valley Railway. 16 miles of rural England from Bridgnorth to Kidderminster through Hampton Loade, a lovely riverside village, Highley and Arley – both beautiful country stations. Special event days include Santa Steam Specials in December. There is a dining service on selected departures.

Open: Sat and Sun Oct - April, May – Sept open every day.
Admission: D.
How to get there: Ample parking at Kidderminster and Bridgnorth stations. Limited parking at other stations. Kidderminster station is adjacent to the mainline station. Disabled passengers in particular are advised to book in advance.

Stone House Cottage Gardens

Stone, Kidderminster
Tel: (01562) 69902
www.shcn.co.uk

Over 3,000 species of plants in a small, walled garden.

Open: March – Sept Wed – Sat 10am – 5.30pm.
Admission: A.
How to get there: Off the A448, behind Stone church.

Harvington Hall

Harvington, Nr Kidderminster
Tel: (01562) 777846
www.harvingtonhall.org.uk

Medieval and Elizabethan moated manor house with the finest series of priests' hiding places in the country. Restored herb garden and chapel.

Open: Mar & Oct, Sat & Sun. April- Sept, Wed-Sun
Admission: B
How to get there: 3 miles east of Kidderminster

Avoncroft Museum of Historic Buildings

Stoke Heath, Bromsgrove
Tel: (01527) 831 886
www.avoncroft.org.uk

An open air museum of buildings including a working windmill. Fascinating.

Open: March – Nov daily 10.30am – 4pm. April – June, Sept & Oct 10.30am – 4.30pm (weekdays)/ 5pm (weekends).
Admission: B.
How to get there: Off A38, S Bromsgrove. Bus: hourly from Bromsgrove town centre.

Hanbury Hall

School Road, Droitwich
Tel: (01527) 821 214
www.nationaltrust.org.uk

William and Mary style house with antiques, fine art and porcelain. Recently recreated Victorian parterre.

Open: House Sun – Wed 1pm – 5pm, Sat 11.30am – 3.30pm; Garden Sun – Wed noon – 5.30pm, Sat 11am – 4pm.
Admission: B.
How to get there: Signposted from J5 of M5.

Worcester Cathedral

Worcester
Tel: (01905) 28854
www.cofe-worcester.org.uk

Worcester Cathedral stands on the banks of the River Severn, England's longest river. It holds the Royal tombs of King John and Prince Arthur – Henry VIII's elder brother. As well as medieval cloisters, a Norman crypt and Victorian stained glass, take time to climb to the top of the tower for the magnificent views of the surrounding countryside.

Open: daily 7.30am – 6.30pm.
Admission: voluntary.
How to get there: Worcester City Centre

Worcestershire County Museum

**Hartlebury Castle,
Hartlebury, Kidderminster**
Tel: (01299) 250 416
www.worcestershire.gov.uk

Restored cider mill, costumes, gypsy caravans, examples of local crafts, housed in the north wing of the Bishop's Palace.

Open: Feb – Nov, Mon – Thurs 10am -5pm, Fri & Sun 2pm – 5pm, bank hols 11am – 5pm.
Admission: A.
How to get there: J6 M5, 4 miles S of Kidderminster on the A449 to Worcester.

The Commandery

Sidbury, Worcester
Tel: (01905) 361 821
www.worcestercitymuseums.org.uk

Worcester was both the starting and finishing points for the English Civil war. The 16th century, timber-framed Commandery sits on the banks of the canal and houses room settings and exhibitions focusing on the Civil War and the Battle of Worcester.

Open: Mon-Sat 10-5pm. Sun 1.30-5pm.
Admission: B
How to get there: Worcester city centre.

The Elgar Birthplace Museum

Crown East Lane, Lower Broadheath, Worcester
Tel: (01905) 333 224
www.elgar.org

The composer's birthplace and new Elgar Centre. Memorabilia, special events.

Open: daily 11am – 5pm. Closed 23 Dec – 19 Jan. **Admission: B.**
How to get there: 3 miles W of Worcester.

Witley Court

Great Witley, Worcestershire
Tel: (01299) 896 636
www.english-heritage.org.uk

Early Jacobean mansion damaged by fire and now in ruins but not devoid of atmosphere. Using the audio tour, hear how an extravagant former owner hung jewels on the Christmas tree as gifts for lady guests. Wonderful grounds for a picnic on a sunny day. Impressive fountain featuring Perseus and Andromeda. One of the finest baroque churches with remarkable decoration. Tea room.

Open: April – Sept 10am – 6pm. Oct 10am – 5pm. Nov & Dec, Wed – Sun 10am – 4pm.
Admission: B.
How to get there: A443, 10 miles NW Worcester. Train: Droitwich Spa station 9 miles.

Burford Gardens

Tenbury Wells
Tel: (01584) 810 777
www.burford.co.uk

Home to the National Clematis Collection – the garden has over 350 varieties.

Open: All year.
Admission: B.
How to get there: 8 miles south of Ludlow.

Hereford Cathedral

**5 College Cloisters,
Cathedral Close, Hereford**
Tel: (01432) 374 202
www.herefordcathedral.co.uk

A wonderful example of some of the finest architecture from Norman times to the present. There's the restored Shrine of St Thomas of Hereford, the Early English Lady Chapel, the old Chained Library and the new library, completed in 1996 to hold the Mappa Mundi, the oldest complete world map in existence.

Open: Summer: Mon-Sat 10-4.15pm, Sun 11-3.15pm. Winter: Mon-Sat 11-3.15pm, Sun closed.
Admission: B
How to get there: Hereford city centre.

Hampton Court Gardens

Hope under Dinmore, Leominster
Tel: (01568) 797 777
www.hamptoncourt.org.uk

Recently completed gardens in the grounds of a fortified medieval manor house. Walled gardens, canal, pavilions, a maze with a secret tunnel, a waterfall in a sunken garden. River and woodland walks.

Open: April – Oct, Tues – Sun, Bank Hol Mons 11am – 5pm.
Admission: B.
How to get there: Off A417, nr A49 between Hereford and Leominster.

South-East of Birmingham

(Solihull, Stratford-upon-Avon, Warwick & Warwickshire, The Cotswolds)

National Motorcycle Museum

Coventry Road, Bickenhill, Solihull
Tel (01675) 44 33 11
www.nationalmotorcyclemuseum.co.uk

Tragedy befell this remarkable museum when, in 2003, it was ravaged by fire destroying many priceless exhibits. It is being restored and the collection being rebuilt.

Open: From Dec 1, 2004
Admission: Telephone for details
How to get there: On A45. J6/M42.

Baddesley Clinton

Rising Lane, Baddesley Clinton, Knowle, Solihull
Tel (01564) 783 294
www.nationaltrust.org.uk

A romantic, moated manor house dating from the 15th Century. Little has changed since 1634. Regaling children with tales of persecuted priests (there are priest-holes) will keep them interested.

Open: March – Nov, Wed – Sun, from 1.30pm.
Admission: C.
How to get there: 6m S of J5/M42. 15 miles SE Birmingham off A4141 Warwick-Birmingham road.

Packwood House

Lapworth, Solihull
Tel: (01564) 783 294
www.nationaltrust.org.uk

A small 16th Century house created by Graham Baron Ash. Famous for its yew trees which represent the Sermon on the Mount.

Open: March – Nov, Wed – Sun, noon – 4.30pm.
Admission: B (Discounted tickets for Baddesley Clinton and Packwood combined).
How to get there: 2 miles E of Hockley Heath off A3400, 11 miles SE of Birmingham.

COVENTRY

Coventry Cathedral

Priory Row, Coventry
Tel: (024) 7622 7597
www.coventrycathedral.org

The charred ruins of the blitzed 14th century cathedral are next to Sir Basil Spence's spectacular new cathedral. Graham Sutherland's tapestry of Christ dominates the altar and Jacob Epstein's remarkable *St Michael defeating the Devil*.

Open: Easter – Oct 8.30am – 6pm, Nov – Easter 8.30am – 5.30pm.
Admission: A.
How to get there: Coventry city centre. Train from New St, Birmingham or Birmingham International.

The Doom Paintings

at The Holy Trinity Church, Priory Row
Tel: (024) 7622 0418
www.holytrinitycoventry.org.uk

Located near the cathedral, this fine church contains a rare medieval fresco, discovered by accident after a fire in 1986 burnt away a layer of whitewash. Now cleaned and restored, a spectacular work of art depicting Christ passing judgement has been revealed. It is thought to relate to an earthquake in Coventry in 1426 leading to the belief that the end of the world was nigh.

Open: daily 9.30am - 3.30pm.
Admission: Free
How to get there: as Coventry Cathedral

Coventry Transport Museum

Millennium Place, Hales Street, Coventry
Tel: (024) 7683 2425
www.transprt-museum.com

Coventry was home to some of Britain's best known car manufacturers and is still a major manufacturing centre. More than 200 cars and commercial vehicles, 200 cycles and 90 motorcycles make this the largest collection of British transport in the world.

Open: Daily 10am – 5pm. (Closed Dec 24 – 26).
Admission: Free
How to get there: Coventry city centre.

Coventry Clock

Broadgate

Next to the cathedral quarter, the clock is a tribute to Lady Godiva, Coventry's most famous celebrated citizen. She's famous for her protest against her husband's crippling tax policy by riding naked through the streets of the city in support of the ordinary people of Coventry. Every half hour can be seen the legendary Lady and Peeping Tom (the only person to see her protest parade).

Kenilworth Castle

Kenilworth
Tel: (01926) 852 078
www.english-heritage.org.uk

The largest castle ruins in England. Henry V rested here after his army's victory at the Battle of Agincourt. Elizabeth I was greeted by nymphs on a floating island when she visited in 1575, establishing Kenilworth as one of the finest Tudor palaces. There's a romantic, red glow on warm summer evenings because of the castle's sandstone walls. Tearoom, audio tour. Nearby is St. Nicholas' Church with its elaborately decorated doorway.

Open: Jan – March 10am – 4pm, April – Sept 10am – 6pm, Oct 10am – 5pm, Nov & Dec 10am – 4pm.
Admission: B.
How to get there: Kenilworth town centre, off A46. Train: Nearest station Warwick (5 miles). Disabled entrance to the north of the castle.

Ragley Hall

Alcester, Warwickshire
Tel: (01789) 762 090
www.ragleyhall.com

The seat of the Marquis of Hertford, Ragley was built in 1680. The house has some fine works of art, magnificent baroque plaster work and a 20th century mural, *The Temptation*. There are 400 acres (157ha) of parkland, designed by Capability Brown, a maze, lake and an adventure playground.

Open: April - Sep.
Admission: C.
How to get there: Off A435/A46

Coughton Court

Nr. Alcester
Tel: (01789) 400 777
www.coughtoncourt.co.uk

A fine Tudor house and the home of the Throckmorton family since 1409. Once shielded by huge elm trees, now you get a panoramic view of the house from the A435. A Catholic family, the Throckmortons - and the property - have suffered from their beliefs. There are strong connections with the infamous Gunpowder Plot of 1605 and in 1688, part of Coughton was destroyed by a fire-raging mob. Formal walled garden, two churches, a lake and a riverside walk.

Open: Mid March – Oct, Low season weekends only. 11.30am – 5pm.
Admission: C.
How to get there: 2 miles N Alcester on A435.

STRATFORD-UPON-AVON.

The Shakespeare Houses

Tel: (01789) 204 016
www.shakespeare.org.uk

Five houses in and around Stratford, all linked to the world's most famous playwright; Anne Hathaway's Cottage was his wife's home before they married, Mary Arden's house was his mother's farmhouse cottage, built c.1514 and a working farm until the 1960s. Shakespeare's birthplace is in the centre

Holy Trinity

of town and has been recreated in authentic 16th century style, Nash's House was owned by Thomas Nash, the first husband of Shakespeare's grand-daughter Elizabeth Hall, and adjoining it is New Place Garden, the site of the house where Shakespeare died. Hall's Croft is the grandest of the Shakespeare Houses. It dates from c.1614 and is where his eldest daughter, Susanna lived with her husband, Dr John Hall.

Open: daily, times vary.
Admission: D.
How to get there: Stratford town centre.

Royal Shakespeare Theatre

Waterside, Stratford-upon-Avon
Tel (info): (01789) 403 404
Tel (ticket hotline): 0870 609 1110
www.rsc.org.uk

The Royal Shakespeare Theatre and the neighbouring Swan theatre are home to the Royal Shakespeare Company, the world's largest classical theatre company. Regular productions of Shakespeare and contemporary drama. Guided tours.

Open: Daily.
How to get there: Town centre, J15/M40. Train: From Birmingham Snow Hill & Moor St stations.

The Royal Shakespeare Company perform more plays to more people than any other theatre company in the world.

The Teddy Bear Museum

19 Greenhill Street, Stratford upon Avon.
Tel: (01789) 293 160.
www.theteddybearmuseum.com

In an Elizabethan house, there are hundreds of bears some of them old and some of them famous.

Open: Daily 9.30am – 5.30pm.
Admission: A.
How to get there: Stratford town centre.

Harvard House and the Museum of British Pewter

High Street, Stratford upon Avon.
Tel: (01789) 204 016.
www.shakespeare.org.uk

Built in 1596, it is a magnificent example of an Elizabethan town house. It was the home of Katherine Rogers, the mother of John Harvard whose bequest founded Harvard University. Examples of British pewter over 2,000 years. Interactive area for children.

Open: May-Sept
Admission: B
How to get there: Stratford town centre.

Boating on the River

Swan's Nest Boat House, Swan's Nest Lane, Stratford-upon-Avon
Tel: (01789) 267 073
www.avon-boating.co.uk

30 minute river trips daily between April and October leaving from the Bancroft Gardens by the RSC Theatre or you can row yourself.

Open: daily 9am – dusk.
Admission: B – D.
How to get there: Stratford town centre.

Holy Trinity Church

Old Town, Stratford-upon-Avon

Shakespeare's final resting place, this peaceful honey-stoned church dates from the 13th century. Surrounded by yews and weeping willows, overlooking the river, it is a tranquil place away from the town centre crowds.

Butterfly Farm

Tramway Walk, Swan's Nest Lane
Tel: (01789) 299 288
www.butterflyfarm.co.uk

Hundreds of the most beautiful, colourful butterflies in Europe's largest butterfly farm. A section devoted to creepy-crawlies including deadly spiders and scorpions.

Open: Summer 10am – 6pm, Winter 10am – dusk.
Admission: B.
How to get there: On the south bank of the river by the park.

The Falstaff's Experience

Sheep Street
Tel: (01789) 298 070
www.falstaffsexperience.co.uk

A theatrical glimpse at the ghostly and ghastly goings on in old Stratford.

Open: daily 10.30am – 5.30pm.
Admission: B.
How to get there: Stratford town centre.

Brass Rubbing Centre

Avonbank Gardens, Stratford-upon-Avon
Tel: (01789) 297 671
www.stratford
brassrubbing.co.uk

Great fun for children and adults. Easy and rewarding. With over 200 brasses including medieval, Celtic and modern ones.

Open: Summer, daily 10am – 6pm; Nov – Feb, Sat & Sun only, 11am – 4pm.
Admission: A.
How to get there: In the gardens between the theatre and the Holy Trinity Church.

Jephson Gardens
Royal Leamington Spa

Recently restored gardens include a glasshouse for exotic plants, a sensory garden and a nectar garden for bees and butterflies. Tea room and restaurant.

Open: Daily.
Admission: free.
How to get there: Opposite the Royal Pump Rooms.

Charlecote Park
Warwick
Tel: (01789) 470 277.
www.nationaltrust.org.uk

Shakespeare was caught poaching deer here – or so the story goes. A majestic house, Charlecote's mellow, Tudor exterior belies an early Victorian interior. The deer park was landscaped by Capability Brown. Licensed Orangery restaurant, shop.

Open: March – Oct, Fri – Tues, House: noon – 5pm. Grounds: 11am – 6pm.
Admission: C.
How to get there: 5 miles E Stratford-upon-Avon.
Train: 5 miles from Stratford train station on Birmingham Moor Street & Snow Hill line.

Warwick Castle
Warwick
Tel: (0870) 442 2000
www.warwick-castle.co.uk

A magnificent, medieval castle with so much to see. In 'Kingmaker', experience the preparations for Richard Neville, Earl of Warwick's final battle in 1471. Spy on Daisy, Countess of Warwick at one of her spectacular dinner parties with her rich and famous guests. There's an armoury display, dungeons and torture chamber, towers and ramparts and a ghost tower. Medieval times are brought vividly to life. Victorian rose garden and Peacock Garden, mill and engine house. Special summer events and medieval banquets.

Open: April – Sept 10am – 6pm. Nov – March 10am – 5pm.
Admission: D
How to get there: 2 miles from J15/M40.

The Master's Garden
Lord Leycester Hospital, High Street Warwick
Tel: (01926) 491 422

An historic walled garden behind medieval timber-framed buildings.

Open: March – Sept (check dates) Tues – Sun and Bank Hols 10am – 4.30pm.
Admission: A.
How to get there: Warwick town centre.

Lord Leycester Hospital

Hatton Country World

Dark Lane, Hatton, Warwick
Tel (01926) 843411

Hatton Country World consists of a free to enter shopping village (majoring on arts and crafts) and Hatton Farm with its traditional farmyard animals and a Guinea Pig Village, based on local Warwickshire beauty spots and home to no less than 300 guinea pigs!

Open: Open daily 10 – 5pm; (27 Dec – 1 Jan incl. 11 – 4pm). Closed Christmas & Boxing Days.
Admission: Farm: B
How to get there: Train: Hatton/Warwick Parkway (then walk/taxi). Car: off A4144.

Arbury Hall

Arbury, Nuneaton
Tel: (024) 7638 2804

The home of the Newdegate family for over 400 years. In the 18th century, this beautiful Elizabethan house became the finest example of Gothic revival in England. The novelist George Eliot was born on the estate. Art, furniture, porcelain. Gardens.

Open: Easter – Sept 2pm – 5.30pm.
Admission: C.
How to get there: Junction 3 off M6 follow A444 to Nuneaton.

Heritage Motor Centre

Banbury Road, Gaydon, Warwick
Tel: (01926) 641 188
www.heritage-motor-centre.co.uk

The world's largest collection of historic, British cars with demonstrations of off-roading and go-cart track. Mesmerises enthusiasts regardless of age.

Open: daily 10am – 5pm.
Admission: C.
How to get there: Signposted from J12/M40.

Upton House

Banbury
Tel: (01295) 670 266
www.nationaltrust.org.uk

This National Trust house contains a wonderful collection of English and European old masters. The house was formerly owned by the 2nd Viscount Bearsted, Chairman of Shell, and has a fascinating collection of the company's commercial art between 1921 and 1946. The gardens include a lovely 1930s' water garden and the National Collection of Asters (that's Michaelmas daisies to the uninitiated).

Open: April – Oct, Sat – Wed, 1pm – 5pm.
Admission: C.
How to get there: Signposted from J12/M40. On the A422, 7 miles NW of Banbury, 12 miles SE of Stratford-upon-Avon.

Helpful Contacts:

Stratford Tourist Information Centre
Tel: (01789) 293 127

Leamington Tourist Information Centre
Tel: (01926) 742 762
www.shakespeare-country.co.uk

Stratford-upon-Avon and District Hotels and Caterers Association:
www.stratford-shortbreaks.co.uk

City Sightseeing/ Guide Friday.
Tel: (01789) 294 466.
www.city-sightseeing.com

Upton House

If you like...

Shopping

The opening of the Bullring finally placed Birmingham as one of Europe's great shopping cities. Not that the Bullring is all there is. Far from it. Birmingham has everything a shopaholic needs or wants and within easy reach.

It's a bustling, busy city. The shopping areas are well contained along or radiating from New Street, High Street and Corporation Street. There are lots of arcades and small malls whilst the main market area is the other side of the Rotunda in the city's Eastside sector.

With much of the area either traffic-free or allowing only limited access to buses and delivery vehicles, walking around is, on the whole, relaxing.

The Great Western Arcade is a quaint shopping arcade that is over 125 years old. Mailbox provides for the chic end of the market with Caxtongate and City Plaza offering designer labels.

On a more realistic note, like all cities there are rogue elements. Take care of your personal possessions, don't leave bags undone or unattended and avoid putting wallets in pockets as with any city there are some proficient pick-pockets about.

Central Quarter

SHOPPING CENTRES/MALLS

Caxtongate
Cannon Street/New Street

Central Quarters fashion district with 21 designer shops including Legends, Ted Baker, Jigsaw and the Orange Studio brasserie.

City Plaza
47 Cannon Street

Glass domed shopping centre just off New Street.

Martineau Place
Corporation Street/Bull Street

Some 30 stores, cafes and restaurants beneath a canopy of sails.

The Great Western Arcade
Colmore Row

A delightful, covered shopping arcade dating from 1875. (See page 21)

The Burlington Arcade
New Street

Newly refurbished and restyled with a handful of specialist boutiques. (See page 21)

The Pallasades
above New Street Station

High street names including Woolworths, Argos and Boots.

The Pavilion Central
38 High Street

Brand name stores and lots of places to eat and drink. Right in the heart of the city's shopping heart.

Priory Square
2, Priory Walk, Dale End

A selection of shops and an open market.

Oasis Market
112-114 Corporation Street
Tel: (0121) 233 4488

Hardly your mainstream shopping centre, but for the past three decades those seeking an alternative lifestyle and individuality have made this their shopping home. Cult clothing, candles, jewellery, posters and piercing studio.

DEPARTMENT STORES

House of Fraser
Corporation Street
Tel: (0121) 236 3333

Formerly Rackhams, this is Birmingham's longest-standing, exclusive, department store. In 1861, retail drapers Wilkinson & Riddell, who were at 78 Bull Street, took on two new sales assistants - John Rackham and William Matthews. They took over and extended the shop into Temple Row, renaming it Rackhams. When Corporation Street was built in 1898, Rackhams was extended into the North Western Arcade. Harrods bought it in 1955, along with the land on which it stands. The current store opened in November, 1960 and has since been extensively re-modelled.

Beatties
Corporation Street
Tel: (0121) 644 4000

The only home grown department store – James Beattie founded the business in nearby Wolverhampton in 1877, with just £300 capital. The Birmingham store, opened in 2001, provides fashions, housewares and cosmetics.

MARKETS

Priory Market
Priory Square
Tel: (0121) 236 5303

Mainly clothes and household goods.

Open: Mon-Sat: 9am – 6pm

Farmers' Markets
New Street/Victoria Square
Tel: (0121) 303 5449

Birmingham Farmers' Markets sell home and locally grown produce.

Open: First and third Wednesday of every month 10am – 6pm.

Eastside

SHOPPING CENTRES/MALLS

Bullring

Birmingham's pride and joy, this wonderfully designed centre claims to be Europe's biggest enclosed city centre complex. 140 shops, cafes and restaurants, together with works of art and uplifting views of St Martin's Church, make this one of Birmingham's great success stories (See page 26-28).

The Custard Factory
Gibb Street

Not so much a shopping centre as an arts complex. You will find designer jewellery and glass, arts, crafts and fashion and even clothes for boarders and bikers. (See page 30).

The Arcadian Centre
Hurst Street

As much restaurants and entertainment as shopping but being at the heart of Birmingham's Chinese Quarter, there are plenty of traditional Chinese stores with herbal remedies, specialist travel and even an estate agent specialising in Chinese takeaway outlets (See page 34).

DEPARTMENT STORES

Selfridges
Upper Mall East, Bullring
Tel: (0870) 837 7377

The Armadillo is just one of the names applied to the curvaceous, 185,000 sq ft (17,186sqm) Selfridges store. (See page 27)

Debenhams
Bullring
Tel: (0121) 622 8000

The first of Debenhams' '2010' flagship stores to be built in Britain. (See page 27)

MARKETS

Bull Ring

The new markets complex houses five retail markets – the Rag Market, the Indoor Market, St Martin's Market, Irish Market and Farmers' Market.

There has been a market at the Bull Ring since 1154 when it was the city's village green and the place where stall holders and barrowboys, 'quack' doctors and pedlars all plied their wares.

However, the idea of it being a pleasant, open-air forum is erroneous. By the 16th century it was a claustrophobic street market that was dirty and noisy.

It was also the site of two medieval fairs: There was the June or Pleasure Fair and the Michaelmas or Onion Fair – a six day festival with rides and menageries. Unfortunately, it was all too risqué for Victorian society and the fairs were stopped in 1875.

Although the fairs were banned, traders and stall holders along with soap box orators maintained the area's reputation as a centre for bargains and entertainment right up to World War Two.

The new Bull Ring may not have the 'quack' doctors but the unique atmosphere generated by independent, free-spirited traders will be there to be enjoyed by the estimated 20 million customers who visit every year.

Indoor Market

Edgbaston Street, Birmingham
Tel: (0121) 622 0203

Nearly 100 stalls trading in clothing, linens, confectionery, meat, poultry, fruit, vegetables and carpets and much more. Fishmongers sell sea, fresh water, shellfish and exotic fish.

Open: Monday – Saturday 9am – 5.30pm.

The Open Market

Edgbaston Street, Birmingham
Tel: (0121) 303 0300

More than 150 covered stalls sell a wide variety of food produce from every continent as well as dairy produce, plants, shrubs and fancy goods.

Open: Tuesday, Friday & Saturday 9am – 4.30pm.

St Martin's Market

Edgbaston Street, Birmingham
Tel: (0121) 303 0300

At the heart of the Bull Ring Markets. 400 varied stalls and a vibrant, cheerful atmosphere from crafts, jewellery, fabrics, china, household goods to clothing new, old and designer wear all under one roof.

Open: Tuesday, Friday and Saturday 9am – 4.30pm.

Birmingham Flower Market

Pershore Street

Full of colour and fragrance. The market opens at 4am on Mon and Thurs. The only time to appreciate the full, floral glory is mid-summer (See page 35)

Antique Fair

St Martin's Market, Edgbaston Street
Tel: (0121) 303 0300

Morning markets are held from 7.30am and afternoon from 4.00pm, most months from June – December inclusive. Telephone for further details.

Convention Quarter

SHOPPING CENTRES/MALLS

The Mailbox

Wharfside Street

A stylish multi-use 1.5million sq ft (140,000 sq m) building with 13 restaurants, two hotels, 200 luxury apartments, 40 exclusive designer shops including Emporio Armani, Hugo Boss, DKNY, Harvey Nichols and many more. (See page 43)

Brindleyplace

Technically not a shopping centre at all but containing a few useful food, pharmacy and newsagency-type shops (handy for conventioneers at the ICC) and a few specialist art and gift galleries (handy for lovers of art and those same conventioneers looking for something unusual to take home).

DEPARTMENT STORES

Harvey Nichols

The Mailbox
Tel: (0121) 616 6000

One of the world's most famous stores, with cos-

metics, shoes, fashions and a great selection of fine food and wine. Plus, the must have accessory: a Harvey Nichols' shopping bag.

CHRISTMAS IN BIRMINGHAM

Great efforts have been made in recent years to attract (even) more people to Birmingham during the run-up to Christmas. Shops stay open later and pre-Christmas Sunday shopping becomes the norm.

The Christmas lights are switched on in mid-November with activities for families and Christmas shoppers. (Tel: (0121) 767 4141 for information.)

The largest authentic German Christmas market outside Germany or Austria, with traders from Birmingham's twin city of Frankfurt, occupies Victoria Square and New Street. The farmers' market in New Street, on Wednesdays, normally becomes weekly during December.

Most of the theatres also put on special Christmas entertainment. The Rep., Centenary Square, has established an excellent reputation for its traditional and inspiring Christmas productions whilst the Hippodrome, Hurst Street, turns to traditional panto.

Birmingham Cathedral also holds a number of carol services. Symphony Hall normally has a series of seasonal productions, including those specifically for children.

Frankfurt Christmas Market

Tel: (0121) 303 1991
Third week in November – Christmas, 10am – 8pm

Jewellery Quarter

Rings, necklaces, bracelets and watches can all be found here. Have something made to your own, individual design by craftsmen in this unique area. Workshops will also undertake repairs. (See pages 44 - 49)

MARKETS

Antique Markets

Regent Street/Vittoria Street
Tel: (0121) 605 7000

Antique markets are occasionally held at Regent Street/Vittoria Street.

Specialist Stores

ALTERNATIVE MEDICINES

Dr and Herbs

Great Western Arcade
Tel: (0121) 236 8882

Traditional Chinese herbal medicines and internet links to Chinese doctors.

Birmingham Centre for Chinese Medicine

245 Alcester Road South, Kings Heath,
Tel: (0121) 441 2757

Acupuncture, herbal medicine, massage, manipulation, breathing and movement exercises, and dietary advice

ARTS AND COLLECTIBLES, PAINTINGS, SCULPTURE AND FRAMING

The Artlounge

The Mailbox
Tel: (0121) 685 2555

Contemporary paintings and sculpture

Temple Gallery

Great Western Arcade
Tel: (0121) 643 9099

Number 9 the Gallery

9 Brindleyplace
Tel: (0121) 643 9099

Highly original and friendly service.

The Halcyon Gallery

International Convention Centre, Broad Street
Tel: (0121) 248 8484

Original and limited editions

New Gallery

St Pauls Square
Tel: (0121) 2330800

Contemporary art

City Art Galleries

Frederick Street
Tel: (0121) 212 1218

Affordable original art

BOOKS

Books Etc

Star City
Tel: (0121) 328 2763

Mainstream

Borders Books and Music Limited

The Bullring
Tel: (0121) 616 1094

Mainstream

Bonds Book Shop

High Street, Harborne
Tel: (0121) 427 9343

Independent and friendly

Midlands Arts Centre Bookshop

Cannon Hill Park
Tel: (0121) 440 6722

Arts and travel a speciality and open daily 8am - 7pm (6.30pm Sunday)

Nostalgia and Comics

14-16 Smallbrook Queensway
Tel: (0121) 643 0143

What it says on the shop front

Ottakar's

75 The Parade Sutton Coldfield
Tel: (0121) 321 2333

Mainstream

Waterstone's

24 High Street
Tel: (0121) 633 4353

128 New Street
Tel: (0121) 631 4333

Both mainstream in fine surroundings

CHOCOLATES

Choucoute

Great Western Arcade
Tel: (0121) 233 1300

Chocolate fantasies

COOKERY AND HOMEWARE

The AGA Shop

The Mailbox
Tel: (0121) 632 1311

Stylish and traditional

Descamps

The Mailbox
Tel: (0121) 643 0542

French style

Domus Optima

The Mailbox
Tel: (0121) 632 1446

Furniture and lighting

The Iron Bed Company

The Mailbox
Tel: (0121) 643 5514

Traditional and modern

Table Works

The Mailbox
Tel: (0121) 632 1277

Sophisticated individuality

Lee Longlands

Broad Street
Tel: (0121) 643 9101

Fine furnishings on a fine scale

FASHION: UNISEX

A2

9 Ethel Street
Tel: (0121) 643 3989

Cool gear

Cult Clothing

25 Temple Street
Tel: (0121) 643 1051

Underground wear

Diesel

8-9 Lower Temple Street
Tel: (0121) 632 5575

Well engineered

Nicholl's

1 Temple Row
Tel: (0121) 687 5557

Designer labels

Yo Yo

7 Ethel Street
Tel: (0121) 633 3073

Retro fittings

Cerruti

The Mailbox
Tel: (0121) 687 2233

Italian flair

Crew Clothing
The Mailbox
Tel: (0121) 632 1313

Sports inspired

DKNY
The Mailbox
Tel: (0121) 600 7200

US for you

Emporio Armani
The Mailbox
Tel: (0121)632 1150

Relaxed style

Polo Ralph Lauren
The Mailbox
Tel: (0121) 616 5915

Preppy wear

FASHION: WOMEN'S

Coast
(Just off New Street)
Tel: (0121) 643 8066

Dress sense

Eda
**Unit 10 Lower Wharfside
Street, The Mailbox**
Tel: (0121) 632 1220

Upmarket underwear

Hobbs
Cannon Street
Tel: (0121) 643 6263

Smart Fashions

Hugo Boss
The Mailbox
Tel: (0121) 632 6012

Classic to contemporary

Iceberg
The Mailbox
Tel: (0121) 632 1288

Streetwise

Jaeger Womenswear
The Mailbox
Tel: (0121) 633 4381

The original designer label
for women

Jesire
The Mailbox
Tel: (0121) 643 4700

Retro clothing for all ages

Nitya
The Mailbox
Tel: (0121) 643 3880

Eastern-inspired

FASHION: MEN'S

Autograph
15/17 Ethel Street
Tel: (0121) 633 3540

Men sign here for design-
er gear

Life
36 Stephenson Street
Tel: (0121) 633 0792

Small store but perfectly
formed fashion

Limeys
14 Stephenson Street
Tel: (0121) 633 0792

Casually smart

Love
Stephenson Street
Tel: (0121) 643 2624

Birmingham original

Messori
The Mailbox
Tel: (0121) 687 1111

Italian sophisticated

Reiss
32 New Street
Tel: (0121) 632 6961

Own-brand fashions

Slater Menswear
Caxton Gate, Canon Street
Tel: (0121) 633 3855

Remarkable value and
helpful staff

Gieves & Hawkes
The Mailbox
Tel: (0121) 632 5295

Saville Row comes to
Birmingham

Jaeger Menswear
The Mailbox
Tel: (0121) 643 1462

The original designer label
for men

Thomas Pink
The Mailbox
Tel: (0121) 632 1301

Shirts. And more shirts

FASHION:
CHILDREN'S

Scallywags
Great Western Arcade
Tel: (0121) 236 7153

Upmarket wear

Baby Bratz
Great Western Arcade
Tel: (0121) 212 1854

The Pavilions
Tel: (0121) 643 7555

Stylish

FLORISTS

Ethos Urban
Six, Brindleyplace
Tel: (0121) 616 6182

Edmund Street
Tel: (0121) 200 0601

Flowers and original gifts

Petals of Piccadilly
17 Piccadilly Arcade, New St.
Tel: (0121) 643 2468

Long established but still
fresh

Water Garden
ICC, Broad Street
Tel: (0121) 644 6022

Creative arrangements

GIFTS

Zen

4 The Waters Edge, Brindleyplace
Tel: (0121) 643 3933

Unusual and original

Parchment

The Mailbox
Tel: (0121) 632 1100

Greetings cards and paper

Blaze

Great Western Arcade
Tel: (0121) 233 0289

The Pen Shop

Great Western Arcade
Tel: (0121) 236 8089

Writing aids

Vom Fass

Great Western Arcade
Tel: (0121) 233 1933

Liqueurs, whiskies and olive oils, all bottled to order and personalised too

HAIR

Obsession Salon & Spa

The Mailbox
Tel: (0121) 665 4600

Hair salon and day spa

Toni & Guy Essensuals

The Mailbox
Tel: (0121) 643 3311

Contemporary styling and colours

JEWELLERY

The Jewellery Quarter

(See pages 44 - 49)

Too many to mention: Britain's highest concentration of jewellery retailers and manufacturers

Faye

The Mailbox
Tel: (0121) 632 1456

Celeb-style jewellery

Diane Cross

Great Western Arcade
Tel: (0121) 236 3857

MAPS

The Stationery Office

68-69 Bull Street
Tel: (0121) 236 9696 (Books)
Tel: (0121) 236 7017 (Maps)

Maps galore and books too. Travel a speciality

MOVIES/VIDEO

Cinephilia

Woodbridge Road, Moseley
Tel: (0121) 449 6000

Arguably the best video/DVD store

New Street Ramp

MUSIC: RARE AND NOT SO RARE

Dance Music Finder

2nd Floor, Smithfield House, Moat Lane, Digbeth
Tel: (0121) 622 5885

Current and past dance music

Depot Records

9 Piccadilly Arcade, New Street
Tel: (0121) 643 6045

Merchandise equipment and records too

Hard to Find Records

10 Upper Gough Street
Tel: (0121) 687 7773

What it says on the shop front

HMV

**Pavilion Central
38 High Street**
Tel: (0121) 643 2177

CDs, videos, computer games and more

Reddington Rare Records

Smithfield House, Digbeth
Tel: (0121) 622 7050

Vinyl and CDs

Swordfish Records

14 Temple Street
Tel: (0121) 633 4859

Vinyl and CDs

Tempest Records

83 Bull Street
Tel: (0121) 236 9170

Garage and deephouse

Tower Records

5 Corporation Street
Tel: (0121) 616 2677

CDs, videos, computer games and more

Virgin Megastore

98 Corporation Street
Tel: (0121) 236 2523

CDs, videos, computer games and more

OUTDOOR PURSUITS

Fat Face

The Mailbox
Tel: (0121) 632 1310

Activities in the extreme

Snow and Rock

14 Priory Queensway
Tel: 0845 1001012

Gear that is not for the faint hearted

SHOES

Sims Footwear

Great Western Arcade
Tel: (0121) 643 4456

Best foot forward

Left®

Great Western Arcade
Tel: (0121) 236 8322

Laser measured/hand-made

Shelly's

41 Corporation Street
Tel: (0121) 633 7432

Extensive selections

Belle Scarpe

The Mailbox
Tel: (0121) 632 1177

Italian for feet

Tim Little

The Mailbox
Tel: (0121) 632 1421

Adventurous shoe design for men

The Anatomical Boot & Shoe Co.

25 Colmore Row
Tel: (0121) 236 7768

Tradition rules

SHOE REPAIRS

Timpsons

21 Great Western Arcade
Tel: (0121) 233 1606

Conveniently located

John Evans

111 Linden Road, Bournville
Tel: (07901) 1725473

Almost sole surviving independent cobbler - nearly 60 years without a break

Open: Thur/Fri 9.30 - 5.30;
Sat 9.30 - 2pm

TOBACCONIST

John Hollingsworth

Great Western Arcade
Tel: (0121) 236 7351

Pipe dreams

TRAVEL OUT OF CITY CENTRE

Carlson Wagonlit Travel (U.K) Ltd

102, New St
Tel: (0121) 631 5020

American Express

Bank House 8, Cherry St
Tel: 0870 600 1060

Thomas Cook Travel

Unit 58, Northwalk, The Pallasades
Tel: (0121) 253 6700

WINE MERCHANTS

Connolly's (Wine Merchants) Ltd

Arch 13, 220 Livery Street
Tel; (0121) 236 9269

Cavernous selection with knowledgeable advice. Ask about Kippers with White Port!

Shopmobility

The Access Committee for Birmingham

The Shopmobility Centre, Snowhill Railway Station,
7 Colmore Row.
Tel: (0121) 236 8980

Also at The Palasades Shopping Centre
Tel: (0121) 643 4035
www.disability.co.uk/
shopmobs.htm

and Level 2 Car Park, Bullring
Tel: (0121) 616 2942,
(0121) 616 2960

Mobility aids with friendly and helpful service.

A free service that loans electric scooters and manual and electric wheelchairs. Good idea to phone in advance.

Open: daily 9am – 4.30pm.

Touchwood

Beyond the centre
South-East

Touchwood

Solihull
Tel: (0121) 709 6999
www.touchwood-solihull.co.uk

Solihull's bright and busy new shopping mall. Parking on site may be difficult on Saturdays – but there are other car parks in the town centre within a pleasant short walk. There's a choice of restaurants, bars and cafes and a multi-screen cinema. Stores include major retailers John Lewis, H & M, Next and some smaller independents. The library and arts complex is next door.

Open: Mon – Fri from 9.30am. Sat from 9am and Sun from 11am. How to get there: Solihull town centre. Train: Solihull station from Birmingham Snow Hill & Moor Street.

North-West

Merry Hill Shopping Centre

Brierley Hill
Tel: (01384) 481 141
www.merryhill.co.uk

An enormous shopping mall with more than 200 shops including Debenhams, Next and Principles plus cinemas, waterside restaurants and bars. Free parking.

Open: Mon – Fri 9am – 9pm, Sat 9am – 8pm, Sun 11am – 5pm. How to get there: Signposted on all main routes.

The Fort Shopping Park,

20 Fort Parkway
Tel: (0121) 386 4442
www.thefort.co.uk

Free parking for over 2,000 cars, this slightly out-of-town shopping mall features a range of high-street stores from Boots to Bhs. A winner of the National Loo of the Year award!

Open: Mon – Fri 9.30am – 8pm, Thurs 9.30am – 9pm, Sat 9am – 7pm, Sun 11am – 5pm. How to get there: Off A38 Tyburn Road or A452 Chester Road and the A47 Heartlands Spine Road. Between J5 & J6/M6.

If you like...

Eating and Drinking

Britain's attitude to food was born out of a pragmatic approach to availability and sound nutritional principles. Back in the 1940s, the link between a nutritious and balanced diet and a healthy nation had been recognised. The government's 2,000 British Restaurants across the country served a wholesome meat dish, a dessert and a cup of tea or coffee for 1/2d (6p). These sound but unadventurous principles resulted in British food having the reputation of being worthy but boring and nutritious but visually unimaginative.

Not so now.

Along with the rest of Britain, Birmingham has suddenly become alive to food culture – from a host of different backgrounds. One legacy of the city's eclectic and open attitude to outside influences is a hugely diverse cuisine – there are restaurants to suit every palate, every taste and every pocket.

Thai and Malaysian cuisine, Chinese, Caribbean, Continental and American, not to mention Indian and Birmingham's own Balti plus, of course, French and yes, English too.

Lunchtime tends to be from 12noon to 2.30pm. If you want a formal lunch then getting to the restaurant before 2pm is advisable. Dinner is served from 6.30pm although 7.30/8pm is more common.

However, there are plenty of bars and pubs that serve food from the time they open until way into the evening.

A word of warning: it's said that running a restaurant or cafe bar is one of life's more risky business ventures. We've listed those that have been around for some time and might therefore be expected to survive, plus - because newcomers are always welcome - some more recent arrivals. In any event, a phone call to book is advised.

Restaurants

Central Quarter

La Galleria

Paradise Place
Tel: (0121) 236 1006

Good Italian food, relaxed atmosphere. Close to the Rep Theatre so you may see a famous face.

Open: Mon – Sat noon –
2.30pm; Bistro 5.30pm – 11pm;
Restaurant 6.30pm – 11pm.
££ (Bistro)
£££ (Restaurant).

San Carlo Ristorante Pizzeria

4 Temple Street
Tel: (0121) 633 0251

Lively restaurant, highly regarded food and brisk but sometimes brusque service.

Open: Mon – Sun noon – 11pm.
£££

Metro Bar & Grill

73 Cornwall Street
Tel: (0121) 200 1911
www.metrobarandgrill.co.uk

Popular, fashionable restaurant with 2* award in the Michelin Red Guide. Excellent, modern, British cooking and stylish surroundings under a roof.

Open: daily, food served Mon - Fri
noon – 2.30pm, 6.30pm – 9.30pm
(Sat 6pm – 11pm). **£££**

Bushwackers

**Lower Ground Floor and
Basement, Exchange
Building, Edmund Street**
Tel: (0121) 236 4994

Australian-influenced restaurant and bar with a themed menu in a smart part of town. Towards the end of the week, by night a nightclub.

Open: Mon – Wed noon – 8pm;
Thurs & Fri noon – 2am. **££**

Hotel du Vin

25 Church Street
Tel: (0121) 200 0600

Yes it's a hotel but it's a wholesome restaurant too with great food served in a great atmosphere.

Open: daily, 12 noon - 1.45pm,
6pm - 10pm . **££ - £££**

Rajdoot

75-79 George Street
Tel: (0121) 236 1116

A member of an award-winning, long-established, chain of restaurants. North Indian cuisine.

Open: Mon – Fri noon – 2pm;
Daily 6.30pm – 11.15pm. **££**

Michelle's La Bastille

220 Corporation Street
Tel: (0121) 236 1171
www.michelles.co.uk

Nouvelle cuisine, brasserie in style.

Open: Sat – Fri Bar: 11am –
10pm, Restaurant: noon –
12.30pm, 6pm – 10pm. **££**

Berlioz

6 Burlington Arcade
Tel: (0121) 633 1737

Classical room with classic service; fine food and space to breathe.

Open: Mon - Sat 12 noon - 2.30pm,
6.30pm (6pm Sat) - 10pm. **£££**

Athens

31 Paradise Circus
Tel: (0121) 643 5523

Sophisticated it isn't, fun it is with good Greek food and the opportunity to show your belly or see someone else's thigh!

Open: 5.30pm - late. **££**

The Coconut Lagoon

12 Bennett's Hill
Tel: (0121) 643 3045

Singapore-style, serving foods from southern India and receiving great reviews.

Open: 12noon - 2.30pm
5pm - 11pm. **££**

Chinese Quarter

Chung Ying Cantonese Restaurant

16 – 18 Wrottesley Street
Tel: (0121) 622 5669

Choose from a huge menu.

Open: Mon – Sat noon – mid-night. Sun noon – 11pm. **££.**

Cafe Soya

Arcadian Centre
Tel: (0121) 683 8350

Inexpensive, bright and breezy with lots going on.

Open: 12noon - 10pm
closed Wednesday

Chung Ying Garden Cantonese Restaurant

17 Thorp Street
Tel: (0121) 666 6622

Famed for its excellent set meals.

Open: Mon – Sat noon – mid-night. Sun noon – 11pm. **££**

The Big Wok

5 Wrottesley Street
Tel: (0121) 666 6800

Oriental buffet restaurant. Unpretentious, lively, noisy, the Big Wok is a huge, licensed canteen. Eat as much as you like at lunchtime or evening.

Open: noon – 11.30pm. **£.**

Maharaja Indian Restaurant

23-25 Hurst Street
Tel: (0121) 622 2641

Established over 30 years ago, this highly regarded restaurant in the heart of theatreland specialises in north Indian and Mughlai cuisine. Booking advised.

Open: Mon – Sat, noon – 2pm and 6pm – 11pm. **££**

Teppanyaki Japanese

**Arcadian Centre,
Ladywell Walk**
Tel: (0121) 622 5183

An established and popular restaurant. Food is cooked at the table.

Open: Mon – Fri noon – 2pm; Mon – Sat 6pm – 11pm. **£££.**

52° North

**Arcadian Centre,
Hurst Street**
Tel: (0121) 622 5250

Fashionable restaurant bar attracting footballers and theatregoers.

Open: Mon – Wed 5pm – 1am; Thur – Fri 5pm – 2am; Sat noon - 2am; Sun noon - 11pm. **££-£££.**

Convention Quarter

Paris Restaurant

**Wharfside Street,
The Mailbox**
Tel: (0121) 632 1488

Few restaurants in Birmingham have achieved such critical acclaim in such a short period. Patrick McDonald and Steve Smith deserve praise.

Open: Tue – Sat noon – 2.15pm; 7pm - 9.30pm Tues - Thurs, 10pm Fri, Sat. **£££**

Blue Mango

**5 Regency Wharf,
Gas Street Basin,**
Tel (0121) 633 4422

Indian food in nautical surroundings with a 1930s' feel.

Open: Mon – Fri noon – 2.30pm;. 6pm - 11pm; Sun closed **£££.**

Jimmy Spice's

Regency Wharf, Gas Street Basin
Tel: (0121) 643 2111

Lunch buffet. Smart setting. Friendly service.

Open: buffet lunch Mon – Sat 12pm – 2pm. Mon – Thurs (dinner), 5.30pm – 11pm; Fri & Sat 5.30pm – midnight; Sun 5.30pm – 10pm. **££**

Shogun Teppanyaki

**The Water's Edge,
Brindleyplace**
Tel (0121) 643 1856

Restaurant with a reputation for wonderful food. Japanese cooked by showman like chefs at your table.

Open: Mon – Sat: noon – 11pm, Sun noon – 7pm. **£££.**

Shogun

The Mailbox,
Tel (0121) 632 1253

Great sushi conveyor and stainless steel tables where food is cooked before you.

Open: Mon – Sat: noon – 11pm, Sun noon – 7pm. **£££.**

Le Petit Blanc

Nine Brindleyplace
Tel: (0121) 633 7333

Smart dining, Raymond Blanc's restaurant is considered one of the city's top eating places. Good food with good service and not horrendously expensive.

Open: Mon – Sat noon – 11.30pm. Sun noon – 3pm, 5.30pm – 10.30pm. **£££**

Tin Tin Cantonese Restaurant

**The Water's Edge,
Brindleyplace**
Tel: (0121) 633 088

Lively at all times. The Sunday lunch buffet is excellent value for money.

Open: Lunch daily, noon – times vary. Dinner, Mon - Sat 5.30pm – 11.30pm (noon Sat) and Sunday 12.30pm – 11pm. **££**

Bank Restaurant & Bar

4 Brindleyplace
Tel: (0121) 633 4466

Stylish/modern, award-winning bar and restaurant.

Open: Mon – Fri 7am – 10.30am; noon – 2.45pm; 5.30pm - 10.30pm. Sat 11am – 3pm, 5.30pm – 11pm; Sun 11am – 5pm **££-£££**

Cielo

Brindleyplace
Tel: (0121) 632 6882

Sophisticated Italian eaterie in smooth surroundings.

Open: Mon – Sat 12noon – 2pm; 5.30pm - 11pm; Sun all day **££-£££**

Thai Edge

**7 Oozells Square,
Brindleyplace**
Tel: (0121) 643 3993

Attractive decor, authentic food. Sunday buffet lunch.

Open: Lunch, Mon – Sat noon – 2.30pm. Dinner, Mon – Thurs 5.30pm – 11.30pm. Fri & Sat: 5.30pm – midnight. Sun noon – 3pm; 5.30pm – 11pm. **££**

Cafe Lazeez

**Wharfside Street,
The Mailbox**
Tel: (0121) 643 7979

Contemporary Indian meets traditional in minimalist surroundings.

Open: Mon – Sat 11am – 11pm; Sun 11am- 3pm. **££**

Shimla Pinks

Broad Street
Tel: (0121) 633 0366

The restaurant that is credited with taking Indian food upmarket. Stylish decor with plush sofas and wooden floors. Excellent mood lighting. Prices reflect the environment.

Open: Mon – Fri noon – 3pm, Mon – Thurs 6pm – 11pm, Fri and Sat 6pm – 11.30pm. **££**

Ipanema

**Nine Brindleyplace,
60 Broad Street**
Tel: (0121) 643 5577
www.ipanema.birmingham@ipan
emarestuarants.com

À la carte Restaurant in the evening with snacks served during the day. Live music. Terrace on Broad Street. Salsa nights Tues and Fri.

Open: Sun and Mon noon – 12pm, Tues – Sat noon – 2am, Sun noon – 10.30pm. **££**

Denial

**120-122 Wharfside Street,
The Mailbox**
Tel: (0121) 632 1231

Another award winner. Canal-side terrace and restaurant serving moderate English cuisine.

Open: Mon – Thurs noon – 10pm, Fri and Sat noon – midnight. **££**

Zinc

**Regency Wharf,
Broad Street**
Tel (0121) 200 0620

Contemporary as you would expect from Sir Terence Conran with modern European food & balcony overlooking canal.

Open: Sun – Wed: 10am – midnight, Thurs 10am – 1am. Fri/Sat 10am – 2am. **£££**

Hard Rock Cafe

263 Broad Street
Tel (0121) 665 6562

Every great city has one. American food. American service.

Open: Daily: 11.30am till late. **££**

Santa Fe

The Mailbox
Tel (0121) 632 1250

New Mexico meets canal side setting.

Open: Mon – Sat: 12 noon – midnight, Sun 12 noon – 11.30pm. **££**

Zizzi

The Mailbox
Tel (0121) 632 1333

Friendly, fun Italian with wood-fired ovens.Good for chicken too.

Open: Mon – Sat: 12noon - 11pm, Sun 12noon - 10.30pm. **££**

Jewellery Quarter

The Jam House

3 St Paul's Square
Tel: (0121) 200 3030

Jools Hollands' stylish, informal restaurant with live music.

Open: Mon & Tue 5pm – midnight, Wed & Thur 5pm – 2am, Fri noon – 2am, Sat 6pm – 2am. **£££**

Henry's Cantonese Restaurant

27 St Paul's Square
Tel: (0121) 200 1190

One of the most highly regarded Cantonese restaurants. 'Henry' is both the proprietor and the chef.

Open: Daily noon – 2pm & 6pm – 11pm. **££**

La Toque D'Or

27 Warstone Lane, Hockley
Tel: (0121) 233 3655

Fine French food served with finesse.

Open: Tues-Fri noon – 2pm, Tues – Sat 7pm – 9.30pm. **££**

The Bucklemaker

**30 Mary Ann Street,
St. Paul's Square**
Tel (0121) 200 2515

Long-time established and still serving good food in the cellars of what was once a Georgian silversmiths.

Open: Mon – Fri 12 noon – 2.30pm; 5.30pm – 10.30pm; Sat 7pm – 10.30pm. **£££**

The Mongolian Bar

Ludgate Hill
Tel: (0121) 236 3842

Fun place to dine. All you can eat stir-fry. Plenty of choice for vegetarians.

Open: Mon – Sun, 6pm – midnight. **££**

Mechu

59 Summerow
Tel: (0121) 212 1661

Restaurant/bar and club/late lounge. Contemporary food. Champagne and cocktail bar. Friendly service, buzzing atmosphere. Sunday lunch: 2 courses £12.95, 3 courses £14.95. Music in the late lounge.

Open: Thurs – Sat noon – 2am, Sun – Wed noon – 12pm. **££.**

Outer Birmingham South-West

Franzl's Austrian Restaurant

151 Milcote Road, Bearwood
Tel: (0121) 429 7920

Unlikely setting for this long established taste of the Alps. Lederhosen optional.

Open: Tues – Sat 7pm – 10.30pm. **££.**

Mangos Caribbean Restaurant

3 Bournville Lane, Stirchley
Tel: (0121) 458 2690

Unprepossessing part of Birmingham but don't let this put you off. Excellent food.

Open: Tues – Sat 6pm – 10pm. **££**

The Jafrany

36 The Mill Walk, Northfield
Tel: (0121) 475 6233
www.thejafrany.co.uk

Getting to this light, bright Indian restaurant is fun – through a ford and a very tight tunnel. Delicious, Bengali-style cuisine awaits - the Chicken Achary and home-made pistachio kulfi are recommended.

Open: Daily 5pm – 11pm. **££**

Xaymaca

34 Bristol Street, Birmingham
Tel: (0121) 622 3332
www.xerestaurant.co.uk

The only Caribbean restaurant in the heart of the city. Cocktails and limbo dancing.

Open: Tues – Sat from 6pm, Sat from 7pm. **££**

Jessica's

1 Montague Road, Edgbaston
Tel: (0121) 455 0999

Once found never forgotten; one of Birmingham's finest. Highly recommended by diners and critics alike.

Open: Mon - Sat 12.30 - 2pm, 7 - 10pm. **£££**

Bay Tree Restaurant

27 Chad Square, Hawthorne Road
Tel: (0121) 455 6697

Modern French cuisine. Closed Sunday evenings.

Open: Mon – Fri: noon – 2.30pm; 7pm – 10.30pm; Sat 7pm – 10.30pm; Sun noon – 2.30pm. **£££**

Michelle's Brasserie Français

69 High Street, Harborne
Tel: (0121) 426 4133

Traditional French restaurant. Well-established.

Open: Mon – Sun noon – 2pm. Mon – Sat 6pm – 10pm. **££**

Outer Birmingham South-East

Bistro Lyonnais

13 St Mary's Row, Moseley Village, Moseley
Tel: (0121) 449 9618

M. Errou is a saucier, creating mouth-watering, authentic dishes.

Open: Tues – Sun 12.30pm – 2pm, daily 6.30 – 11.30pm. **££**

Little Italy

2-4 St Mary's Road, Moseley
Tel (0121) 449 8818

Bustling atmosphere, no frills, unlicensed restaurant

(take your own wine & beer). Italian owner. Excellent food.

Open: Daily, noon – 11pm. **££**

Zorba's Greek Restaurant

359 – 361 Olton Boulevard East, Acocks Green
Tel: (0121) 706 4709

Entertainment, dancing. A popular venue for party people. Can be difficult to chat above the laughter.

Open: Mon – Sat 6pm – late. **££**

Around the NEC and airport

Turners

Crowne Plaza, NEC
Tel: (0121) 781 4000

Fine views across Pendigo Lake, fine food and fine wines in chef Brian Turner's exceedingly good restaurant.

Open: Daily 12noon - 2.30pm; 5.30pm -10.30pm; Sat closed; Sun 12noon – 3pm. **£££**

White Lion

High Street, Hampton-in-Arden, Solihull
Tel: (01675) 442 833

Traditional inn and restaurant in one of the area's most charming villages. Close to the NEC. Simple

Turners, Crowne Plaza

food, served in attractive dining room. Traditional Sunday lunch.

Open: daily from noon. **£££.**

The Moat Manor

Four Ashes Road, Dorridge, Solihull
Tel: (01564) 779988

Excellent value for money – beautifully cooked food, well presented and a dining room that is elegant but not imposing. Moat Manor is tucked away at the end of a long drive by the side of the riding school.

Open: Mon – Sat noon – 2.30pm, 7pm – 10.30pm, Sun noon – 2.30pm. **££/£££.**

Nuthurst Grange

Nuthurst Grange Lane, Hockley Heath
Tel: (01564) 783 972
www.nuthurst-grange.com

Formal elegance, delicious food but not inexpensive.

Open: Mon – Sat noon – 2pm, 7pm – 9.30pm, Sun noon – 2.30pm. **££/£££.**

Da Corrado

1097 Stratford Road, Monkspath, Shirley
Tel: (0121) 744 1977

Good Italian restaurant with friendly service. Weekly specials.

Open: Mon – Sat noon – 2pm; 6.30pm – 11pm. **£££.**

Loch Fyne Seafood Restaurant

The Bank House, High Street, Knowle, Solihull
Tel: (01564) 732 750
www.lochfyne.com

Stylish, brasserie-style restaurant. Menu based mainly on fresh seafood from Scotland. Doesn't sell any of the top 20 endangered species.

Open: Mon – Sat 9am – 10pm, Sun 10am – 10pm. 2 course lunch special. **£££.**

The Forest,

Dorridge, Solihull
Tel: (01564) 772120
www.forest-hotel.com

A Les Routiers Central England Restaurant of the Year. Contemporary restaurant, bar and hotel. Delicious sandwiches or full à la carte menu.

Open: Mon – Sat noon – 2pm, 6.30pm – 10pm. **£££.**

Longfellows

255 Hampton Lane, Catherine-de-Barnes, Solihull
Tel: (0121) 705 0547

Small, intimate English restaurant. Specialises in game and seafood. Good vegetarian selection also.

Open: Lunch Tues – Fri, Dinner Tues – Sat. **££.**

The Orange Tree

Warwick Road, Chadwick End
Tel: (01564) 785 364
www.theorangetree.co.uk

Open-plan, friendly restaurant with Italian theme. Delicious food and delightful atmosphere. Authentic pizzas, succulent spit-roast chicken. Large garden for summer evenings.

Open: noon – 2.30pm, 6pm – 9.30pm. **£££.**

Outer Birmingham North-West

Jonathan's Restaurant

16 Wolverhampton Road, Oldbury
Tel: (0121) 429 3757

Well-established Victorian style restaurant. serving traditional English cuisine. The Secret Garden bistro offers a stylish but less expensive alternative.

Open: Mon – Fri noon-3pm, Mon – Thu 6pm – 10pm, Fri & Sat 6pm – 10.30pm, Sun noon – 3pm. **£££**

Wing Wah The Wing Yip Centre

278 Thimble Mill Lane, Nechells
Tel: (0121) 327 7879

Award-winning restaurant. Eat all you want from the comprehensive lunch and dinner buffets.

Open: Mon – Sat 11am – 11pm. **££**

Tipping

There are no hard and fast rules about tipping. In restaurants and cafes, a tip of around 10% will be welcome. (Annoyingly, some restaurants not only add a service charge – which should be indicated on the menu – but then leave a blank space in the credit card bill; watch out for this ploy and always fill in the total box.)

Tipping in a pub is not normal although bar staff might appreciate the offer of a drink (which they may or may not take at the time you are there). A tip of about 10% in hairdressing and beauty salons is normal. Taxi drivers will also expect tips, particularly on longer journeys, of about 10%. As in most countries, it is normal to tip porters and concierge staff in the more upmarket hotels.

Restaurants

Breakfast in Birmingham

The English are renowned for the emphasis they put on the first meal of the day. From birth, they're told to eat well at breakfast for the optimum in health and temper. A good breakfast is said to improve mental ability and concentration. Realistically though, the English now tend to have a hurried weekday breakfast and linger over it a little longer at the weekend.

The typical cooked English will include eggs (fried, scrambled or poached), grilled or fried bacon, fried bread, sausages, mushrooms, tomatoes and black pudding. But you could also include kidneys, a little steak (at posh establishments) and fried potatoes. Or opt for smoked haddock topped with a poached egg or, more traditional still, kippers.

All this is followed by toast and rough cut marmalade, served with tea or coffee.

Alternatively, opt for a croissant or pastry with coffee.

You'll find most cafes including fast food outlets, serve some form of breakfast. Here's the pick of those that are special, reasonable or downright good value.

Central Quarter

The Burlington Hotel,

Burlington Arcade,
126 New Street
Tel: (0121) 643 9191

Posh breakfast in grand surroundings.

Hotel du Vin

25 Church Street
Tel: (0121) 200 0600

Not just for hotel guests, plenty of choice in relaxed surroundings.

The Orange Studio

7 Cannon Street
Tel: (0121) 634 2804

Trendy ground-floor internet cafe.

Druckers

100 Great Western Arcade
Tel: (0121) 236 6292

Cosy cafe, popular with shoppers, and really good coffee.

Starbucks

125 Colmore Row
and New Street

Not exactly British, but we include them because, as far as we know, no one else has thought to offer paninis with cheese & Marmite or sausage, egg & baked beans.

Hudson's Coffee House

122 – 124 Colmore Row
Tel: (0121) 236 9009

Breakfast in style in the traditional coffee house located in a grade 1 listed building. Waiters in tail coats, a fine collection of coffee, teas and good honest food.

Open: Mon – Sat 10am - 5pm, closed Sun.

Bagel Nation

Colmore Row
Tel: (0121) 233 3636.

Hardly British but delicious.

Croissant

110 New Street
Tel: (0121) 643 8697.
32 Martineau Place
Tel: (0121) 233 2400.

Eat in/takeout; savoury and sweet croissants of all varieties.

Victorian Restaurant

Great Western Arcade
Tel: (0121) 236 8312.

Traditional English at reasonable prices.

Open: Mon – Sat 7.30am – 4pm

Convention Quarter

City Café

1 Brunswick Square,
Brindleyplace
Tel: (0121) 643 1003.
www.cityinn.com

Trend-setting restaurant bar and terrace. Part of the City Inn Hotel. Weekend brunches a speciality.

Breakfasts include porridge, smoked haddock, a selection of cheeses and pastries along with cereals, fresh fruit and traditional English breakfast. Open to non-residents.

Open: Mon – Fri 6.45am – 9.30am. Sat 7am – 10am, Sun 7.30am – 11am. Brunch served Sat & Sun 11am – 4pm.

Costa Coffee

Central Square, Brindleyplace
Tel: (0121) 643 4020

In the main square, next to the fountains. Every coffee you can think of and a range of delicious cakes, pastries and panninis.

Open: Mon – Fri from 8am , Sat from 10am and Sunday 11am.

All Bar One

The Water's Edge, Brindleyplace
Tel: (0121) 644 5861

Try a steak sandwich or an All Bar One breakfast served all day Sat and Sun.

Open: daily from noon.

Floating Coffee Canal Boat

The Waters Edge, Brindleyplace.
Tel: (0121) 633 0050.

A floating bistro. Breakfast and light bites during the day.

Open: daily 9am – 4pm.

Café Ikon

1 Oozells Square, Brindleyplace
Tel: (0121) 248 3226.
www.ikon-gallery.co.uk

On the ground floor of the Ikon art gallery serving a selection of croissants and continental pastries, from 10.30am.

Open: Tues – Sun

Baguette du Monde

Brunswick Arcade, Brindleyplace
Tel: (0121) 633 7766

A bustling 'buy to go' sandwich bar that's popular with local office workers.

Open: Mon-Fri 8.30am – 3pm.

Russell & Porters

The Water's Edge, Brindleyplace.
Tel: (0121) 643 4994.
www.russellandporters.com

A great choice of fillings and breads and a self-service salad bar.

Open: Mon – Fri 7am – 3.30pm, Sat 9am – 3pm.

Denial

120-122 Wharfside Street, Mailbox
Tel: (0121) 632 1232

One of the trendiest places for a weekend breakfast in the city. Muffins, traditional English breakfast, vegetarian options.

Open: Saturday/Sunday from 10am (last breakfast 5pm).

Tesco

Five Ways, Ladywood Middleway
Tel: (0845) 6779259

Supermarket cafes are great value for the full English breakfast at reasonable cost. Not the most plush surroundings but the choice is there: eggs, bacon, sausages, hash browns, beans and fried bread for a completely full feeling. It'll often be enough to carry you through to dinner.

Open: All day breakfast served 7am – midnight.

Jewellery Quarter

Café Neo

87 Spencer Street, Birmingham
Tel: (0121) 236 3555

Eating a traditional English breakfast at reasonable prices in the garden of the former 'Jeweller's Café' is a grand start to the day. Diners include local jewellery trade workers.

Open: Mon – Fri 7.30am – 3.30pm, Sat 9am – 3pm.

Chinese Quarter

The Green Room

Arcadian Centre, Hurst Street
Tel: (0121) 605 4343

A popular cafe/bar with a range of bagels to suit all.

Open: Mon – Fri noon – 10.30pm, Sat noon – 1.30am.

Eastside

Druckers

Café 1 Upper Mall West, Bullring
Tel: (0121) 643 7190

Something of a Birmingham institution, not the full works but delicious pastries.

The Kitchen

The Custard Factory, Gibb Street
Tel: (0121) 224 7504

Breakfast in stylish surroundings.

Open: Mon - Fri 9am - 8pm, Sat 10am 8pm.

Bullring Markets

Various cafes in the midst of the markets, serving traditional breakfasts at just about any time of the day.

Outer Birmingham South-West

Selly Sausage

539 Bristol Road, Birmingham
Tel: (0121) 471 4464

A bustling and lively place frequented by students in need of a hangover cure. Traditional breakfast at low prices a speciality. Vegetarian options.

Open: Mon – Fri 8am – 4pm, Sat and Sun 9am – 5pm.

If you like...

Baltis

Intrigue surrounds the origins of the balti - the spicy, aromatic dish served in a single bowl - that has become synonymous with Birmingham.

It is claimed that the Pakistani and Kashmiri communities first introduced the balti to Birmingham back in the 1970s.

Others believe that the balti (a convenient method of cooking as so few utensils are used) originated from mountain tribesmen from Baltistan – a Himalayan valley in west Kashmir, and some distance from Birmingham's 'Balti Triangle'.

Either way, its popularity as a dish has earned it a place in The Oxford English Dictionary.

Balti restaurants are big business and an essential part of the local economy. The typical balti house can use 2,000 lbs (907kg) of cooking onions and 300 lbs (136kg) of chicken breast in less than a week.

However, to the thousands of people who each day flock to Birmingham's Balti Triangle (the area between the Stratford Road and Moseley Road in Sparkbrook, Sparkhill and the edge of Moseley) its origins and contribution to the economy are less important than the taste and experience. The surroundings may not have the same glitz and glamour as the city centre – but that is one of the attractions.

There are some 50 specialist balti restaurants to choose from in just this one area - and many more are scattered throughout the city.

Sophisticated eating it is not. However, if you want a good meal in fun surroundings, then there can be nothing better than a good balti. The more traditional restaurants display the menus under glass on the table. Most do not serve alcoholic drinks - instead bring them with you. In consequence, there are many wine and beer stores in the area.

Start by asking the waiter for a pile of poppadoms. These wafer thin 'crisps', each about 6-inches (15cms) diameter, are served with chutneys, onions and spicy sauces.

If you are feeling hungry, try one of the many varied starters: perhaps katlama, samosas or bhaji.

And then to the main course: the balti itself. Ask the staff for guidance - and use our Balti Dictionary to help. Order naan bread for dipping, or perhaps a chapati. For those feeling really adventurous, try a side dish of vegetables: aloo, sag or vegetable pakora.

And if you're still hungry, you can always try an Indian sweet. Kulfi and Barfi for instance.

All can be washed down with water, wine, beer (there is even a special beer brewed locally by Aston Manor Brewery called, appropriately and somewhat unimaginatively, Balti Beer) – or a liquid yoghurt drink.

Whilst in the balti area take a little time to visit one of the many supermarkets and food stores. Many of the spices used in balti cooking can be found there and the aroma fills the air. You'll also see huge sacks of rice and dried pulses, vast displays of fresh and preserved fruits and exotic vegetables.

Sweet centres are just that. Normally made on the premises, the sweets are made from exotic ingredients ranging from buffalo milk to extraordinarily rich chocolate.

Textile shops are in abundance selling materials and finished items: sarees (a length of cloth several yards/metres long and wrapped around the body) worn by Hindu women or shalwar kameez (loose trousers and knee-length tunics respectively) worn by Sikh and Muslim women.

The Balti Triangle

There are more than 50 restaurants. We list some of the more popular.

1 Adil

148 Stoney Lane, Sparkbrook.
Tel: (0121) 449 0335

Popular, award-winning balti house.

Open: daily noon – midnight. Car park opposite, an off-licence next door. **£**

2 Al Frash

186 Ladypool Road, Sparkbrook.
Tel: (0121) 753 3120

Another award winning restaurant. Welcoming with some interesting choices.

Open: Sun – Thurs 5pm – midnight, Fri 5pm – 1am, Sat 5pm – 3am. **£**

3 Channi's

795 Stratford Road Sparkhill,
Tel: (0121) 778 6465

Traditional-style restaurant also serving Patrani Fish for which 24 hrs notice required.

Open: daily 12.30 - 2.30pm; 5.30pm - late. **£**

4 Imran

246 - 266 Ladypool Road, Sparkbrook
Tel: (0121) 449 1730

One of the longest and best loved restaurants especially known for its Tandoori Fish.

Open: daily noon - late (2am Fri/Sat). **£**

5 Jyoti

569/571 Stratford Road, Sparkhill,
Tel: (0121) 766 7199

Vegetarian restaurant with dishes from South India and Gujarat. No smoking. Friendly atmosphere.

Open: Tues – Thurs 6pm – 9.15pm, Fri noon – 1.45pm, 6pm – 9.15pm, Sat 1.30pm – 9.15pm, Sun 1.30pm – 8.30pm. **£**

6 Kings Paradise

321 Stratford Road, Sparkhill
Tel: (0121) 753 0006 / 2212

Another long-standing restaurant, with smart decor and serving generous portions.

Open: daily 12noon - 2.30pm; Sun 12noon - midnight; 5.30pm - 1am (2am Fri/Sat). **£**

7 Lahore Karahi

357-363 Ladypool Road. Moseley
Tel (0121) 449 9007

There are over 30 dishes on the buffet 'eat as much as you like' menu. Off licence close by and own car park. Lamb balti a speciality.

Open: Sun – Thurs noon – midnight, Fri and Sat noon – 1am. **£**

8 Punjab Paradise

377 Ladypool Road, Sparkbrook
Tel: (0121) 449 4110

Long established, two storey restaurant. Well worth a visit for the neo-classical décor alone. Family naan the size of a small duvet. Attended parking.

Open: 5pm – 1am (2am Fri & Sat). **£**

9 The Royal Al Faisal

136 – 140 Stoney Lane, Sparkbrook,
Tel: (0121) 449 5695

The Royal Al Faisal is the original - dating back to 1978 and since then customers have included HRH Prince Charles. Introduced the family naan (karak) to Birmingham. Great buffet selection.

Open: 12 noon – midnight daily. **£ - ££**

10 Royal Naim

417-419 Stratford Road,
Tel: (0121) 766 7849

twice the winner of the best british baltihouse. informal. highly regarded food.

Open: Fri and Sat noon – 2am, Sun – Thurs noon – midnight. **£**

11 Saleems

256-258 Ladypool Road, Sparkhill
Tel: (0121) 449 1861

Bright and light restaurant. Asian sweets a speciality.

Open: from lunch 'til late daily. **£**

If getting to the Balti Triangle is impossible, there are a few good Balti restaurants dotted throughout the region.

Eastside

Mokhoms Kashmiri Balti

Digbeth,
Tel: (0121) 643 7375

Great food & friendly service close to the Bullring.

Open: Daily 6pm – midnight (Fri, Sat 2am). **££**

North-East

Streetly Balti

188 Chester Road, Streetly
Tel: (0121) 353 2224

Small restaurant with friendly staff and consistently high quality food.

Open: Mon – Thur 5.30pm – midnight; Fri & Sat 5.30pm – 12.30am. **£**

South-East

Titash International Balti

2278 Coventry Road, Sheldon
Tel: (0121) 722 2080

Good value restaurant. Close to the NEC and airport.

Open: daily 5.30pm – 12.30am **££**

Kasbah Bar and Restaurant

327 Highfield Road, Hall Green
Tel: (0121) 778 1958

Not technically a balti but serves excellent Indian food. Friendly service. Chill out area with chess set and large bar. Licensed.

Open: Mon – Sat 5pm – 11pm, Sun 5pm – 10.30pm. **££**

The Balti Triangle

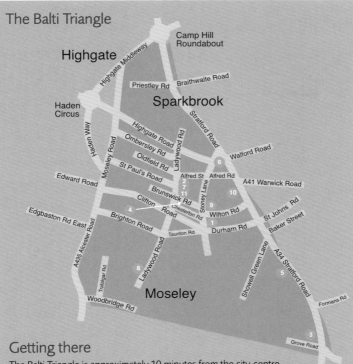

Camp Hill Roundabout

Highgate

Haden Circus

Sparkbrook

Priestley Rd Braithwaite Road

Highgate Middleway

Highgate Road

Ombersley Rd

Oldfield Rd

St Paul's Road

Moseley Road

Haden Way

Edward Road

Brunswick Rd

Clifton Road

Chesterton Rd

Brighton Road

Taunton Rd

Edgbaston Rd East

A435 Alcester Road

Trafalgar Rd

Ladywood Road

Woodbridge Rd

Moseley

Ladywood Rd

Stratford Road

Walford Road

Alfred St   Alfred Rd

A41 Warwick Road

Stoney Lane

Wilton Rd

Durham Rd

St Johns Rd

Baker Street

Showell Green Lane

A34 Stratford Road

Formans Rd

Grove Road

Getting there

The Balti Triangle is approximately 10 minutes from the city-centre, by taxi or bus. Bus services 2, 4, 6 and 31 travel down the A34 Stratford Road. Disembark in the vicinity of the A41 Warwick Road junction. Alternatively bus service 50 travels along Moseley Road. Disembark near Clifton Road.

A Balti Dictionary

Aloo - Potato

Bhaji - Usually a starter of spicy, deep-fried rings – often onion or mushrooms

Bhindi- Vegetable known as okra or 'Ladies Fingers'

Chana: - Chick peas

Chappatis - Unleavened, circular bread

Dal: Spicy - Dried lentils

Dhansak - Hot, sweet dish with lentils and tomatoes

Dopiaza - Lots of onions in this medium hot dish

Gobi - Cabbage or cauliflower

Gosht - Lamb

Jalfrazies - Cooked with onions and peppers

Katlama - Pastry with mince and fried

Keema - Mince

Kofta - A spicy meatball

Korma - Mild dish made with nuts and cream

Methi - Fenugreek leaves, slightly bitter

Mughlai - Saffron flavoured

Murghi - Chicken

Naan - Leavened bread

Pakora - Spicy, deep-fried vegetable starter (variations include meat)

Paratha - Bread stuffed with spicy potato

Pathia - Hot, sweet and sour dish

Peshwari Naan - Naan stuffed with almonds and fruit

Poppadom - Large, spicy 'crisps'. Eat with chutneys and sauces

Saag / Sag - Spinach

Samosas - Deep-fried meat or vegetable, triangular pastry starter

Sheeskh - Kebab: Spicy, skewer cooked minced lamb

Shaslik - Cubes of lamb and chicken on skewers

Tandoori - Style of cooking, marinated in spices and cooked in a clay oven

Tikka - Usually chicken or lamb cubes, marinated in yoghurt and cooked on a skewer.

Cafes, Pubs and Bars

Licensing hours

The sale of alcohol is restricted to licensing hours, normally 11am (12 noon Sunday) until 11pm (unless the premises hold a special extended licence). Premises charging an admission fee, such as nightclubs, may hold a licence until 2am. It is not unusual for licensed premises to open earlier than the licensing hours, for serving coffee, tea etc. Hotel residents should be able to obtain an alcoholic drink at any time of the day at the hotel bar.

Central Quarter

Carpe Diem
48 Great Charles Street, Queensway
Tel: (0121) 212 2345

A watering hole for city slickers during the week.

Open: Mon – Thurs 10am – 8pm, Fri 10am – 11pm.

Chi
61 Newhall Street
Tel: (0121) 233 3150

Slick, stylish and swanky on three levels with a 60ft bed and jacuzzi in the private bar!

Open: Mon – Thur 12noon – 12 midnight;
Fri - Sat 12noon – 2am.

Digress
21-22 Newhall Street
Tel: (0121) 200 0980

Popular and smart with good food.

Open: 12noon – 2am

The Orange Studio
7 Cannon Street,
Tel: (0121) 634 280

Coffee and web-surfing on the ground floor with an attractive, light and airy bar-cum-cafe restaurant on the first. Pleasant outside terrace.

Gabriel & Raphael's
45 Pinfold Street
Tel: (0121) 643 5666

City centre wine and champagne bar. Relaxed atmosphere, smooth jazz.

Open from lunchtime, a great place to chill out, late. Happy hour 4pm – 8pm

Old Joint Stock
Temple Row West
Tel: (0121) 200 1892

A former bank, this distinctive pub includes chandeliers, illuminated busts and a magnificent cupola.

Open: Mon – Sat 11am – 11pm

Utopia
Innovation Square, Church Street
Tel: (0121) 233 3666

Comfortable brown leather settees and seats in business–like surroundings. Good menu too.

Open: Mon – Sat 11am – 11pm

Bennetts
8 Bennett's Hill
Tel: (0121) 643 9293

A former bank with architectural touches.

Open: Licensed hours

Bushwackers
The Exchange, Edmund Street
Tel: (0121) 2364994

Busy wine bar and restaurant with music Thursday, Friday and Saturday nights.

Open: Mon to Wed midday to 8pm, Thurs to Fri 12noon to 2am, Saturday 7pm to 2am

Bacchus bar
Burlington Arcade, New Street
Tel: (0121) 616 7991

Dungeons meet Roman and Medieval in a display of architectural diversity below ground.

Open: Mon to Fri and Sun 12noon to 11.30pm; Sat 11am to 11.30pm

Convention Quarter

Pitcher and Piano
The Water's Edge, Brindleyplace
Tel: (0121) 643 0214.
www.pitcherandpiano.com

Comfortable armchairs and loads of light wood make this a relaxing place to eat and drink.

Open: Mon – Fri 12noon – 11pm, Sat & Sun 11am – 11pm.

The Pit Stop
The Water's Edge, Brindleyplace
Tel: (0121) 644 5981

A lively pub with a retro feel.

Open: Mon – Sat 12noon – 11pm. Sun 12 – 10.30pm

Cube
The Water's Edge, Brindleyplace
Tel: (0121) 616 7911

Open: Mon – Sat 12noon – 2am. Sun 7pm – 10.30pm

Walkabout Inn
Regency Wharf, Broad Street
Tel: (0121) 632 5712
www.walkabout.eu.com

Australian-style bar famed for serving copious amounts of food at reasonable prices. TVs, music, comfy armchairs and wooden benches. Next to Surfers Paradise nightclub – appeals to 25+.

Open: Mon – Thurs: 12noon – 1am; Fri & Sat. 12noon – 2am; Sun 12noon – 10.30pm

The Tap & Spile
Gas Street
Tel: (0121) 632 5602.

Pub grub like gammon and chips in an old, canal-side building. Stone floors, wooden tables and chairs. Food 12noon – 8pm with a choice of baguettes from Monday to Friday 12noon – 3pm.

Open: Licensed hours

Wine REPublic
Centenary Square, Broad Street
Tel: (0121) 644 6464

Attached to the Rep Theatre, and with terraces overlooking Centenary Square.

The Sports Cafe

Broad Street
Tel: (0121) 633 4000

The pool lounge has 20 tables; there's a happy hour, music, dancing and TVs.

Open: until 2am.

James Brindley

Bridge Street
Tel: (0121) 644 5971

Pub with outside area overlooking canal.

Open: Licensed hours

All Bar One

The Water's Edge, Brindleyplace
Tel: (0121) 643 8633

Frequented by office workers and club-goers, with good people-watching from the patio area.

Open: Mon to Thurs, 12noon to 11pm (Fri/Sat midnight); Sunday, noon to 10:30pm

Bar Epernay

The Mailbox
Tel: (0121) 632 1430

Champagne and quality food with piano accompaniment.

Open: Mon - Thur 11am - 11pm; Fri - Sat 11am - 12am; Sun 12noon - 10.30pm

Bar Estilo

The Mailbox
Tel: (0121) 643 3443

Spanish theme with some surprising English additions.

Open: Mon - Sat 10am - 11pm; Sun 10am - 10.30pm

The Living Room

Regency Wharf, Broad Street
Tel: (0870) 44 22 539

Discreet, friendly service and delicious food. Highly regarded and with bar staff who perform cocktail stunts that put Tom Cruise in the shade.

Open: Mon – Wed noon – 11pm, Thurs noon – 11.30pm, Fri and Sat noon – 12pm, Sun noon – 10.30pm. **£££**

Jewellery Quarter

Après

39 Summer Row
Tel: (0121) 212 1661

Sports bar, DJs, food served. Relaxed - somewhere to chill out.

Open: daily, 9am – 2am. Happy hour 5pm – 8pm.

Rose Villa

Warstone Lane/Vyse Street
Tel: (0121) 236 4394

Fabulous tiled surroundings with panelled front saloon. Traditional ales and foods.

Open: Licensed hours

Chinese Quarter

52 Degrees North

Arcadian, Hurst Street
Tel: (0121) 622 5250

Fashionably chic restaurant and bar. The place to see celebrities. Cocktails a speciality.

Open: Mon – Wed 5pm – 1am, Thurs-Fri 5pm – 2am, Sat 12noon-2am, Sun 12noon -11pm

Arca Bar

The Arcadian Centre
Tel: (0121) 666 7777.

Minimalist setting attracting the young crowd.

Open: Mon – Wed 11am – 1am, Thurs – Sat 11am – 2am, Sun 6pm - 12.30am

Sobar

The Arcadian Centre

Hurst Street
Tel: (0121) 693 5084
www.sobar.co.uk

Oodles of noodles in swanky setting.

Open: 11am - 2am; Sun 12noon - 12 midnight

Baracuda

Hurst Street
Tel: (0121) 622 6878

Great atmosphere with excellent DJs.

Open: Mon - Fri 4pm - 2am; Sat 7pm - 2am

Barocco

The Arcadian, Hurst Street
Tel: (0121) 246 7862

Moroccan in feel and looks but British in content.

Poppy Red

The Arcadian,Hurst Street
Tel: (0121) 687 1200

Fine food in pleasant surroundings and good value lunches.

Open: Mon - Tue 12noon - 11pm; Wed - Sat 12noon - 2pm; Sun 12noon - 10.30pm

Old Fox

Hurst Street
Tel: (0121) 622 5080

Well kept beers, good value food and theatre drinks too.

Open: Licensed hours

Eastside

Arts Cafe

St Martin's Church in the Bullring
Tel: (0121) 600 6028

Popular with shoppers, this unexpected treasure serves really good food in artistic surroundings.

Open: Mon – Sat 10am – 5pm.

The Old Crown Inn

High Street, Deritend
Tel: (0121) 248 1366/7/8

The oldest pub in town dating back to 1368.

Open: Licensing hours.

The Anchor Inn

308 Bradford Street
Tel: (0121) 622 4516

Well preserved and with many of its original features, this Edwardian pub is traditional in style and serves a vast range of beers plus huge chip butties.

Open: Licensing hours.

Warehouse Cafe

54-57 Allison Street
Tel: (0121) 633 0261

Vegetarian heaven. Located above the Friends of the Earth HQ, this cafe is popular with locals. Tasty baguettes.

Open: Mon – Fri, noon to 3pm and Fri & Sat, 6pm – 9pm.

Medicine Bar

The Custard Factory, Gibb Street
Tel: (0121) 693 6333

Music and food in major arts venue.

Open: Mon - Sat 11am - 2am

The Kitchen

The Custard Factory, Gibb Street
Tel: (0121) 224 7504

All-day menu including pastas, salads and organic foods to pitta breads & burgers

Open: Mon - Fri 9am - 8pm, Sat 10am- 6pm

If you like...

Cathedrals, Churches, Places of Worship

It is unlikely that Birmingham had a church before 1086 as there is no record of a resident priest in the Domesday Book although both Aston and Northfield had priests mentioned.

Records were haphazard before 1538 when Thomas Cromwell ordered every parish to record in writing the baptisms, marriages and burials wherever there was an officiating priest.

Headstones didn't appear until the 17th century; the earliest was found in Northfield, dated 1651 although the earliest now surviving there is that commemorating the life of John Palmer, who died 4th February 1682.

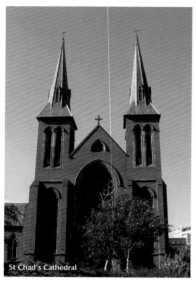

St Chad's Cathedral

Religious intolerance has been prevalent for as long as there has been religion. A reaction to the bigotry was in the design of St. Peter's Roman Catholic Church; built in 1786, near Broad Street (Convention Quarter). It was the first catholic parish church to be built after the Reformation and was deliberately designed to look like a factory in an effort to conceal its true purpose.

When St Peter's was demolished to make way for the International Convention Centre on Broad Street, 1163 bodies were revealed with 586 in a single, mass grave. It is thought they were the unfortunate casualties of an outbreak of bubonic plague in the early 1600s. It has been suggested that the pestilence killed around a quarter of Birmingham's population of the time.

Religion has played a key role in society's development. In terms of architecture and social and political history, it provides a rich seam of information.

It is worth noting that the churchyard is often older than the church. Looking at the ground level can reveal how old the burial area is – church walls and paths may be lower as a result of centuries of burying people one on top of the other.

If you look at a churchyard, the south side is invariably higher than the north where the shadow of the church falls across the graves. This is because the north side is least popular as legend has it the Devil lurks in the shadows.

To revive Britain's flagging wool trade, in 1678 it became law that all bodies were wrapped in a woollen shroud. The penalty for flouting it was a £5 fine.

Carrying a body along the lychpath – lych is an Old English word for dead body – to its final resting place was a task performed carefully, especially by local farmers as wherever a corpse was carried, a new public right of way was created.

One man was kept very busy thanks to Birmingham's enthusiastic desire to maintain and build more churches. Julius Alfred Chatwin was involved in the design, restoration and expansion of more than 30 churches in the district.

Central Quarter

Birmingham Cathedral (St Philip's),
St Philip's Place

Wonderful, English Baroque, St Philip's became the cathedral for the new diocese of Birmingham in 1905. Although consecrated in 1715, the tower was incomplete until 1725 when George I donated £600 towards its construction. (See page 23).

St Chad's Cathedral,
St Chad's Queensway

Commanding neo-gothic Roman Catholic cathedral designed by Augustus Welby Pugin. (See page 23).

Convention Quarter

Birmingham Hebrew Congregation,
Singer's Hill

A Grade II listed building designed by H Yeoville Thomason. (See page 43).

Jewellery Quarter

St Paul's Church,
St Paul's Square

Built in 1777-9 with the belfry and spire added in 1823, complete with private pews. (See page 47).

Eastside

St Martin in the Bullring,
The Bullring

Recently restored and now occupying a prominent position. (See page 28).

Birmingham South-West

The Oratory,
114 Hagley Road, Edgbaston.

Baroque-style church built in 1907-10 as a memorial to Cardinal Newman, founder of the English Oratory. (See page 53).

St Laurence Church,
Rectory Road, Northfield

A perfect example of early English architecture. (See page 55).

King's Norton Church,
King's Norton village

The church of St Nicholas dates from the 13th century. (See page 55).

The Serbian Orthodox Church of the Holy Prince Lazar,
131 Cob Lane, Bournville

Constructed in the 1960s based on a 14th century design (See page 54)

Birmingham South-East

Birmingham's Central Mosque,
Belgrave Road

An impressive central dome and minaret. (See page 56)

St Agatha's Church,
Stratford Road, Sparkbrook

Grade 1 listed building with neo-gothic architecture. (See page 56)

Birmingham North-East

Aston Parish Church, (St Peter & St Paul's)
Aston Hall Road, Aston

An unusually large, Gothic church which was known as Aston Juxta Birmingham until around 1911. It has a number of effigies and at least two 17th century tombstones including one dated 27th December, 1660. (See page 59)

If you like...

Parks, Gardens & Open Spaces

Birmingham has more than 8,000 acres (3,237ha) of parkland resulting in its claim to the title of Britain's greenest city. Viewed from the air or a high-rise building and its trees and open spaces become much more visible.

Although the city centre currently lacks the open parks found in cities like London, New York or Paris, there are grand plans to create a park in the city's Eastside.

And it takes botany and horticulture seriously with not one but two botanical gardens. The city has won four Britain in Bloom awards and a record 18 of the Chelsea Flower Show's prestigious gold medals. There are 40 listed conservation sites.

Take time to travel a little further afield to find not only peace but also pace when you come across one of the many weekend summer festivals which make the parks their homes.

Central Quarter

St Philip's,
St Philip's Place

If it's a sunny day, join local office workers and sit in the recently restored churchyard to eat a lunchtime sandwich and soak up the sun.(See page 23).

Convention Quarter

St Thomas' Peace Garden,
Bath Row

A place of serenity and tranquillity between the city centre and Five Ways. (See page 43).

Jewellery Quarter

St Paul's Square
Surrounding 18th century church. (See page 47).

Birmingham South-West

Cannon Hill Park,
Edgbaston Road, Edgbaston

Boating lakes, playgrounds, tennis courts, conservation areas, cycle route, bandstand and lots of geese. (See page 52).

Birmingham Nature Centre,
Pershore Road, Edgbaston

Lots of wildlife and great for children. (See page 52).

Birmingham Botanical Gardens,
Winterbourne Road, Edgbaston

Glasshouses, grounds and tranquillity. (See page 52).

University of Birmingham Botanic Garden at Winterbourne,
58 Edgbaston Park Road, Edgbaston

Edwardian garden with woodland walks. (See page 53).

Lickey Hills Country Park,
Warren Lane, Rednal

Walks and wildlife in woodland and heathland. (See page 55).

Birmingham South-East

Moseley Bog,
Yardley Wood Road, Moseley

Inspiration to the young J.R.R. Tolkien. (See page 56).

King's Heath Park,
Vicarage Road, King's Heath

Source of inspiration to many as home to BBC Gardeners' World gardens. (See page 56).

Sarehole Mill,
Cole Bank Road, Hall Green

The working watermill dates back to 1542. (See page 57).

Birmingham North-East

Castle Bromwich Hall Gardens,
Chester Road, Castle Bromwich

Walled gardens and holly maze. (See page 59).

Sutton Park,
Park Road, Sutton Coldfield

One of Europe's largest urban nature reserves. (See page 59)

If you like...

Museums & Galleries

When it comes to art and preserving its cultural heritage, Birmingham takes its role seriously.

Sir Edward Coley Burne-Jones (1883-1898), the British painter who was apprenticed to Rossetti, was born in Pershore Street, Birmingham. His work was inspired by the romance of myths and legends and he was later to join William Morris (1834–1896) in founding the Arts and Crafts movement. His work is characterized by slender, elongated forms.

It's no surprise then that the Pre-Raphaelite collection at the city's Museum and Art Gallery is considered the best in the world. If you're a Burne-Jones enthusiast, watch out for when the Holy Grail Tapestries are exhibited - they are well worth a visit as are the windows in both St. Philip's and St. Martin in the Bull Ring.

Modern art is featured at the new Waterhall Gallery and there are several small, private galleries dotted around the city. To see one of the finest small galleries in Europe then make your way to the Barber Institute at Birmingham University. You'll find an outstanding collection of old masters, modern paintings, sculpture and drawings.

There are many museums celebrating not only the city but the region's industrial heritage. The Pen Room in the Jewellery Quarter is quirky and fascinating and The Museum of Science and Discovery is interactive heaven.

The huge Sea Life Centre on the canal-side at Brindleyplace is a tour of discovery into life beneath our waters.

Aston Hall is a remarkable example of a house from the Jacobean period and the National Trust back-to-back properties in Hurst Street offer a real insight into early city living.

Going just a little further afield, and detailed in the appropriate geographic sections, takes you to the pleasures of the Black Country Living Museum – allow a day to make the most of everything this recreated village has to offer. Visit the New Art Gallery in Walsall on the same day as the town's Leather Museum to appreciate fully the complementary and contrasting approaches to art and craftsmanship.

Central Quarter

Birmingham Museum & Art Gallery,

Chamberlain Square

BMAG's collection covers fine art and applied arts, archaeology and ethnography as well as local and industrial history. Founded in 1885, the museum's Fine Art and Applied Art Collections include paintings and drawings, British Watercolours and Arts and Crafts. Most visitors enter the museum through the rich, ruby red Round Room, designed by Birmingham architect H. Yeoville Thomason. Pride of place is given to the Birmingham-born artist David Cox including his remarkable Rhyl Sands. Further paintings include Albert Moore's Dreamers, Sir Lawrence Alma-Tadema's Pheidias and one of the most popular landscapes of the Victorian era, Benjamin William Leader's masterpiece, February Fill Dyke. The Renaissance and Baroque period produced some of the largest paintings in the collection including Botticelli's rare but damaged Florentine altarpiece and Orazio Gentileschi's early masterpiece - The Rest on the Flight into Egypt. Other major Italian Baroque paintings include Guercino's Erminia and the Shepherd and Benedetto Gennari's Holy Family commissioned for St James's Palace. Galleries contain objects from Ancient Egypt and the ancient Near East, Greece and the Roman Empire. The neighbouring Gas Hall Gallery has a constantly changing programme and the Waterhall Gallery contains Birmingham's collection of Modern Art. (See page19).

Eastside

ThinkTank:The Birmingham Museum of Science & Discovery,

Curzon Street

Lots of fun, education and thought-provoking exhibits and hands-on displays for children and adults alike. (See page 29).

Convention Quarter

The Halcyon Gallery

International Convention Centre, Broad Street

Tel: (0121) 248 8484

Friendly, commercial gallery featuring original paintings, sculpture and limited editions.

Ikon Gallery

1 Oozells Square.
Tel (0121) 248 0708.   www.ikon-gallery.co.uk

Based in a refurbished, neo-gothic school building, the Ikon is an internationally renowned showcase for contemporary art by national and internationally-regarded artists. (See page 41)

De-stress through music

Check out the dates and times for CBSO stress-busting Rush Hour Concerts. Venue: Symphony Hall Level 3 Foyer. Start: approx 5.30 - 6pm. Duration: 1 hour. Why spend time in traffic queues when you can use that time relaxing and soaking up the finest in classical music? Tel: (0121) 780 3333 for further information.

Number Nine the Gallery

1-2 Cumberland Street, Nine Brindleyplace:
Tel: (0121) 643 9099.
www.numberninethegallery.com

A dynamic, commercial gallery with enthusiastic and knowledgeable staff, where the work on display – glass, ceramics, sculpture – is for sale.

The National Sea Life Centre,

The Water's Edge
Tel: (0121) 633 4700

Life beneath the oceans and seas in all its glory. One of the largest inland aquaria in Europe. (See page 41).

The Jewellery Quarter

Royal Birmingham Society of Artists,

4 Brook Street
Tel: (0121) 236 4353
www.rbsa.org.uk

One of the UK's oldest art societies with a regular programme of exhibitions. (See page 47).

St Paul's Gallery,

94 Northwood Street
Tel: (0121) 236 5800

The largest commercial, contemporary gallery outside London, featuring rising stars in the art world. (See page 47)

The Museum of the Jewellery Quarter

75 – 79 Vyse Street.
Tel: (0121) 554 3598.
www.bmag.org.uk

Fascinating insight into jewellery making from the Middle Ages to the present. (See page 48).

The Pen Room

Unit 3, The Argent Centre, 60 Frederick St., Hockley.
Tel (0121) 236 9834.
www.bptha.xoasis.com.

Writing implements through the ages with demonstrations and displays. (See page 47).

The Pen Room

Birmingham South-West

Barber Institute of Fine Arts,

The University of Birmingham, Edgbaston
Tel: (0121) 414 7333.
www.barber.org.uk

Works by Turner, Gainsborough, Reynolds, Rubens, Van Dyck and Murillo's magnificent *Marriage Feast at Cana*. (See page 53).

Lapworth Museum,

Birmingham University, Edgbaston
Tel: (0121) 414 7294

Free entry to this dig at the past. (See page 54).

Photograph below shows Charles Lapworth, who gave his name to the museum, trained as a school teacher in Oxfordshire. His interest in geology started after moving to Scotland. Whilst living in Birmingham, he spent many years studying the rocks of the Midlands and Welsh borders taking groups of students, amateur and professional geologists on field excursions.

Birmingham North-West

Soho House

Soho Avenue, Handsworth
Tel: (0121) 554 9122.
www.bmag.org.uk

The meeting place for The Lunar Society: the exclusive institution attended by the great thinkers of the 18th century. (See page 58).

The New Art Gallery Walsall,

Gallery Square, Walsall
Tel: (01922) 654 400
www.artatwalsall.org.uk

New, £21 million gallery with works by Epstein and Van Gogh. (See page 64).

Walsall Leather Centre Museum,

Littleton Street West, Walsall
Tel (01922) 721 153

The history or leatherwork through the ages. (See page 64).

Birmingham North-East

Aston Manor Road Transport Museum

208-216 Witton Lane, Aston
Tel: (0121) 322 2298.
www.amrtm.org

Museum of restored commercial vehicles including lorries, trams, buses and vans. (See page 59).

Aston Hall,

Trinity Road, Aston
Tel: (0121) 327 0062.
www.bmag.org.uk

Elaborate ceilings, magnificent carved oak staircase, priceless furniture and Victorian toys. (See page 59).

Further Afield

Compton Verney, Kineton, Warwickshire
Tel: (01926) 645500
www.comptonverney.org.uk

This 18th century mansion has recently opened as a £64m art museum. The Robert Adam designed house and the Capability Brown designed gardens provide a fabulous setting for six differing collections.

Open: 10am – 5pm daily
Admission: C

A 1950 LEYLAND PD2/1 54-seater from Birmingham City Transport.

Aston Hall

Transport/Public Art

Displays of street public art can be seen at several road and rail interchanges. The first four were commissioned in 2001. There are now 26 pieces to be seen including:

Olton	Saxon King on a Horse
Soho Road, Handsworth	The Tulip Tree
Washwood Heath Road, Saltley	Circular Dance
Soho Hill, Hockley Circus	Coin Stack
Stechford Lane, Washford Heath	Star Gazer
Cotteridge	Feathers of Freedom
Longbridge	The Genie of Industry
Stratford Road, Springfield	Bullrushes
Winson Green	Wooden man
Bristol Road, Edgbaston	Garden
Hagley Road, Bearwood	Voyage
Walsall Road, Great Barr	Beech Beacon
Solihull Station	Trees

If you like...

Sport & Recreation

Birmingham stages more World and European championships, in more sports than any other UK city. It is also one of only three UK cities to hold the National City of Sport title, awarded by the Sports Council.

Birmingham and the Midlands is home to seven Football League Clubs. The first 12 teams that comprised the football league back in 1888 included Aston Villa and West Bromwich Albion. Both have gone on to win the prestigious FA Cup. It is also home to Warwickshire County Cricket Club - and boasts of being the home of lawn tennis.

Municipal facilities - that's those owned by the City Council - are open to the public. Membership is normally required for private health centres and golf courses or guest fees are payable. Many of the more luxurious hotels offer leisure and health facilities including swimming pools although most are small.

Convention Quarter

LivingWell Health Club

3 Brunswick Arcade, Brindleyplace
Tel: (0121) 633 4645 www.livingwell.co.uk

A beautiful health club with fitness studios, gymnasium, sauna, steam room, a 20m pool with spa and a beauty suite. There's a bar for relaxation after all the strenuous exercise.

Open: Mon – Fri, 6.30am – 10.30pm, Sat & Sun 8.30am – 10pm.

Community Hall, National Indoor Arena

King Edward's Road
Tel: (0121) 644 7134.

Community Hall is an opportunity for ordinary people to train where the best have competed. It's a sports venue for all within the prestigious NIA. Gym, sauna, massage, reflexology and various classes.

Open: Mon, Tues, Thurs, Fri 9am – 11pm, Wed 7 am – 11pm, Sat and Sun 9am – 5pm.

Chinese Quarter

Megabowl

Pershore St
Tel: (0121) 666 7525

A 26 lane bowling alley, licensed bar, American pool tables and amusement arcade.

Open: daily noon – 11.30pm.

Planet Ice

Pershore Street
Tel: (0121) 693 2400
www.planet-ice.co.uk

Ice rink with public sessions, group tuition and special events including ladies' nights. Bar and gallery.

Open: 10am - 10.30pm (Check as some sessions are restricted or there may be hockey matches).

Eastside

Rock Face, A B Row,

Jennens Road
Tel: (0121) 359 6419 www.rockface.co.uk

Climbing centre with walls of various difficulties from beginners to experienced climbers. Lessons for children.

Open: Mon – Fri 10am – 10pm, Sat – Sun 10am – 8pm.
How to get there: Close to Millennium Point.

Birmingham South-West

Harborne Church Farm Golf Course

Vicarage Road, Harborne
Tel: (0121) 427 1204

9 hole course and putting green. Advance booking recommended.

Lickey Hills

Rose Hill, Rednal
Tel: (0121) 453 3159

18 hole golf course and putting green. Advance booking recommended.

Edgbaston Cricket Ground

Edgbaston
Tel: (0121) 446 4422
www.thebears.co.uk

World renowned sports stadium, venue for one day cricket, home to Warwickshire County Cricket Club. The new steel and glass building is the Edgbaston Cricket Centre. Opened in 2000, it has state-of-the-art facilities for budding county internationals.

Edgbaston Priory Club

Sir Harry's Road, Edgbaston
Tel: (0121) 440 2492

Lawn tennis originated in Edgbaston in 1865. Two Wimbledon singles champions have also come from this prestigious tennis club: Ann Jones (1969) and Maud Watson, the first ever, nearly 100 years earlier. Annual women's international tournament held in June.

Birmingham Squash Rackets Club

121a Rotton Park Road, Edgbaston
Tel: (0121) 455 0181

Non-members need to be accompanied by a member.

Open: daily from 10am.

Birmingham South-East

Stirchley Superbowl

Pershore Road, Stirchley
Tel: (0121) 458 4444

20 lane bowling alley with licensed bar.

Open: daily 10am – 11.30pm

Moseley Road Baths

Moseley Road, Moseley
Tel: (0121) 464 0150

Swimming architectural gem (although it could do with a good refurbishment).

Open: Variable but generally 7am-8pm weekdays; Sat: 9am-4.30pm; Sun: 8am-12.30pm.
Admission: A.

David Lloyd Leisure Health & Fitness Club

Monkspath Leisure Park, Highlands Road, Shirley
Tel: (0121) 712 1600

Air conditioned gym, aerobic dance studio, equipment for toning and muscle development. Spa, sauna and pool. Membership required.

Open: Mon – Sat 6.30am – 11pm, Sun 7am – 10pm.
How to get there: Near J4/M42.

David Lloyd Leisure Health & Fitness Club

247 Cranmore Boulevard, Shirley
Tel: (0121) 733 5300

Health and fitness specialising in racquet sports. Membership required.

Open: Mon – Sat 7am – 11pm, Sun 8am – 10.30pm.
How to get there: Near J4/M42

Cocks Moors Woods Leisure Centre

Alcester Road South, Kings Heath
Tel: (0121) 464 1996

Public leisure pool with wave machine and slide. Fitness room, gym and a variety of classes.

Open: phone to check.

The Ackers Trust

Golden Hillock Road, Small Heath
Tel: (0121) 772 5111
www.ackers-adventure.co.uk

Outdoor activity centre with skiing, snowboarding (dry-slope), climbing, canoeing, kayaking, rope courses, archery, orienteering. Group and private lessons.

Open: Mon – Fri 10am – 9pm, Sat and Sun 10am – 5pm.

Hall Green Stadium

York Road, Hall Green
Tel: (0870) 840 8502

Greyhound racing is the second largest spectator sport in Britain. Hall Green is home to The William Hill Blue Riband and the Midland Flat Championship events. Racing on Tues, Fri & Sat evenings. Hotel and restaurants.

Birmingham City FC

St. Andrew's Ground
Tel: (0121) 202 5204
www.bcfc.com

BCFC, nicknamed the Blues, was founded in 1875 by an enthusiastic group of cricketers who wanted something to do in the winter. In 1906 the club moved to St. Andrews. The ground has a capacity of 30,000. Tours of the ground and pitch are available.

Billesley Indoor Tennis Centre

Wheelers Lane, Billesley
Tel: (0121) 464 4222.

Coaching for all abilities – adults and children. Pay and Play. Health and fitness gym.

Open: Mon – Fri 7am – 10pm, Sat and Sun 8am – 10pm.

Moseley Rugby Football Club

University of Birmingham, Munrow Centre, Edgbaston
Tel: (0121) 414 2780

Founded in 1873 the team adopted its signature red and black colours in 1874. Moseley originally played its home matches at The Reddings until the end of the 1999-2000 season.

With the start of the 2000-2001 season, Moseley moved to a new home on the University of Birmingham campus. A member of the English National League, it is among the top 40 clubs in England.

Old Edwardians RFC

Streetsbrook Road, Solihull
Tel: (0121) 744 6831

Rugby and cricket club. Bars and crèche.

Birmingham & Solihull RFC

Sharmans Cross Road, Solihull
Tel: (0121) 705 0409

Now the Pertemps Bees, as a result of a three-year sponsorship deal, this (currently) First Division rugby club results from a merger in 1989 between Birmingham RFC and Solihull RUFC, both formed in the 1940s.

Birmingham North-West

David Lloyd Leisure Health & Fitness Club

Shady Lane, Great Barr
Tel: (0121) 325 0700

Gym, fitness classes, tennis courts, fitness coaching. Membership required.

Open: Mon – Sat 7am – 11pm, Sun 8am – 10pm.
How to get there: Just off J7/M6.

Athletics

Alexander Stadium, Perry Barr
Tel: (0121) 344 4858

Home to the city's top athletics club Birchfield Harriers. Caters for all ages, disciplines and standards from Olympic champions to recreational runners.

Hilltop Golf Course

Park Lane, Handsworth
Tel: (0121) 554 4463

18 hole course and putting green. Advance booking recommended.

Warley Golf Course

The Pavilions, Lightwoods Hill, Smethwick
Tel: (0121) 429 2440

18 hole course and putting green. Advance booking recommended.

Greyhound Racing Perry Barr Greyhound Racing Stadium

Aldridge Road, Perry Barr
Tel: 0870 840 7411/2

Live greyhound racing. Fun night out.

Open: Thurs, Fri & Sat evenings, Wed and Sun afternoons.

West Bromwich Albion F.C.

The Hawthorns, West Bromwich
Tel: (0121) 525 8888
www.wba.co.uk

Nicknamed the Baggies, West Bromwich Albion is one of the oldest names in English football, and one of a small group of clubs to have won all three major domestic honours. Formed in 1879 as West Bromwich Strollers, it became Albion a year later, and in 1888 joined their neighbours Aston Villa and Wolverhampton Wanderers among the original 12 members of the Football League.

Birmingham North-East

STARCITY,

Watson Road, Birmingham
Tel: (0870) 844 66 00
www.starcitym6j6.com

A 22 lane bowling alley, American pool and Holmes Place Health Club with gym, pools and fitness classes.

Open: Daily.
How to get there: 10 minutes drive from city centre. Off J5 and J6/M42. STARCITY is adjacent to The Fort Shopping Park.

Wyndley Leisure Centre

**Clifton Road,
Sutton Coldfield**
Tel (0121) 464 7741

Public leisure pool, fitness suite, sunbeds, beautician, athletics track, badminton and squash courts.

Open: daily 7am-11pm.

Pype Hayes Golf Course

**Eachelhurst Road,
Sutton Coldfield**
Tel: (0121) 351 1014

18 hole course and putting green. Advance booking recommended.

Aston Villa FC

**Trinity Road,
Villa Park, Aston**
Tel: (0121) 327 5353
www.avfc.co.uk

Formed in 1874 they later became one of the twelve founder members of the Football League. Villa Park became the club's home in 1897. Since then the grounds have become the regular site of FA Cup semi-finals, hosting games at the 1966 World Cup and the European Championships. Their first match was against a rugby team – they won 1-0. Nicknamed 'The Villains'. The Aston Villa ground includes an impressive museum, tour of the pitch and - for the real enthusiasts - 48 hour city breaks that include a ticket to a home match. Telephone for details of Sunday tours also.

Birmingham Bullets (Basketball)

8 Aston Hall Road, Aston
Tel: (0121) 246 6022

A taste of the USA. Many of the players are from there.

Out of town but nearby

Solihull Ice Rink

Hob's Moat Road, Solihull
Tel: (0121) 742 5561

Home to the Barons Ice Hockey team. Skating lessons, bar, cafe.

Open: 11am – 4pm during school holidays plus some evening sessions.

Stratford Racecourse

**Luddington Road,
Stratford-upon-Avon**
Tel: (01789) 267 949
www.stratfordracecourse.net

Open: Easter – September. Off B439, 1 mile from the town centre.

Warwick Racecourse

Hampton Street, Warwick
Tel: (01926) 491 553
www.warwickracecourse.co.uk

Full racing calendar all year round. A short walk from Warwick Castle.

Open: all year.

Marriott Forest of Arden Hotel & Country Club

Maxstoke Lane, Meriden
Tel: (01676) 522 335
www.marriotthotels.com/cvtgs

Two, 18 hole courses – the Arden Championship and the Aylesford. Hosts the British Masters until 2005. Members and residents only.

Stonebridge Golf Centre

Somers Road, Meriden
Tel: (01676) 522 442
www.stonebridge.co.uk

Leading pay-as-you-go centre. Floodlit driving range, challenging 18 hole course, bar and restaurant and conference centre.

Ardencote Manor Hotel & Country Club

Lye Green Road, Claverdon, Warwick
Tel: (01926) 843 111
www.ardencote.co.uk

Country manor hotel with 9 hole course, gym, pool bar and restaurant.

Dunstall Park Racecourse

**Dunstall Park Centre,
Wolverhampton**
Tel: 0870 220 2442.

Britain's first floodlit racecourse. All-weather racing throughout the year

with themed Saturday evening meetings. On-site Holiday Inn hotel and exhibition hall.

Speedway Wolverhampton Wolves

**Ladbroke Stadium,
Sutherland Avenue,
Wolverhampton**
Tel: (01902) 870 400
www.wolverhampton-speedway.com

Top speedway action.

Open: March – October, Mon from 7.30pm.

Alison Nicholas Golf Academy

**Queslett Park, Booths Lane,
Great Barr**
Tel: (0121) 360 7600

9 hole academy course with teaching facilities, 58 bay all-weather driving range. Bar.

The Snowdome

**Leisure Island, River Drive,
Tamworth**
Tel: 0870 500 0011
www.snowdome.co.uk

It's not much if you're used to blizzards but the 558ft (170m) real snow slope offers skiing, snowboarding, tobogganing and adrenalin tubing. Lessons can be booked. Bar and restaurant.

Open: daily 8.30am – 11.15pm.

The De Vere Belfry

Wishaw
Tel: (01675) 470 301
www.deveregolf.co.uk

Golfing heaven. Internationally renowned club and Ryder Cup host. The Brabazon course, the PGA National Course and the Derby course. Restaurant, bar and conference facilities.

Mallory Park Circuit,

Kirkby Mallory
Tel: (01455) 842 931
www.mallorypark.co.uk

Watch or join in with car and motorbike racing schools.

Open: daily.

If you like...

Walks and trails

There are plenty of opportunities to walk around the city centre. The quarters and districts are reasonably distinct and moving from one to another is easily achieved without having to resort to too many subway passes.

There are also organised walks and trails; having a professional guide can make sightseeing that bit easier but beware, commentary is invariably in English - with or without the Birmingham accent.

Birmingham may be home to the car but it is at its best when explored by foot - or canal. A walk by the canal for instance, away from the crowds of Gas Street Basin, reveals a different world and a water-borne community. The backs of factories, the disused wharfs and trees spreading outer branches across the water - decked with makeshift swings erected by local children - give a different perspective to the industrial city.

Then there are ghost walks and, of course, the Tolkien Trail (although unless you are particularly hardy, a car or public transport is recommended).

Central / Jewellery Quarter

Ghost Walk

A former mayor of Birmingham is reputed to still watch over the city. Whether or not you see him on this one-hour walk is likely to be dependent on your imagination. You will also hear about the landlady who, to this day, haunts the area where she met her maker – in Paradise Street of all places - and the last man to be publicly hanged in Birmingham. For reservations, see below.

Graveyard Walk

City walks around Warstone Cemetery in the Jewellery Quarter bring the area and its residents to life. Walks last around 1 hour. Specific evenings.

Tickets must be purchased in advance from the Tourism and Ticket shop, The Rotunda, 150 New Street, or by phone on (0121) 202 5000 (postal charge applies). Private group walks for 10 or more persons are also available.
E-mail: birmingham.walks@btopenworld.com.

Cost: B. Call for details. Tailored walks for groups of 10+.

Jewellery Quarter Pavement Trails

The Findings Trail

Designed by jeweller, Laura Potter, the Heart starts the trail from Newhall Street, past the Assay Office and the RBSA gallery and along Graham Street and back into town past the Sikh Gurdwara Temple and near the old Elkington Building where electroplating was invented. There are 30 pavement slabs made from stainless steel based on a 'finding' – a jewellery hallmark tag. Each plaque has a glass cat's-eye to reflect light day and night, symbolising the qualities of a gemstone. (See page 46).

The Charm Bracelet Pavement Trail

The start of the trail is the Key at the bottom of Newhall Hill. Walk past the site of one of the largest public gatherings when, in 1832, 200,000 Chartists met to campaign for parliamentary reform, crossing over after the Assay Office just past Legge Lane and up Frederick Street to the Chamberlain Clock. Designed by local artists, Renn and Thacker. Each giant charm contains a fact and at the end at Newhall Hill is a charm bracelet padlock, which is lit at night. (See page 46).

Central / Convention Quarter

Pub Walks

Various walks from one pub to the next have been devised, amongst them The Classic Pub Walk by Marigold Lankester, B.A., a Blue Badge Guide. (See page 99) Including Crown, 182 Corporation Street; Old Royal, 53 Church Street; Edwards, 36-37 Broad Street; James Brindley, 12 Bridge Street and Bacchus Bar, Burlington Arcade, New Street.

Birmingham South-West / South-East

In Tolkien's Footsteps

Birmingham Visitor Information Centre Guided Tours
Tel: (0121) 202 5099
www. tolkiensociety.org
(Owing to the distance, a car is advisable, but see also page 164 for details of Tolkien by bus)

With the trilogy of films helping to popularise the works of author J.R.R. Tolkien, walking in his footsteps has become a popular activity - although not as easy as it should be.

An eminent scholar and the author of books on Anglo-Saxon and Middle English, Tolkien's celebrity lies in his wonderful fantasy novels; glorious trips into the imagination that engage adults as much as children.

J.R.R. Tolkien was born in South Africa in 1892 although both his parents came from Birmingham. It was whilst on holiday visiting his grandparents in the now suburban village of Kings Heath with his mother Mabel and younger brother, Hilary, that his father died.

The family stayed and the young John Ronald Reuel went to King Edward's School which was, at the time, in New Street in the city centre. They lived at 264, Wake Green Road (a private residence), Sarehole, near Hall Green then moved to Moseley, Kings Heath and Ladywood.

Mabel died in 1904 and the two boys went to live with their aunt. They were unhappy times and the brothers moved into lodgings in Duchess Road. Tolkien was only 16 and it was here he fell in love with Edith Bratt who later became his wife. In an effort to put an end to the relationship, his guardian, Father Morgan, moved the two boys to Highfield Road, Hall Green, Tolkien's last home in Birmingham.

Whilst in Highfield Road, Tolkien learned he had been awarded a place at Exeter College, Oxford, a move that took him into a world of scholastic studies and away from Birmingham forever.

His memories of growing up in and around Birmingham – the people and the places – were

important foundations for what were to become best-selling fantasy novels. J.R.R. Tolkien died in 1973, aged 81.

Two Towers

Waterworks Road, Edgbaston

Also known as Perrott's folly. 96ft (30m), seven storey, octagonal tower with battlements built in 1758 by John Perrott. Birmingham University has used it as an observatory. It is close to a second, Victorian tower, part of Edgbaston Waterworks. Together they are reminiscent of 'Minas Morgul' and 'Minas Tirith', the famous 'Two Towers of Gondor'. (Care should be taken by tourists visiting this area).

Speaking Brummie

Whilst you are walking around Birmingham, listen out for what others in Britain claim to be the country's least popular accent.

But beauty, as they say, is in the eyes – or ears – of the beholder.

A study conducted by Birmingham University PhD student Steve Thorne, concluded that the Brummie accent is a lilting melodious tone which impresses overseas visitors.

"Contrary to popular belief, there is nothing wrong with Birmingham speech – Birmingham English is not an inferior variety, nor is it inherently ugly. Non-native English speakers unaware of the social connotations which Brummie possesses for British English speakers do not discriminate on the same grounds. This strongly suggests that attitudes towards the Birmingham dialect are influenced by factors such as social snobbery, negative media stereotyping, the poor public image of the city of Birmingham, and the north/south geographical and linguistic divide," said Mr Thorne when the study was released in 2003.

Many features of contemporary Birmingham speech were used in Shakespeare's works and can be traced back to Anglo-Saxon settlers in the area in the sixth century, according to the study.

Sarehole

A place of exploration for the young Tolkien and his brother, Sarehole was translated into 'The Shire', the home of the hobbits. The working watermill is now a museum – the imaginative boys nicknamed the miller's son the 'White Ogre' as he was often chasing them off. During the 1960s, Tolkien contributed to a public appeal to restore the Mill. (See page 57).

Across the road at 264, Wake Green Road is where Tolkien is said to have spent his happiest days. This is a private home. No access is possible.

Moseley Bog

A mile or so down the road is Moseley Bog, a local nature reserve. It's not hard to see how the Bog would influence a creative mind. There are entrances on Yardley Wood Road and via Wake Green Road playing fields. (see page 56).

Churches

Following Mabel's conversion to Catholicism, the family worshipped at St. Anne's church in Alcester Street. When they started praying there, it was a relatively new church as it was built in 1884 to replace Cardinal Newman's original chapel.

Open: service times. Tel: (0121) 772 2780.

Mabel found immense solace in her faith, spending time at The Oratory on the Hagley Road. Father Francis Xavier Morgan became the boys' guardian following their mother's death. (See page 53).

Blue Badge Guides

Heart of England Tourist Guides Association.

Tel: (0121) 711 3225
www.touristguide-bluebadges.co.uk

Blue Badge tourist guides are registered and trained. They cover Birmingham and the counties in the Heart of England area. Special interests include industrial heritage and medieval history. Corporate events, coach tours and individual guided tours. Many are linguists.

Rates: on request.

If you Like...

Theatres, Cinemas, Comedy and Music

OK, so Birmingham may not be able to compete with London when it comes to theatres but nightlife in the city is thriving.

It is the only city outside London to have its own symphony orchestra and ballet company. Most recently, it has attracted the Royal College of Organists to establish themselves in Birmingham's Eastside quarter.

The symphony orchestra - the CBSO - and the Royal Ballet, the latter based at Birmingham Hippodrome Theatre, have done much to attract worldwide attention to Birmingham's cultural output.

In addition, Birmingham has established a fine reputation for its Jazz Festival (first two weeks of July) and Birmingham Screen Festival (March). More recently, Artsfest (September) has become the UK's largest concentration of free events.

Birmingham is also the birthplace of the repertory theatre movement. The present Repertory Theatre, Centenary Square, is well respected for its productions whilst the (original) Old Rep stages both professional and amateur theatre.

Birmingham also hosts major concert tours - particularly at the NEC Arena and National Indoor Arena. Symphony Hall, at the International Convention Centre, hosts world-class orchestras and performers.

And if you fancy a good laugh (this is, after all, the home of comedian Jasper Carrott) there is a host of comedy clubs, including established venues such as The Glee Club and Jongleurs, and also local pubs (but phone first to check listings).

Central Quarter

The Alexandra Theatre

Station Street
Tel: 070 607 6533
www.cclivelive.co.uk

When it was first opened in 1901, it was known as The Lyceum – it didn't last long, the curtain came down later that same year. It re-opened, this time as the Alexandra. The unprepossessing exterior conceals a lovely Edwardian theatre.

Odeon

New Street
Tel: (0870) 505 0007
www.odeon.co.uk

It was originally The Paramount back in 1937 and changed its name to The Odeon in 1942. When it was built, there was seating for 2,440 people. The Compton Organ was installed in 1965. New Street Odeon is now a modern, multiscreen cinema showing latest releases.

The Old Rep Theatre

Station Street
Tel: (0121) 236 4455
www.birminghamstage.net

Small theatre with professional resident company. Stages some acclaimed pieces.

Birmingham Repertory Theatre

Centenary Square
Tel: (0121) 200 2000
www.birmingham-rep.co.uk

Next to the ICC and at the heart of Centenary Square, Birmingham Rep was built in 1971 and flaunts a lot of the features that epitomised design at the time – a functional appearance, large windows, little noticeable decoration. The auditorium seats 900. The theatre is respected for the calibre of its productions, its innovative approach to drama and making theatre accessible to all. Recently refurbished bar/restaurant Wine REPublic.

Eastside

IMAX Theatre

Millennium Point, Curzon Street
Tel: (0121) 202 2222
www.millenniumpoint.org.uk

Huge, 16m x 20m cinema screen. Amazing, vivid, 2D and 3D films – calling them educational is simply inadequate – with 'A' class celebrity narrators. Just to get some idea of the scale, the screen is more than five stories high with a width of four double-decker buses. In addition to vast-scale IMAX films (which can really take your breath away) the theatre also shows general release films, blockbusters and classics. Niche films, not normally shown in high street cinemas, also get an airing. These are not 3D large screen format and so only take up a proportion of the screen – but are still impressive.

Major arts festivals

Birmingham Screen Festival, March
Tel: (0121) 643 0631
www.birminghamscreenfestival.com

Birmingham International Jazz Festival, July
Tel: (0121) 454 7020
www.birminghamjazzfestival.com

ArtsFest, September
www.artsfest.org.uk

Comedy Festival, September
www.icBirmingham.co.uk/comedyfestival

The Birmingham Book Festival, October
Tel: (0121) 236 5622
www.lit-net.org/bbf/

Chinese Quarter

The Hippodrome

Hurst Street
Tel: (0870) 730 1234
www.bhip.ws

The Hippodrome first opened its doors in 1899 as the Tower of Varieties and Circus. In 1900 it was renamed the Tivoli Theatre and became The Hippodrome in 1903. The home of Birmingham Royal Ballet and the DanceXchange (0121 689 3174), it was recently refurbished and includes several bars and the Hippodrome Restaurant (0121 689 3181). The season often includes productions by major opera companies. Traditional Christmas pantomimes are real spectacles.

The Glee Club

Arcadian Centre
Tel: (0121) 693 2248
www.glee.co.uk

Still the city's leading comedy venue. Big names on the comedy circuit come here. Recently refurbished to include a nice, new bar. Large single-sex groups have to pay a 'good behaviour' deposit.

Convention Quarter

Broadway Plaza

Ladywood Middleway, Edgbaston

An entertainment hub on the site of the city's former children's hospital. Multi-screen 'Film City', Bowlplex with 20 lane alley, 13 table pool pit, Video World, Stadium Bar and Grill, health and fitness club with restaurants, bars and shops around a central piazza. Car parking for 1,400.

The Crescent Theatre

20 Sheepcote Street, Brindleyplace
Tel: (0121) 643 5858
www.crescent-theatre.co.uk

A 340 seat auditorium with an intimate atmosphere. Canal-side location with easy access to bars and restaurants.

The city's Artsfest is an annual arts showcase with the UK's largest concentration of free events. Over 11,000 come to the events.

Hard Rock Café

263 Broad Street
Tel: (0121) 665 6562

An air guitartist's delight, decorated with guitars owned by Richie Sambora, Bob Dylan, Paul Weller, Leslie West and Jimmy Page amongst others.

Open: daily from 12noon with live music on Wed and Fri (£3 entrance charge on Wed).

Jongleurs Comedy Club

Quayside Tower, Broad Street
Tel: (0870) 787 0707
www.jongleurs.com

One of the new kids on the block to keep The Glee Club on its toes. Next to the Rococo Lounge.

Open: Thurs – Sat 7pm – 2am.

Oscar Deutsch (1893 – 1941) was born in Balsall Heath, the son of a scrap metal merchant. His magnificent, art-deco Odeon Theatres spread to many British towns and cities. The Odeon in New Street had the UK's second largest auditorium before it was transformed into a multi-screen complex.

The National Indoor Arena (NIA)

Broad Street
Tel: (0121) 780 4444
www.necgroup.co.uk/thenia

Venue for major rock concerts and even clasical events, the NIA also incorporates the smaller Academy.

O'Neills Irish Bar

Broad Street
Tel: (0121) 616 7821

Live music Fridays and Sundays with some quality acts. Last Saturday each month is Northern Soul night. Tuesday is student night in the music room. Saturday night DJs until 2am.

Symphony Hall

ICC, Broad Street
Tel: (0121) 780 3333
www.necgroup.co.uk/symphony

Opened in 1991, Symphony Hall is recognised as one of the most acoustically perfect concert halls in the world. It is home to the City of Birmingham Symphony Orchestra.

Symphony Hall is positioned on 2,000 rubber 'shock absorbers' preventing external vibration reaching the hall.

UGC Cinema

Broad Street, Five Ways, Edgbaston
Tel: (0870) 907 0723

12 screen cinema. Walking distance from Centenary Square.

Jewellery Quarter

The Jam House

3 St. Paul's Square
Tel: (0121) 200 3030.

The inspiration of Jools Holland its restaurant combines world-class rhythm 'n' blues with good food and a chance to dance.

Open: Mon – Fri noon – late, Sat: 6pm – 2am. **££**

Birmingham is the centre for the UK's Asian music industry, it's the UK centre for Garage and the base for the UK's first South Asian Music Performance and Dance company, SAMPAD

Birmingham South-West

Birmingham Botanical Gardens

Westbourne Road, Edgbaston
Tel (0121) 454 1864

Music alfresco on Sunday afternoons during the summer. (See page 52)

Birmingham Cheeky Monkey

The Station, 7 High Street, Kings Heath
Tel (0121) 444 1257

Pub-style comedy club.

Birmingham Comedy Kav

The Patrick Kavanagh, Woodbridge/Trafalgar Roads, Moseley
Tel (07092) 252 844

Comedy Club in traditional pub surroundings.

The MAC Arts Centre

Cannon Hill Park, Russell Road, Edgbaston
Tel: (0121) 440 3838
www.mac-birmingham.org.uk

The MAC is in Cannon

Hill Park, two miles from the city centre. It's a 'hands-on' type of venue showing popular and art house films; there are dance, drama and music studios, puppet theatre and courses to learn everything from textiles to circus skills. Bustling and popular with local people.

Open: Daily 9am – 9pm. Admission: Variable. Some courses and activities are free.

Bear Tavern

Bearwood Road,
Tel (0121) 429 8413

Comedy Club.

Birmingham South-East

The NEC Arena

Junction 6, M42
Box Office: (0870) 909 4133
www.necgroup.co.uk

Located in the busiest exhibition centre in Europe. The 12,000-seat Arena has hosted shows by the greatest stars in the entertainment universe including Pavarotti, Tom Jones and Eric Clapton.

The Red Lion,

Vicarage Road, King's Heath
Tel: (0121) 441 6941

The city's premier folk music venue.

Ty's Jazz & Spice

132 Stratford Road, Sparkbrook
Tel: (0870) 066 0868
www.tys-jazzspice.co.uk

Great combination of live jazz and ‹ delicious Kashmiri food.

Open: Tues – Sat 5pm – late.
£££ (inc. jazz club fee).

Birmingham North-East

The Drum

Potters Lane, Aston
Tel: (0121) 333 2444

The Drum is one of the UK's biggest African, Asian and Caribbean arts centres. Dedicated to promoting performance and visual arts.

> In 1855, Alexander Parkes, the son of a Birmingham locksmith invented semi-synthetic plastic, which six years later, was developed into celluloid.

Warner Village Cinemas

STARCITY, Watson Road, Birmingham
Tel: (0870) 240 6020
www.warnervillage.co.uk

Billed as 'the Midland's biggest entertainment destination', STARCITY aspires to a Las Vegas-style ambience. The cinema complex is huge – the largest in the UK. There's an advance booking service, a fully licensed bar and comfy, reclining seats that have loads of leg-room.

> The character George Dixon in the 1949 film *The Blue Lamp* and the TV series *Dixon of Dock Green* was named after producer Sir Michael Balcon's old school, The George Dixon School, Edgbaston

If you like...

Clubs and Casinos

Birmingham's nightlife has improved immeasurably in recent years. Although focused around Broad Street in the Convention quarter and the Arcadian in the Chinese Quarter, you should not ignore some of the more specialist offerings, such as in Digbeth, Eastside.

Clubs

Most tastes are catered for: pop and rock; music from the seventies and eighties; jazz, soul and funk, hip-hop, techno and electronica as well as salsa.

Phone or visit websites for the latest information especially to check out whether you can get on a club's guest list. The advantages can include no queuing to get in and access to the VIP lounge or Champagne lounge.

Most clubs do not get under way until 10pm although you may find that if you arrive earlier, entrance is free or at a reduced price. Most are open until 2am or later. During the week, a number of clubs have free entrance for women.

Casinos

The city's casinos are particularly popular with the Chinese community. Even if you do not intend to spend (or lose) too much money, they provide some fascinating people watching. At present, casinos are required to operate the '24 hour rule' which means that 24 hours must lapse between receipt of application and participation (this law is due to be changed as part of the government's proposal to de-regulate the industry). You are advised to telephone in advance of your visit. Most casinos open around 2pm and remain open till between 4am and 6am the following morning.

Adult entertainment

Birmingham has achieved something of an unwanted reputation for its table (or lap) dancing clubs. Indeed, some of the city fathers have endeavoured to prevent the development of such clubs, particularly in the mainstream entertainment areas. The reputable city-centre clubs have the same rule: you can watch but don't touch. Opening hours vary. Most are late afternoon going through till 2am

The gay scene

Birmingham's gay nightlife is predominantly focused around the streets in the Chinese Quarter where there are a number of stylish clubs and bars as well as lifestyle shops. The whole area enjoys a village-like atmosphere.

Clubs

Central Quarter

Hush Club

55 Station Street
Tel: (0121) 242 6607

Open only to members and guests and particularly suited for those late nights when other clubs have closed.

The Academy

Dale End
Tel: (0121) 262 3000

Major venue for big bands on tour. Twinned with the Shepherd's Bush Empire and Brixton Academy, this sizeable venue is particularly popular with students.

Snobs

29 Paradise Circus, Queensway
Tel: (0121) 643 5551

Little in the way of a dress code and lots in the way of fun, particularly for youngsters.

Convention

The Works

182 Broad Street
Tel: (0121) 633 1520.

Large, purpose-built night club (can hold 2,400 clubbers), opened in 2001. Three rooms focus on different styles from dance and party to funk house.

APT/Polaris

Broad Street, Five Ways
Tel: (0121) 643 9722

APT is the restaurant; Polaris the night club. Both boast decor that is smart and cool and will prove popular with a mixed age range. Open from noon until 2am Monday – Saturday (and Sunday 5pm – 12.30am). You can go for more discreet dining by booking one of the restaurant's many private booths.

Stoodi Bakers

192 Broad Street
Tel: (0121) 643 5100

You'll see a lot of younger clubbers and 'pretty people'.

Flares

55 Broad Street
Tel: (0121) 632 5500

A blast from the Birmingham club scene past. Old name but new club. Very 70s. Small dance floor. Mixed age range. Fun. Expect to queue to get in. Prices depend on day and time.

Bakers

162 Broad Street, Five Ways
Tel: (0121) 633 3839
www.bakerstheclub.co.uk

Resident DJs including Dave Pearce (Radio 1), Jon Hollis and Andy Cleeton.

Bobby Brown's the Club

52 Gas Street
Tel: (0121) 643 2573

Off Broad Street, three bars, bistro and club in what was a canal side warehouse. A favourite with over 25s.

Jewellery Quarter

Miss Moneypenny's

1 James Street
Tel: (0121) 693 6960

Trendy mainstream club with VIP lounge.

The Jam House

1 St Paul Square
Tel: (0121) 200 3030

The inspiration of jazz musician Jools Holland, this is, without doubt, the best live music venue in Birmingham. A vast mix of pop and jazz of the type popularised by Jools Holland's late night TV programmes - and there is always the chance of big name celebrities joining the club's jazz pianists.

Chinese Quarter

Zanzibar

Hurst Street
Tel: (0121) 643 4715

Present-day music played with loads of decibels.

Sobar

The Arcadian Centre, Hurst Street
Tel: (0121) 693 5084/5087

Drinking and eating venue that stays open till 2am Friday to Sunday.

Eastside

Air

Heath Mill Lane, Digbeth
Tel: (0121) 693 2633

Three rooms - Oxygen, Nitrogen and Carbon - make for a heady mix. Mixed age range (pockets of 30+ spotted). Trance, progressive, hard house, rave, techno, dance. Not cheap – around £10 depending on membership and time of night. Strict dress code – no denim or leisurewear allowed.

Medicine Bar

The Custard Factory, Gibb Street,
Tel: (0121) 693 6333

A wide variety of music according to the day of the week and the day in the month. Located in Birmingham's leading arts venue.

The Sanctuary

High Street, Digbeth
Tel: (0121) 246 1010

One of the top student venues in well used surroundings, and certainly less sophisticated than Broad Street, but where the music, particularly drum and bass, rules.

Birmingham South-West

Liberty's

184 Hagley Road
Tel: (0121) 454 4444
www.libertysnightclub.co.uk

Mainstream club appealing particularly to 25+ clubbers. Courtesy bus runs from Broad Street. VIP lounge, restaurant.

Tower Ballroom

Reservoir Road, Edgbaston
Tel: (0121) 454 0107

Still going strong after several decades so it must be getting something right. A favourite with mature clubbers. Band at weekends, good resident DJ. Revolving stage, fantastic tribute nights.

Birmingham North-East

The Bel Air at The De Vere Belfry

Wishaw
Tel: (01675) 470 301
www.devereonline.co.uk

A sophisticated nightspot in the world famous De Vere Belfry resort. Four bars, restaurant.

Casinos

Central Quarter

Gala Casino

84 Hill Street
Tel: (0121) 643 1777
www.galacasino.co.uk

Free membership (24 hour rule applies). Blackjack, American roulette, casino stud poker, free car jockey service, cafe, à la carte restaurant.

Convention Quarter

Grosvenor Casino

Broad Street, Five Ways
Tel: (0121) 631 3535

Big and bold as befits its Broad Street location.

Chinese Quarter

China Palace Casino

16-18 Hurst Street
Tel: (0121) 622 3313

Free membership (24 hour rule applies). Blackjack, roulette, stud poker. Car Park. Buffet restaurant and bar.

Birmingham North-East

StarCity Casino

StarCity
Tel: 0800 3283332
www.starcitycasino.co.uk

Billed as 'The Vegas Experience', this is Britain's biggest casino with 40 gaming tables – and should you tire of the gaming, there is always dinner and cabaret plus a late night Champagne Show at 11.30pm.

Adult Entertainment

Convention Quarter

The Rocket Club

258 Broad Street
Tel: (0121) 643 4525
www.therocketclub.com

An 'executive gentlemen's club'. No membership required.

Chinese Quarter

Legs 11

30 Ladywell Walk
Tel: (0121) 666 7004

Table dancing club, stage shows, personal dances. Only escorted women welcome. Open plan, no private booths. Strictly no contact between customers and dancers. No membership required.

Birmingham South-West

Spearmint Rhino Gentlemen's Club

64 Hagley Road, Edgbaston
Tel: (0121) 455 7656
www.spearmintrhino.com

World famous table dancing club. No membership required.

The Gay Scene Pubs and Bars

Chinese Quarter

Angel's Cafe Bar

131 Hurst Street
Tel: (0121) 244 2626

Large bar, pool tables and DJ. Serves food.

Boots Bar

77 Wrentham Street
Tel: (0121) 622 1414
www.come.to/bootsbar

Amsterdam-style bar for skins, leather and uniform. Also has a cruise maze. Men's bar. Not for the faint-hearted.

Clone Zone

Hurst Street
Tel: (0121) 666 6640

Gay lifestyle shop selling books, clothes, cards, CDs, DVDs etc.

DV8

Essex Street
Tel: (0121) 666 6366.

Large warehouse-style club. Two dance floors and three bars on two levels and outside area.

Open: Thurs – Sun 10pm – 4am

Equator

Hurst Street
Tel: (0121) 622 5077

A 'best new bar on the scene' winner. Stylish decor with comfy sofas to lounge on. Serves food and has regular drinks promotions. Quiz nights and late licence certain Saturdays.

The Fountain Inn

Wrentham Street
Tel: (0121) 622 1452

Real ale pub with a beer garden. A leather and denim place, popular with men.

Missing

Hurst Street
Tel: (0121) 622 1718

Cabaret bar.

The Nightingale

Essex House, Kent Street
Tel: (0121) 622 1718
www.nightingaleclub.co.uk

Large club and bar. 3 floors and 5 bars. Two discos, restaurant and games room and garden. Winner of 'Best Midlands Gay Venue' 2002.

Open: Daily from 5pm.

PK @ The Wellington

72 Bristol Street
Tel: (0121) 622 2592

Traditional pub.

Route Two

Hurst Street
Tel: (0121) 622 3366

The city's largest gay bar. Fun pub. Cabaret/DJs most nights.

Saathi

Cobs, 127 Sherlock Street
Tel: 07799 201267
www.saathi.org.uk

The region's major Asian gay venue. Asian gay night every 2nd Friday monthly although everyone's welcome.

Open: from 10pm.

The Village Inn

154 Hurst Street
Tel: (0121) 622 4742

Traditional bar and garden terrace.

52 North

The Arcadian, Hurst Street,
Tel (0121) 622 5250

and Route 66

139 Hurst Street,
Tel (0121) 622 3366

are both regarded locally as "gay-friendly" as are several of the bars and restaurants in The Mailbox, Convention Quarter.

Convention Quarter

The Jester

Holloway Circus
Tel: (0121) 643 0155

One of the oldest gay bars in the city. Mixed crowd. Circular bar downstairs. Cabaret.

Jewellery Quarter

Subway City

Livery Street
Tel: (0121) 233 0310.

Away from the main gay area, Subway City has several bars and levels with games room, restaurant and chill-out area. A heavier style club than either DV8 or The Nightingale.

Open: 10pm – 4am.

The National Exhibition Centre

Both the National Exhibition Centre and The International Convention Centre/National Indoor Arena in the city-centre (see next page) have had a major impact on the economic prosperity of Birmingham and the region. Some 22,000 full-time jobs have been created. Each year, visitors spend more than £700 million.

When The National Exhibition Centre (NEC) opened in 1976, it immediately dwarfed any other exhibition facility in the UK - including London's Earl's Court and Olympia combined.

Since that time, it has become Europe's busiest exhibition centre, staging more than 180 exhibitions each year, ranging from world-famous public shows such as Crufts Dog Show and the British International Motor Show to international trade exhibitions like IPEX and Spring Fair. In 2003, it hosted the world's largest peripatetic exhibition, ITMA.

The NEC site is not, in fact, in Birmingham - but neighbouring Solihull. Not that you would notice - for the urban conurbation is seamless. The NEC is often described as an exhibition village. Set in 628 acres (254ha), it has its own roads, several on-site hotels, a lake (sometimes used for exhibition displays), car parks and its own security, traffic and fire-fighting forces. Some 4 million people visit the NEC each year and, with 20 halls, it is the biggest exhibition centre in Britain and 7th largest in Europe.

Most know the NEC for its major large-scale international trade fairs and public exhibitions - but a number of smaller specialist shows have been developed.

The Association of Exhibition Organisers has voted the NEC Best Exhibition Venue Management for several consecutive years. The flat-floored, interconnected halls offer organisers endless possibilities for all types of exhibitions and events, complemented by extensive conference and banqueting facilities.

Its history

The origins of the NEC go back to 1959 when an independent committee reported that trade exhibitions would play an increasingly important part in the promotion of export trade for Britain. Throughout the 1960s, various schemes for a London venue were proposed but none came to fruition. Birmingham produced a feasibility study for an exhibition centre on a 300-acre (121ha) site eight miles from the city-centre.

By the early 1970s, plans started to take shape. A company was formed, the gov-ernment endorsed the scheme and offered a financial grant towards initial marketing. In November 1971, outline planning approval was given. Opened in February 1976 by Her Majesty the Queen, the NEC initially offered 89,000 square metres (960.000 sqft) of exhibition space. The first exhibition was the International Spring Fair - a major giftware trade exhibition. In 1989, three further halls were opened by the Queen since which time further expansion has extended it to 200,000 square metres (2.15 million sqft). Further expansion is planned.

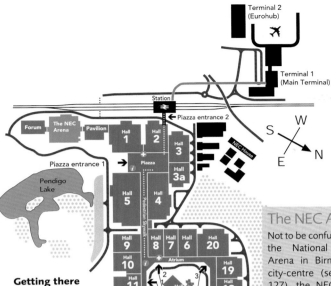

Getting there

The NEC is located eight miles south east of Birmingham city centre.

By road: access is direct from the M42 and M6 motorways which link to the M1, M40 and M6 Toll. There are 22,000 parking spaces and a shuttle bus service operates throughout exhibition periods.

By rail: the NEC is immediately adjacent to Birmingham International Station with its InterCity services from London Euston (90 minutes) to Birmingham New Street in Birmingham city centre (10 to 20 minutes).

By air: the NEC is adjacent to Birmingham International Airport which provides a Skyrail overhead rail shuttle service to Birmingham International station and then by bridgelink direct to the NEC itself.

Facilities

Banks, newsagents, restaurants and cafes, together with business services (such as printing and photography) are available throughout the NEC site.

Hotels

On-site hotels include Crowne Plaza, Hilton Metropole, Express by Holiday Inn and Premier Lodge. (See page 155 for full listing).

Disabled access

The NEC Group publishes a comprehensive leaflet covering all facilities available to visitors with a disability. All levels of the NEC and the NEC Arena are accessible to wheelchair users, by ramps or lifts. Both the Piazza and Atrium main entrances have automatic doors. (See page 127 for additional information).

Information for exhibition visitors

Exhibition visitors are advised to contact the exhibition organiser. The NEC organising team can be contacted on:

Tel: (0121) 780 4141 .
Web: www.necgroup.co.uk/organiser

The NEC Arena

Not to be confused with the National Indoor Arena in Birmingham city-centre (see page 127), the NEC Arena was one of the first large-scale concert venues in the country. Since its opening in 1980, the 12,500 seat arena has staged more than 1,400 concerts attracting more than 14 million people. The legendary rock band Queen was the first to perform. Since that time, the Arena has hosted many of the world's top performers including Shirley Bassey, Whitney Houston, Tina Turner, Elton John, Barry Manilow, Diana Ross, Take That, the Spice Girls, S Club 7, Simply Red, David Bowie and Pavarotti. It has twice been voted Best UK Concert Venue.

It is also used for major sporting events: world gymnastics, wrestling and world figure skating as well as being the home of The Horse of the Year Show. Its size also makes it popular with conference organisers.

The International Convention Centre, Symphony Hall and National Indoor Arena

The International Convention Centre (ICC) which incorporates Symphony Hall, and the separate National Indoor Arena (NIA) are located in Birmingham city-centre in the Convention Quarter.

Operated by the NEC Group, the ICC was opened by H.M. The Queen in 1991, during a meeting of the International Olympic Committee, its first ever full session in Britain. Symphony Hall, an integral part of the building, and the NIA opened that same year.

International Convention Centre

Not the most prepossessing of buildings on the outside, the ICC (developed at a cost of £180 million) is none the less a tribute to its architects and designers - as well as the hundreds that keep it in such pristine condition. The ICC was prompted by the severity of the 1980s industrial recession. Birmingham's unemployment was then twice the national average and its manufacturing economy was badly hit. For a number of years, plans had been discussed to provide a new home for the City of Birmingham Symphony Orchestra (CBSO). The opportunity was taken to combine a major concert venue with a world-class convention facility.

Today, each year it stages more than 400 conferences and related events. It has been the venue for the G8 Summit, the European Summit and frequently hosts the Confederation of British Industry's national conference. Other users have included organisations such as the British Medical Association, Lions International

G8 Summit

Conference, the Law Society, International Red Cross and major corporations such as Ford, Microsoft, Peugeot and Compaq Computers. Without a doubt, the ICC is one of the main reasons for the city centre's resurgence.

Symphony Hall

The 2,200-seat Symphony Hall is home to the internationally acclaimed City of Birmingham Symphony Orchestra. Opened in April 1991, it has been described by critics, performers and public as one of the finest concert halls in the world. Almost every major orchestra has appeared, alongside conductors such as Sir Simon Rattle (who, as conductor of the CBSO, was one of the prime movers), Sir Georg Solti, Valery Gergiev and Daniel

Barenboim. Soloists have included local boy Nigel Kennedy, Dame Kiri Te Kanawa and Evelyn Glennie. Not that it is all classical: Symphony Hall also hosts pop, jazz, folk, world-music and comedy: Bruce Springsteen, Van Morrison, Dudley Moore and Harry Connick Jnr. have all performed beneath the adjustable canopy which is used to tune the hall itself.

Behind the stage can be seen the magnificent organ, completed in 2001.

The National Indoor Arena

The NIA (which, just to reiterate the point made on a previous page, should not be confused with the NEC Arena) is one of the busiest, large-scale indoor sporting and entertainment venues in Europe. More than 4 million visitors have watched some 30 different sports and an extensive variety of entertainment and music. The £51 million development seats up to 13,000 and hosts many international sporting events: the Davis Cup Tennis, the IAAF World Indoor Championships in Athletics (it has the UK's only demountable 6-lane 200 metre track which is dismantled and stored out of season), badminton, judo, power lifting, basketball and wrestling. Concerts, entertainment and business conferences and exhibitions have also been staged: *Disney on Ice*, *Carmen* and *Madam Butterfly* plus concerts by Paul McCartney, Oasis and Coldplay. The TV programme *Gladiators* and the *Eurovision Song Contest* have also been hosted at the NIA. Below the main arena is the community hall which operates a pay and play leisure centre and is used as a warm-up facility during major events.

The NIA Academy, within the NIA itself, creates a more intimate theatre-like auditorium for up to 4,500.

Getting there

The ICC, Symphony Hall and NIA are all at located in the Convention Quarter, approximately 10 minutes walk from Birmingham New Street, Snow Hill and Moor Street stations. Dedicated car parking is available in the adjacent 2,500 space car-park, accessible from St Vincent Street, and King Edward's Road (signposted from Broad St and Queensway).

Facilities

The central concourse includes newsagents, cash dispenser and cloakrooms. A number of retail outlets, including a popular unit specialising in classical music, can also be found .

Hotels

The only hotel with direct access to the ICC is the Hyatt Regency. Many other hotels are within easy walking distance (see p 153 for full listing).

Disabled access

The NEC Group publishes a comprehensive leaflet covering all facilities available to visitors with a disability. All levels of the ICC and NIA are accessible to wheelchair users, by ramps or lifts. The entrance from Centenary Square provides the most convenient access to Symphony Hall. Tactile signs are fitted in the majority of lifts and public areas. Assistance dogs are welcome but are not recommended at loud music concert events. Orange badge holders can park free of charge. Public telephones are available for those with hearing impairments. Those with disabilities attending concerts are advised to call the dedicated ticket line Tel: (0121) 782 3555.

Information for delegates

Convention delegates are advised to contact the Convention Organiser. The ICC organising team can be contacted on Tel: (0121) 200 2000. The National Indoor Arena can be contacted on Tel: (0121) 200 202.

www.necgroup.co.uk/organiser

The Symphony Hall organ

The Symphony Hall organ was built by Johannes Klais Orgelbau, a long-established German firm with one of the finest international reputations.

It stands nearly 65 ft (19.8m) tall, has more than 6,000 pipes which, laid end-to-end would stretch more than two-and-a-half miles. Collectively, they weigh more than 30 tonnes. The pipes are made from a range of woods and metals: oak, fir, pine, and soft metal alloys from tin, lead and zinc. For the biggest 32ft (9.75m) pipe to sound, it takes 1,300 litres of air per minute. This plays the deepest note while the smallest would fit in your pocket!

Birmingham for Business

Birmingham is, first and foremost, a business city. It played a pivotal role in the industrial revolution and today is the capital of a region that is the centre of Britain's industrial heart. This however, is a double-edged sword. Whilst industry was the reason for Birmingham's rise to greatness, the demise of industry also resulted in the perception of Birmingham as a grimy and derelict city.

Even the casual visitor to the city will realise that is no longer the case. The wealth that has been created in the city-centre, through developments such as the International Convention Centre, has slowly spread to encompass most of the city suburbs. New business and industrial parks have been created, many succeeding where run-down industries have failed. It is, as you will hear from any business lobby group, the second largest city in the world's fourth largest economy.

Birmingham is still at the manufacturing heart of the UK (it remains a major automotive centre producing Jaguar, Land Rover, MG Rover and, in neighbouring Coventry, Peugeot cars) but it now concentrates on the value-added end of manufacturing with research and development playing a major role.

Inward investment has been of critical importance. Birmingham is at the centre of a region that has attracted more inward investment than any other European region. This is not surprising when you consider Birmingham's geographical position at the heart of the country, the fact that English is the mother tongue and, for Japanese and US investors in particular, the wealth of golf courses!

Birmingham's financial and professional community has also grown significantly. Some 140,000 are employed in a sector that has become the fastest growing in the city. A further 50,000 jobs are forecast by 2010.

However, it faces increasing competition from Far Eastern and East European countries in particular. Call centres and back office functions are particularly vulnerable.

The city's resurgence has enabled Birmingham to win recognition as one of the world's top corporate destinations with a quality of life superior to locations such as Rome, Milan and Hong Kong - according to a world-wide survey.

Unemployment has fallen by two-thirds over the last 20 years. Output has increased from £8.5 billion to £12 billion over the last 20 years and household disposable income has almost doubled in real terms over the last 20 years. It is forecast that over the next 10 years, some 30 per cent of Birmingham's employment will be in highly skilled occupations.

That is not to say that Birmingham is without problems. There is still a skills shortage and certain sections of the community remain unemployed.

Birmingham statistics

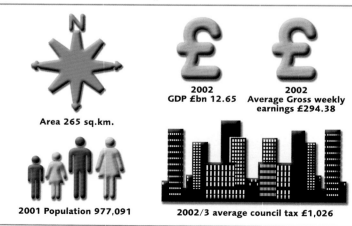

Area 265 sq.km.

2002
GDP £bn 12.65

2002
Average Gross weekly
earnings £294.38

2001 Population 977,091

2002/3 average council tax £1,026

Birmingham's Universities

The city's three universities have a population of some 60,000 students.

Aston University:
www.aston.ac.uk

A key part of the new learning quarter in Eastside, Aston University started life as the Birmingham Municipal Technical School in 1895. In the 1950s, it became the College of Technology, Birmingham - the first college of advanced technology in the country. It became a University in 1966. With more than 7,000 students in its four schools, it is particularly well known for its industrial and commercial partnerships.

University of Birmingham:
www. bham.ac.uk

Established at the turn of the 20th century, the original buildings on the campus at Edgbaston are believed to be the source of the expression "red-brick university". It is a founding member of Universitas 21, a group of top research universities throughout the world. The University of Birmingham is also one of only 25 European institutions to be awarded the distinction of Jean Monnet European Centre of Excellence by the European Commission. It attracts students and staff from around the world; each year, more than 4,500 attend from more than 100 countries.

University of Central England:
www.uce.ac.uk

Birmingham's most recent addition, it was previously Birmingham Polytechnic. Founded in 1843, as a result of the collapse of the Mechanics Institute it was visited by author Charles Dickens. Forced to close in 1853, it was succeeded by the Birmingham Midland Institute. Birmingham Polytechnic was established in 1971 through the merger of Birmingham College of Art (including the School of Jewellery), Birmingham School of Music (including the Conservatoire), Birmingham College of Commerce, South Birmingham Technical College and North Birmingham Technical College. In 1992, Royal Assent was given to The Further and Higher Education Act which enabled all polytechnics to adopt the title "University" if they so chose.

Useful contacts

Advantage West Midlands:
regional development agency
Tel: (0121) 380 3500
www.advantagewm.co.uk

Birmingham and Solihull Learning and Skills Council:
training and skills development
Tel: 0845 019 4143
www.lsc.gov.uk

Birmingham Chamber of Commerce and Industry:
representing businesses based in the city.
Tel: (0121) 454 6171
www.birmingham-chamber.com

Marketing Birmingham:
destination marketing organisation and information for visitors.
Tel: (0121) 603 2000
www.birmingham.org.uk
(see also pages 150-151)

Business Link Birmingham and Solihull:
support for small and medium sized enterprises
Tel: (0121) 607 0809

CBI West Midlands:
industry/commerce membership organisation
Tel: (0121) 454 7991
www.cbi.org.uk

Institute of Directors:
membership organisation
Tel: (0121) 632 2300
www. iod.com

Executives Association of Great Britain – Midlands
forum for developing business relationships
Tel: (01564) 782742
www.eagb-midlands.co.uk

Locate in Birmingham:
inward investment body
Tel: (0121) 303 2222
www.locatebirmingham.org.uk

Birmingham Forward:
access to the city's professional and financial community
Tel: (0121) 632 2200
www.birminghamforward.co.uk

Birmingham Future:
young professional and business support organisation
Tel: (0121) 632 2200
www.birminghamfuture.co.uk

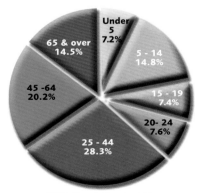

2001 Population by age

Unemployment Rate 7.9%[2]

Average House Price £139,227[1]
Average Residents 2.48
Number of Households 404,000

[1] West Midlands, December 2003. Source: Land Registry

[2] Birmingham, January 2004.
Source: Birmingham Economic Information Centre.

A cultural melting-pot

You can travel the world by spending a few days in Birmingham. Communities as diverse as Asian, Jewish, Irish, Afro-Caribbean, Chinese and, of course, Anglo-Saxon live cheek by jowl.

It is not surprising therefore, that many of the billboards advertising Birmingham have, as the strap line, the words, "Many Worlds ... one great city". Not so long ago, the slogan was "Europe's Meeting Place".

Both are appropriate.

For nearly 1000 years, Birmingham has been the place where people have congregated to trade goods and exchange ideas.

This diversity of population is now potentially one of the city's greatest assets provided it can continue to be harnessed and utilised to full effect.

New communities have been established. The area that, for the purpose of this guide-book, we have designated Chinese Quarter, could just as easily be referred to as the Irish Quarter. Not so long ago, it was known as "Little Italy".

In 1991, the population of Birmingham and neighbouring Solihull was some 1.16 million. In the following decade, the population rose by just 16,000. The dramatic shift though, was in its ethnic profile. The traditional white population declined overall by 7.6 per cent and from a low base in terms of total numbers, some groups, such as black African, rose by 177 per cent (an increase of some 8,000) whilst other Asian groups saw growth of 197 per cent - an additional 17,000 people. By 2001, 43 per cent of children under the age of 15 were of non-white ethnic origin.

As at 2001, some 74 per cent of the population was white but by 2010, this is anticipated to reduce to 63 per cent. Black Caribbean and Indian will then be the largest ethnic groups (respectively 7.5 per cent and 5.3 per cent of the population). And well before 2020, the ethnic majority groups will collectively represent the largest proportion of the Birmingham population.

Such cultural divergence has also led to religious divergence. The most recent census showed nearly one in seven people in Birmingham are Muslim. Sikhs account for nearly three per cent of the population compared to the national average of 0.63

per cent. There are nearly 20,000 Hindus in the city - proportionately far larger than the national average. However, more than half the population is Christian.

Birmingham's cultural diversity is reflected in the arts: the city is the centre of the Asian music industry, the UK centre for Garage Music and the base for the UK's first South Asian Music Performance and Dance company, SAMPAD.

Business is responding to the change in demographics. The city's professional, financial and business support community together with the Learning and Skills Council has, for instance, established a new organisation to provide guidance and support to business to help it effectively manage and value racial diversity. In 2003, more than 80 per cent of people employed in professional and financial service firms were white. With the ethnic population expected to grow by 60,000 by 2010, it recognises that to maintain a competitive edge, businesses need to understand the requirements of the multicultural marketplace by managing and valuing racial diversity ensuring it forms an integral part of the business planning process.

A year in a multi-ethnic community:

Winter

Ed ul Fitr – public holiday in Islamic countries, the celebration marks the end of Ramadan (the spiritual month of fasting).

Birthday Anniversary of Guru Nanak Dev – Sikhs celebrate the birth of Guru Nanak Dev, founder of Sikhism.

Guy Fawkes' Night (Bonfire Night) – November 5: effigies of catholic Guy Fawkes are burnt on bonfires. He attempted to blow up the Houses of Parliament in 1605.

Diwali – Festival of Lights, celebrated by Hindus and Sikhs, commemorating the ancient story of Prince Rama and Sita's homecoming after the defeat of Ravana (the demon king).

Hanukah –Jewish 'Festival of Lights' eight days mid to late December, recalls the Jews' struggle for religious freedom.

Christmas Day – December 25, Christians celebrate the birth of Jesus Christ by going to church, sharing a meal and exchanging presents.

Hogmanay – December 31, with public festivities and fireworks.

Ed ul Adha – four to five-day Islamic festival marking the end of Hajj (the holy pilgrimage to Mecca).

Paranirvana Day – Buddhist festival marking the anniversary of the death of Buddha.

Chinese New Year – determined by the solar/lunar calendar (varying from January to late February), this exciting festival celebrates the earth coming back to life. Fireworks, lantern festivals and special meals are customary.

Burns' Night – January 25, celebrations abound for the anniversary of the birth of Scottish poet Robbie Burns. A special meal with a centrepiece of haggis is traditional.

Spring

Pancake Day (Shrove Tuesday) – celebrated by Christians, a day of penitence and the last chance to feast before Lent, usually on pancakes!

Ash Wednesday – for Christians, this day is the beginning of fasting for Lent, marked with special services where worshippers are dusted with ashes as a symbol of mortality.

Beltane – Pagan fire festival that celebrates the coming of summer and the fertility of the coming year. Traditionally celebrated on April 30th/May 1st.

St Patrick's Day – March 17, when people around the world join in the traditional Irish celebration of the life of St Patrick, who is believed to have converted the Irish to Christianity. The day is marked by parades.

Good Friday – during special services, Christians commemorate the death of Jesus Christ.

Easter Sunday – a day of great joy in the Christian church, Jesus' return to life is celebrated with church services and the sharing of 'easter eggs' - a symbol of new life.

Baisakhi/Vaisakhi – Sikh New Year Festival celebrates the beginning of Sikhism.

St George's Day – April 23 marks the celebration of the life and death of England's patron saint, George, put to death for protesting about the persecution of Christians.

Passover (Pesach) – lasting for eight days, this Jewish celebration commemorates the emancipation of the children of Israel from Egypt. Family and friends gather for Pesach Seder (ritual) meals.

Wesak – the most important day of the year for Buddhists, Wesak celebrates the anniversary of the birth of Buddha.

Summer

Pentecost (Shavout) – Jewish celebration commemorating the giving of the '10 Commandments' to Moses on Mount Sinai. Customs include reading the Torah, eating meals made from dairy products and bringing plants to the synagogue.

Autumn

Rosh Hashanah – two-day Jewish New Year festival commemorating the anniversary of the creation of mankind.

Yom Kippur (Day of Atonement) – the most important day in the Jewish calendar, where God makes the final decision on what the new year will be like for each person. Marked by fasting and services.

Halloween (All Hallows' Eve) – according to medieval tradition, October 31 was the night when the spirits of the dead roamed the earth. Now, regarded as a fun festival for children, with ghostly costumes and sweeties galore!

Sambhain – for most Pagans the end of October is the most important date in the calendar as it marks the beginning of the year.

Source: www.bbc.co.uk/parenting/

Canals and waterways

Birmingham is canal city. No less than eight separate canals converge linking Liverpool in the north-west to London in the south-east and stretching from the River Severn in the west to the River Trent in the east. By the early 1800s, the network was virtually complete: each canal representing the energy, enthusiasm and radical thinking of some of the greatest engineers of the time: James Brindley, Matthew Boulton, James Watt and Thomas Telford.

The driving force of this vigorous and back-breaking work, was Birmingham's rise to industrial prominence. The owners of the extensive coalfields in the Black Country, to the north-west of the city, had to get coal to fuel Birmingham's manufacturing output. Once constructed, canals proved to be a cheap and easy method of transporting thousands of tons each day.

Today, canals are very rarely used by industry but instead form a picturesque backdrop to the city and its regeneration, linking communities with traffic free towpaths (ideal for walking and in parts, cycling) and, of course, viewing Birmingham from a narrow boat.

The canals

The bridge linking the ICC to Brindleyplace (page 41) crosses the **Worcester and Birmingham Canal**. It took more than 20 years to complete to Worcester and includes the UK's longest lock flight at Tardebigge (in Worcestershire). In Gas Street Basin (page 42), a number of the attractively decorated narrowboats are permanent, albeit mobile, homes. Walk for five minutes south-east from Gas Street Basin and you could easily be in the countryside. A further 2 miles (3km) will bring you to the University of Birmingham (Barber Institute of Fine Arts, page 53). A further 2 miles (3km) and you reach Selly Manor and Cadbury World (page 54). Cadbury's narrowboats were still using the canal as late as the early 1960s.

Heading north-west from the ICC and you quickly come to Old Turn Junction where the Worcester and Birmingham Canal meets with the **Birmingham and Fazeley Canal** and the **Birmingham Mainline**. This was the first of the city's canals linking Wednesbury in the Black Country to Newhall Street in Birmingham. It was designed by engineer James Brindley. Walk along the canal for the 3km (2 miles) from the National Indoor Arena (page 42) and you arrive at Soho where Matthew Boulton built steam engines with James Watt from 1796. The canal splits into the Old Mainline and the New Mainline, constructed in the 1820s by Thomas Telford.

The **Birmingham and Fazeley Canal** runs to the north-east, passing under Spaghetti Junction (see page 58) on its way to Tamworth. Planned by canal engineer John

Smeaton, it first passes the National Indoor Arena after which a long flight of locks (known as the Old Thirteen) enable the canal to drop 81 ft (25m) near the BT Tower (page 46). This area was once jammed with horse-drawn boats resulting in 24 hour working and the installation of lighting in the early 1900s. Walking past Spaghetti Junction, you reach the prominent Fort Dunlop building, once a tyre factory, with its nearby (and more recent!) Fort shopping-centre (page 95).

Walk north-west from Spaghetti Junction, and you're on the **Tame Valley Canal**, the most recent of Birmingham's canals completed in 1844.

Walk south from Spaghetti Junction and you are on the **Birmingham and Warwick Junction**, now known as the **Grand Union Canal**. This was opened in 1844 to bypass the city-centre and form a direct link to London. It is linked to the Birmingham and Fazeley Canal by the **Digbeth Branch**, opened around 1799. Nearby is Birmingham's first railway station, Curzon Street (near Millennium Point) (page 30). Opened in 1837, it served trains from Liverpool and later, London.

Finally, there is the **Stratford-upon-Avon Canal**, not readily accessible from the city-centre, joining the Worcester and Birmingham Canal at King's Norton (page 55) and completed in 1816.

A word of warning

Towpath surfaces are generally good but there may be short sections that are uneven or narrow. Ramps can be steep and may prove difficult for those with pushchairs or wheelchairs. Children should be supervised at all times. The water is at least 6ft 6ins (2m) deep. Once outside the city centre, most are not illuminated and should only be used during daylight hours.

Does Birmingham have more canals than Venice?

For many years, that has been the claim. Is it true?

Birmingham City Council claims 114 miles of canals; Cities of Science claim 160 miles (but concede that these are not all within the city boundary). Our reckoning is a much more modest 65.4 miles.

For the purpose of the argument, we will use the smaller figure.

This compares to 28 miles in Venice excluding the off shore islands of Giudecca and San Giorgio Maggiore. But the total area of Birmingham is 265 sq.kms compared to Venice at 7 sq.kms.

Thus, for every square kilometre in Venice there are four miles of canal – compared to just one quarter of a mile of canal per square kilometre in Birmingham. So yes, there are more miles of canal in Birmingham – but the canal network is a lot less intensive.

And only Venice has gondoliers. Or is someone going to claim otherwise?

A few days on the water

Away4awhile

Specialises in full-board, short-break canal cruises where active participation is optional. Routes include Birmingham to Stratford, Warwick to Birmingham and Stratford to Warwick.

Friday to Sunday:
Approx £300 per person
Friday to Monday:
Approx £345 per person
Tel: (0845) 644 5144
Web: www.away4awhile.com

Canal Trips

Find out how the canals made Birmingham into a mighty industrial city with one of the regular sightseeing tours.

Parties Afloat,

Tel: (0121) 236 7057

Regular city centre tour with commentary from Gas Street Basin, near the ICC.

Open: Easter – end Oct.
(Private charter also available).
Admission: B.

Second City Canal Cruises

Tel: (0121) 236 9811/643 7700

Based at the Canal Shop in Gas Street Basin, they operate regular, guided tours from outside the shop.

Sherborne Wharf Heritage Narrowboats

Tel: (0121) 455 6163

From corporate, silver service dining to public, guided tours. 4 times a day from ICC. Commentary.

Open: April – Sept daily,
Oct – March weekends.
Admission: B.

For further information:

British Waterways Birmingham and Black Country Canals
Tel: (0121) 506 1300
Web: www.britishwaterways.co.uk

British Waterways Canal Information Centre
Gas Street
Tel: (0121) 632 6845

Birmingham for little bunnies...

If you're visiting a city with children, getting the balance right between culture and fun is key to the success of the trip for everybody.

There may have to be compromise but it's not always necessary. **ThinkTank** at Millennium Point, Eastside, is interactive fun for everyone. A visit to **Cadbury World** at Bournville can take half a day and everybody learns something about social history and a lot about chocolate – coming away with samples is an added incentive. A bit of trivia is that piling all the Cadbury crème eggs on top of one another would create a chocolate mountain 900 times higher than Everest. **The National Sealife Centre** in the Convention Quarter offers an underwater world in the heart of the city. If your wish is to remain on top of the water, a canal trip (page 133) is both educational and entertaining.

If the weather's good and you've access to a car, there are zoos at **Dudley** and **Twycross**, a safari park and two theme parks – **Alton Towers** and **Drayton Manor**. Visiting the **Black Country Living Museum** will take a day as there's so much to see and do with a Victorian school room, fairground and mine.

Take a ramble in the **Lickey Hills** (page 55) or visit **The Avoncroft Museum of Buildings** - fascinating but your visit will be more pleasant in good weather.

Warwick Castle is great for both adults and children.

The Heritage Motor Centre is great for anyone who gets passionate about machines that have both sleek lines and speed. If you're based at the NEC or the Airport, you can spend an entertaining couple of hours at the **Motorcycle Museum** (page 73) and you don't have to go far to get there.

Convention Quarter

The National Sea Life Centre

One of Europe's largest inland aquaria. Designed by Sir Norman Foster, the walk-through tank is the closest most of us will get to sea life without swimming. The 'discovery trail' is designed to stimulate younger visitors (page 41).

Eastside

ThinkTank: The Birmingham Museum of Science & Discovery

At Millennium Point, it's learning without realising it through hands-on, interactive fun; ideal for children of all ages. Based in Millenium Point (page 29).

Birmingham South-West

The MAC Arts Centre

The MAC is in Cannon Hill Park, two miles from the city centre. It makes culture accessible to children. There are courses (many free) on everything from dance and drama to pottery and circus skills (page 120).

Cadbury World

A great family day out dedicated to the delights and history of chocolate. Lots of free chocolate – guaranteed to satisfy even the sweetest toothed in the family (page 54).

Birmingham Nature Centre

With 134 species of British and European Wildlife, Birmingham Nature Centre provides youngsters with an insight into the lives of animals (page 52).

Birmingham South-East

Birmingham Railway Museum/ Shakespeare Express

Steam locomotives and workshops on the site of an old Great Western Railway steam shed. Children will love 'Henry', a small tank engine (page 57).

Birmingham North-East

STARCITY

M6, Junction 6

We're not talking discreet or sophisticated; STARCITY is the epitome of loud, brash fun. You'll need money – and plenty of it because they'll be tempted at every turn. 22 lane bowling alley with video games, a 'Billy Bubbles' entertainment centre and a 30 screen cinema. A choice of restaurants and bars (page 59).

South-West

West Midlands Safari and Leisure Park

Off A456, 2 miles west, Kidderminster
Tel: (01299) 4021141
www.wmsp.co.uk

Drive-through animal safari park with an amusement area.

Open: March-October, daily.

Avoncroft Museum of Historic Buildings

A fascinating open air museum of buildings including a working windmill (page 71).

Severn Valley Railway

If you want to get to see some of the countryside that surrounds Birmingham and don't want to drive, the Severn Valley Railway could be the ideal solution. It's a day out on a genuine, steam train through 16 miles of beautiful, rural England (page 71).

South-East

Warwick Castle

A magnificent castle. The 'Kingmaker' focuses on the preparations for Richard Neville, Earl of Warwick's final battle in 1471. Spy on the rich and famous guests at one of The Countess of Warwick's spectacular dinner parties. Dungeons, torture chamber, ghost tower. Medieval times are brought vividly to life (page 76).

Butterfly Farm

From the beautiful to the creepy crawlies (page 75).

Brass Rubbing Centre

Adults get to visit the Shakespeare Houses and children get to do the brass rubbing – although it has been known for adults to become as enthralled as their offspring. One advantage is you get to take something home at the end of the day (page 75).

North-West

Black Country Living Museum

Fantastic re-creation of a village complete with bakers, ironmongers and pub; all brought vividly to life by costumed guides. Street games and school room – if your children think their school is strict, let them have a taste what it was like in Victorian England (page 65).

Dudley Zoo & Castle

Partly destroyed castle built on a hill – worth noting if you've got small children who need to be carried. Wonderful views across the countryside and a zoo (page 65).

Ironbridge Gorge Museums

Ten museums and monuments including the amazing Iron Bridge, a Victorian town and a tar tunnel. Enginuity is a new, design and technology attraction. Hands-on and interactive, it brings science to life (page 66).

North-East

Drayton Manor Theme Park

2 miles south of Tamworth
Tel: (01827) 287979
www.draytonmanor.co.uk

The closer of the region's two theme parks (the other is Alton Towers), Drayton Manor has over 100 rides including a zoo and dinosaurland plus lakes and gardens. Shockwave is Europe's first stand up rollercoaster – not for the faint hearted.

Open: April - October

Twycross Zoo

A444, 9 miles north east of Hinkley, M42 junction 11
Tel: (01827) 880250

Home to a world-famous primate collection and the only UK zoo to have a Bonobo – man's closest relative. Pet's corner and adventure playground (undercover soft play area for small children).

Open: All year.

Conkers

Learn about life in the forest and woodlands. A hands-on discovery centre (for children and adults alike) in The National Forest with activities both inside and out (page 69).

Shockwave, Drayton Manor Park

Places for little bunnies to stay

(See also Where to stay page 152)

Convention Quarter

Days Inn Hotel,
Wharfside, The Mailbox
Tel: (0121) 643 9344

Up to two children (under 12) stay free when sharing a room with 2 adults.

The Novotel,
Broad Street
Tel: (0121) 643 2000

Free accommodation for up to two under 16s when sharing with two adults.

Jury's Inn,
Broad Street
Tel: (0121) 606 9000

Facilities: Bar, restaurant, 445 large en suite rooms.

Rooms are large enough to accommodate up to 3 adults or 2 adults and 2 children under 15.

Malmaison
Mailbox, Royal Mail Street
Tel: (0121) 246 5000

Chic location. Family rooms with under 5s staying free.

South-West

Apollo Hotel,
Hagley Road, Edgbaston
Tel: (0121) 455 0271

Free accommodation for up to two under 16s when sharing with two adults.

South-East

The Lodge Hotel,
York Road, Hall Green
Tel: (0121) 777 3480

Facilities: Bar, restaurant, snooker club. On the site of the greyhound race-course.

13 family rooms with double bed, single bed and sofa bed.

The Holiday Inn,
Birmingham International Airport
Tel: (0870) 400 9007

Free accommodation for up to two under 16s when sharing with two adults.

Crowne Plaza,
NEC
Tel: (0121) 781 4000

Free accommodation for up to two under 19s when sharing with two adults.

Solihull Moat House
Tel: (0121) 623 9988

Close to Solihull town centre. Family rooms with free accommodation for children when sharing with 2 adults.

Renaissance Solihull Hotel
Tel: (0121) 711 3000

Family rooms and special rates for children.

North-East

Moor Hall Hotel and Country Club
Tel: (0121) 308 3751

4-star country house hotel in Sutton Coldfield. Family rooms and discounts available.

Charges for meals may apply.

Places for little bunnies to eat

The attitude to children varies tremendously from eatery to eatery. Sometimes, children's menus lack inspiration and finding somewhere that serves more sophisticated food for children can be a challenge but it's not impossible. Have a look at the following....(prices approximate)

Central Quarter

Cafe Uno
126 Colmore Row
Tel: (0121) 212 0599

City centre location. Veggie breakfast, ciabatta sandwiches served daily until 4pm. Menu for children includes a choice of pasta or risotto, dessert and a drink for about £4. Good value for money.

Open: Mon – Sat 10am – 11pm; Sun 11am – 7.30pm.

Birmingham Museum & Art Gallery
Chamberlain Square
Tel: (0121) 303 2834

Magnificent and large art nouveau dining room. Great value afternoon pot of tea for two at only £2 can be enjoyed in the presence of fine art. Occasional musical accompaniment adds to the ambience.

Great for children's meals at about £3 (served daily, noon – 4pm) or half portions of any of the main meals for about £4 (served daily, noon – 2.30pm).

Convention Quarter

Le Petit Blanc
Nine Brindleyplace.
Tel: (0121) 633 7333

A refreshingly welcoming approach to children without being patronising. One of the city's top restaurants. Two course children's menu (up to 11 years) about £6, 3 course about £8. Children can choose from more sophisticated dishes like tagliatelle or goujons of fish.

Open: Mon – Sat noon – 11.30pm. Sun noon – 3pm/5.30pm – 10.30pm.

South-East

Diwan

3 Alcester Road, Moseley.
Tel: (0121) 442 4920

In the 'Balti triangle', this large restaurant is particularly attentive to the needs of children. Another bonus is the truly enormous onion bhajis they serve.

Open: 5.30pm – 1am (2am Fri and Sat), Sun 6pm – midnight.

Places to Picnic

For a nation that has such an unreliable climate, the English are strangely enthusiastic devotees of the picnic.

To appreciate fully the joys of the picnic, picnics are probably limited to sometime between early July and late August – if you're fortunate.

A successful picnic has four essential ingredients: fine weather, delicious food, good company and stunning location.

On the basis that three of the four are out of the hands of any compiler of guide books, we're concentrating on the fourth – the location.

The following include places that are in the most wonderful settings, places that have cultural significance and places that combine the two.

Central Quarter

St Philip's Place

On a summer's day, take a sandwich and join the office workers in the sunshine. On certain days adults and children will enjoy free concerts in the cathedral – a way of lifting the spirits and getting to the cultural heart of the city without spending loads of money (page 23).

Birmingham South-West

Birmingham Botanical Gardens

A 15 acre (6ha) haven of exotic plants and birds not far from the city centre. On Sunday afternoons during the summer there is music from the bandstand. A wonderful place to relax. Adventure playground to keep the children entertained (page 52).

Lickey Hills Country Park

Visitor centre with adventure playground for children and miles of glorious walks right on the edge of the city. Busier on Sundays, when local people go to spend an hour or two walking and during school holiday's when the Lickeys become a magnet for parents who want to occupy their children without spending a fortune (page 55).

South-West

Avoncroft Museum of Historic Buildings

Spend time wandering around actual buildings from bygone eras on the edge of rolling English countryside. There's plenty to do and see (page 71).

Witley Court

Wonderfully romantic atmosphere with the ruins of the early Jacobean mansion – damaged by fire – presiding over glorious countryside. An impressive fountain featuring Perseus and Andromeda is a fine backdrop to a picnic. The adjacent baroque church is wonderful and features one of the first paintings to include a Down's Syndrome child (page 72).

South-East

Ragley Hall

A magnificent stately home set amidst 400 acres (162ha) of parkland. Lakeside picnic area, woodland walk and adventure play area for children with large maze. There are outdoor concerts and firework and light extravaganzas staged during the summer – a great way to round off a picnic in the grounds. Phone for concert details/prices (page 66).

North West

Weston Park

This 17th century house, famed for its fine art and porcelain is set in magnificent grounds, perfect for a picnic on a warm, summer day (page 66).

Made in Birmingham (and a few from beyond)

Over the centuries, Birmingham characters have made significant contributions to the fields of commerce, politics, science, industry, sport and the arts.

Just a few of its famous sons and daughters (and a couple of adopted ones as they spent their most productive or influential period here) and their outputs are featured below:

Joan Armatrading MBE
(1950 -)

The Armatrading family moved to Birmingham in 1958 and Joan taught herself to play the piano and guitar. She shortly met Pam Nestor also a West Indian immigrant and both worked in the touring cast of the celebrated hippy musical *Hair*. Together they wrote songs but Joan went on and produced her debut album *Whatever's For Us* in 1972. Since then she has collaborated with some of the biggest names in the music industry and has had success with a number of her songs including 'Show Some Emotion', 'Me Myself I', 'Walk Under Ladders', 'Drop The Pilot' and 'What Do Boys Dream'.

Thomas Attwood
(1783-1856)

Born in Halesowen, elected High Bailiff of Birmingham in 1811 and with fifteen others met to form the Birmingham Political Union for the Protection of Public Rights Union in December 1829 and consequently united the middle and lower classes in a movement for fair representation in Parliament and became a major influence in the passing of the Reform Act in 1832. Following that he was elected an MP for Birmingham where he served for seven years.

W.H. Auden
(1907 - 1973)

Wynston Hugh Auden was born in York but he was brought up in Birmingham where his father was Schools' Medical Officer and later Professor of Public Health at the University of Birmingham. He was considered the poet of the British left for confronting the social problems of pre-World War II Britain. He moved to the US in 1939 where his work turned to religious themes. He also wrote literary criticisms and opera libretti. He won the Pulitzer Prize for *The Age Of Anxiety* in 1947.

Sir Herbert Austin
(1866 – 1941)

Founded the Austin Motor Company on Bristol Road, Longbridge with Frank Kayser and Harvey Du Cross. By 1914, 1,500 cars a year were coming off the production line. In 1922 the first Austin Seven was built. Herbert Austin became Sir Herbert in 1917.

Bakelite

Bakelite is a heat resistant thermo-setting chemically stable resin invented in 1907-1909 by Dr Leo Baekeland. Bakelite Ltd was formed in 1927 the amalgamation of three suppliers of materials and set up its factory in Tyseley, Birmingham for its manufacture. Bakelite is little used today.

Sir Michael Balcon
(1896-1977)

Born in Birmingham, often regarded as one of the pioneers of the British Film Industry, he also had a talent for producing both comedy and drama. Educated at George Dixon Grammar School in Edgbaston (remember PC George Dixon in the film *The Blue Lamp* and later in the famous BBC TV series *Dixon of Dock Green*?). It was after the First World War that he joined another Birmingham film enthusiast Victor Saville to make short advertising films and then the production of feature films. His films include *The Thirty-Nine Steps* and following becoming Executive Producer at Ealing Studios in 1937 his films went on to include the famous series of Ealing comedies and more latterly *The Cruel Sea*, *The Lady Killers* and *Dunkirk*. He was knighted in 1948.

John Baskerville
(1706 - 1775)

18th century printer and member of the Lunar Society who gave his name to the Baskerville typeface. He wasn't a Birmingham man but moved here as an engraver and then a japanner. Although an atheist, he is now buried in a Warstone Lane churchyard.

Edwin P Bennett MBE
(1873-1954)

Chief Superintendent Edwin P Bennett of the Birmingham City Police is believed to have introduced the one-way traffic system to Birmingham (but don't tell motorists that!). He also played a major part in the breaking up of the criminal gangs and the suppression of the infamous garrison vendetta. He was awarded the King's Jubilee Medal, the King's Coronation Medal and the MBE. He joined the police force on Friday 13th July 1894, was drafted to Ladywood Police where he lived in Room 13, was there for 13 years and when promoted Sergeant was given the number 13 – but was not superstitious!

Edward White Benson
(1829-1896)

Born in Lombard Street, Balsall Heath on 14th July, he was educated at King Edward's School in Birmingham and subsequently became a fellow of Trinity College. In 1883 he became Archbishop of Canterbury and he also served as Prebendary of Lincoln and Chaplain to the Queen.

Birchfield Harriers

Based at the Alexander Stadium at Perry Barr. The club was formed in 1877 and is one of Britain's highest achieving athletics clubs. Ashia Hansen won gold in the 2002 Commonwealth Games, Mark Lewis Francis is a world-class 100m sprinter and Denise Lewis is an Olympic Heptathlon gold medallist.

Alfred Bird
(1811-1878)

In 1837, Alfred Bird invented custard for his wife who was allergic to eggs and could not eat home made egg custard. He then went on in 1843 to invent Baking Powder to make bread without yeast and this subsequently revolutionized home baking. In 1914 Bird's Custard was supplied to His Majesty's forces throughout the First World War and in 1929 the "Three Birds" trade-mark was born. This independent business went on to be part of Kraft General Foods in 1947. One in three of the UK population has Bird's custard in their cupboards. The original Bird's factory in Digbeth, Birmingham is now the largest single complex of creative activity in Europe offering 250,000 sq. ft. (23,225sqm) of affordable workspace for creative industries.

Birmingham Small Arms Company [BSA]

BSA was founded in 1861 by fourteen gunsmiths in Birmingham to supply arms to the British government during the Crimean war. Following the war it branched out into other fields and began to make bicycles and even motorcycles. It produced its first prototype automobile in 1907 and in 1910 purchased the British Daimler Company for its automobile engines. The company produced rifles and Lewis guns as well as shells, motorcycles and other vehicles and by the Second World War had 67 factories. Following the war it bought Triumph making them the largest producer of motorcycles in the world. In its hey-day the company had one of its main facilities in Tyseley, Birmingham.

Black Sabbath

Formed by four friends from Aston, one of whom was frontman, Ozzy Osbourne. Still playing after more than 30 years.

Matthew Boulton
(1728 – 1809)

Boulton, the son of a silver-stamper was born in Snow Hill. In 1773 he went into business with James Watt. For 11 years, Boulton's factory produced and sold Watt's steam engines. Within 15 years, there were over 500 Boulton & Watt machines in Britain's mines and factories. He experienced personal tragedy when his first wife, Mary Robinson, the daughter of a wealthy heiress, died in 1759. He then married her sister Anne, by whom he had two children. Some mystery surrounds her death – said to be by drowning – in 1783.

John Bright
(1811-1889)

John Bright joined the Anti Corn Law League in 1839 and made many speeches attacking the privileged position of the landed aristocracy and argued that their selfishness was causing the working class a great deal of suffering. He encouraged the working and middle classes to fight for free trade and cheaper food. In 1857 he won a bi-election in Birmingham. As a Quaker he was opposed to slavery and became President of the Board of Trade under William Gladstone in 1868. Whilst he retired from the Cabinet in 1870 he remained MP for Birmingham until his death in 1889.

James Brindley
(1716-1772)

A great engineer and whose expertise and imagination carried the canal idea across England. With little formal education he preferred to work his ideas out in his head rather than on paper. One of his famous projects was the Birmingham Canal. During his lifetime he designed some 375 miles of waterways. He died of overwork and diabetes.

Jane Bunford
(1895- 1922)

Born in Bartley Green, she grew into "The Tallest Woman in the World". She eventually grew to a height of 7' 9" (2.36 m).

Sir Edward Coley Burne-Jones
(1833 – 1898)

An apprentice to Rossetti in 1856. His inspiration came from myths and legends and is much in evidence throughout the artistic paintings, tapestries and stained glass. He also collaborated closely with the designer, social-

ist and poet, William Morris.

George Cadbury
(1839-1922)

Born in Edgbaston the son of John Cadbury a tea and coffee merchant in Bull Street, Birmingham. With his brother Richard he took over the Cocoa Factory in 1861. George was particularly interested in social reform and provision of decent housing for working people. He supported Joseph Chamberlain's Municipal Initiatives and rebuilt the Cocoa Factory on a greenfield site in Bournville in 1879 where he began to develop good quality and affordable housing for the workers.

Jasper Carrott OBE
(1945 -)

Born Robert Davis, comedian and raconteur Jasper Carrott picked up the nickname Jasper at school and subsequently added Carrott as his stage name. Educated at Moseley Grammar School, he made his first public appearance at The Boggery Folk Club (originally in Field Lane, Solihull). (He lived in nearby Bickenhill, not far from the airport and used to joke that his house was so close to the runway, it had tyre marks on the roof). He rose to national fame through his TV work which included *Carrott's*

Lib, *The Detectives* and, more recently, *All About Me* (the first series with fellow Brummie Meera Syall). Whilst he has made a stage appearance in Gilbert & Sullivan's *Mikado* in the West End, and had a hit single in 1975 with 'Funky Moped' (B side 'Magic Roundabout'), that sold more than half a million copies, he continues to love standing on the stage and entertaining (a planned week at The Academy, NIA, turned into a sell-out 14 days). He remains an ardent Birmingham City FC fan.

Barbara Cartland OBE
(1901 - 2000)

The prolific writer of romantic fiction – famous for wearing only pink outfits and being the step-grandmother of Princess Diana – was born in Edgbaston.

Sir Arthur Conan Doyle
(1859-1930)

Prolific writer and renowned for his Sherlock Holmes stories. He lived at 63 Aston Road North in Birmingham between 1878 and 1881. In 1880 having completed three years of his medical studies he signed on as ship's surgeon on the Greenland whaler "Hope". He eventually qualified as a doctor in 1885. He is however best known for his writing including *The Hound of the Baskervilles*, *The Adventures of Sherlock Holmes* and in the latter years dedicating himself to spiritualistic studies.

Austen Chamberlain
(1863 – 1937)

The only son of Joseph Chamberlain by his first wife, Harriet, who died in childbirth. Austen became Chancellor of the Exchequer and Foreign Secretary. He was awarded the Nobel Peace Prize in 1925.

Arthur Neville Chamberlain
(1869 – 1940)

Lord Mayor of Birmingham 1915 – 17 and responsible for opening the Municipal Bank in 1911. He was an MP and Chancellor of the Exchequer and prime minister from 1937 – 1940. In 1938 he signed the Munich pact with Adolph Hitler proclaiming it meant "peace for our time." War broke out shortly after.

Joseph Chamberlain
(1836 – 1914)

The founder of municipal government was known affectionately by Brummies as 'Joe' or 'the gas and water socialist'. He entered public life in 1868 as a town councillor and was mayor from 1873 – 1876. He was the first chancellor of Birmingham University. He resigned

from the government over Gladstone's policy of home rule for Ireland.

Henry Clay

He patented the process of making papier mâché in 1772 and was previously one of John Baskerville's apprentices. He died at the Manor House, Northfield.

Lisa Clayton
(1959 -   )

In 1994, Lisa Clayton set out to attempt two world records: fastest sailing around the world by a woman and the first woman to sail single handed and non-stop around the world. She returned after 285 days at sea on her 11.6m boat *The Spirit of Birmingham* in June 1995 having clocked up some 30,000 miles. She has since married Lord Cobham and lives at nearby Hagley Hall.

David Cox
(1783 - 1859)

Born in Heathmill Lane, Deritend. Apprenticed to a painter of miniatures he then moved onto theatrical scene painting in Birmingham and London. Following that he then began water colour painting for which he became famous and moved to Harborne in 1841 where he remained until he died in 1859. He is buried at St Peter's, Harborne where he is commemorated by a stainedglass window.

John Curry
(1949 - 1994)

Born in Birmingham he began skating at the old Summerhill ice rink which is now demolished. He became British Junior Champion in 1967 and Senior Champion in 1970. In 1976 he won the European Championship

and a gold medal performance at the Innsbruck Olympics. He then went on to win the world championships in Gothenburg in 1976.

Lucy Davis
(1973 -   )

To radio listeners, she is the voice of Hayley Tucker in the long running The Archers. To television viewers, she is receptionist Dawn Tinsley in the award-winning The Office - the hit BBC comedy whose credits include two Golden Globe Awards, four BAFTAs and a Silver Rose at the Montreux TV Festival. Her early work included the Carlton TV children's show Woof and the acclaimed comedy, One Foot in the Grave. More recently, she appeared in the TV production of Pride and Prejudice and the horror comedy, Shaun Of The Dead (2004). We'd like this to be the first biography not to mention that she is the daughter of Jasper Carrott – but both are such enthusiasts of Birmingham, we can't.

Alan Dedicoat

Born in Hollywood, Birmingham. Alan went to Edward VI Camp Hill School for Boys and University of Birmingham. Changing from Law he went into the world of show business. He is famous for the "Voice of the Balls" calling out Lottery Numbers in the *National Lottery Draw* each week.

Cat Deeley
(1976 -   )

Born in Sutton Coldfield now a TV presenter, hosting a multitude of shows on MTV, UK and ITV. Her career began by participating in the Clothes Show aged 14 and whilst she did not win she was spotted and signed up by Storm Model Agency.

John Boyd Dunlop
(1840 - 1921)

He is remembered for inventing the first commercially viable pneumatic tyre for his son's bicycle. He patented the idea and then sold the Patent in 1896 for £3.0m! The company set up home at "The Fort" and became the major employer in the city. The Fort is now in the process of being redeveloped to provide a multi use scheme.

Duran Duran

Created in and around the city's Rum Runner nightclub on Broad Street, which was demolished to make way for the Hyatt Hotel. Roger & Nigel Taylor & Nicholas Bates were born in Birmingham. The band is named after Milo O'Shea's character in the film *Barbarella*.

Oscar Deutsch
(1893 - 1941)

Born in Balsall Heath, Birmingham, the son of a Jewish scrap metal merchant, he created the Odeon Cinema chain. Odeon stands for 'Oscar Deutsch Entertains Our Nation' and in the ten years between founding the chain and his death from cancer, 258 Odeons opened throughout the UK. The business was nurtured in Birmingham with the first Moorish style cinema opening in Perry Barr in 1930. In 1941, the year of his death, the chain was taken over by J Arthur Rank.

Dexy's Midnight Runners

UK rock band based in Birmingham and fronted by Kevin Rowland who was born in Wolverhampton.

They had a number one hit with 'Geno' a tribute to Geno Washington and 'Come On Eileen' that was a number one in both the UK and the USA.

John Hall-Edwards

Birmingham's Hall-Edwards pioneered the use of x-rays in the UK several years before Röntgen. On Valentine's Day, 1896 he took the first radiograph for the purpose of an operation. He lost his left arm due to x-ray dermatitis caused by his experiments. There is a plaque commemorating his work at the Children's Hospital, Steelhouse Lane.

Trevor Eve
(1951 -)

Born in Birmingham, studied architecture at Kingston Polytechnic but his true love was acting. Famous for his TV super-sleuth Eddie Shoestring in the late 1970s he then went on with his wife to form Projector Productions and has been behind major television shows in the UK including *Alice through the Looking Glass* and *Cinderella*.

Sid Field
(1904 - 1950)

Appropriately for a comedian, he was born on April Fool's Day, 1904. The Sparkhill-born comedian was a stage and screen star, his films included *That's My Ticket* in 1939.

Fine Young Cannibals
(1985 -)

Originated in Birmingham and featuring the distinctive vocal talents of singer and actor, Roland Gift.

Dr Joseph Sampson Gamgee
(1828 - 1886)

A surgeon at Birmingham's Queen's hospital, he invented cotton wool. He was later immortalised by J.R.R. Tolkien in the *Lord of the Rings* stories. Dr Gamgee lived where Birmingham Repertory Theatre now stands. He also had a house at Five Ways.

Tony Hancock
(1924 – 1968)

The morose comic genius lived in Hall Green and died in Sydney. There is a monument to him in Old Square on Corporation Street, by The Minories Shopping Centre.

Lenny Henry
(1957 -)

One of the Midlands' greatest comedians. He made his TV debut in 1975 when he won the *New Faces* Talent Competition and he has gone on to have many famous TV shows including the *Comic Strip* in 1980, *Chef*, *Lenny Henry in Pieces*. He is famous for being one of the founding figures of *Comic Relief*.

Anne Heywood
(1931-)

Born Violet Joan Pretty in Handsworth changing her name to Anne Heywood led in 1956 to her being given a seven year contract with Rank as an actress. She starred in over thirty films in Italy, Hollywood and Britain, many produced by her husband Raymond Stross.

Sir Rowland Hill
(1795 - 1879)

Born in Kidderminster, he taught astronomy in his father's school in Birmingham. He went on to establish the Hazelwood

School in Edgbaston in 1819 and in 1822 with his brother, published *Public Education* when they proposed making science a required subject, an end to corporal punishment and having gym class once a week. 'Hill the Reformer', as he was known, is perhaps most well known for being the 'father' of the Postage Stamp and his Postal Reform Plan was adopted in the Parliamentary budget in 1839. His work led to the printing and use of the Penny Black in 1840.

Hiatt & Co

In 1780, Mr Hiatt's factory at 26, Masshouse Lane, began making handcuffs and leg irons. It was here the handcuffs used by Britain's first police force in London in 1829 were made. The company also made handcuffs for escapologist, Harry Houdini.

Noddy Holder
(1946 -)

Born in Newhall Street, Walsall, the son of a window cleaner and known originally as Neville. He began his singing career in Working Men's Clubs aged 7 and had his first guitar when he was 10 or 11 years of age and formed his first band a year or so later. He released his first single in 1965 with another Midland hero Steve Bret and The Mavericks and they eventually changed their name

to Slade and became one of the biggest British bands in the 1970s. Noddy's moved on to TV and film appearances playing in the TV comedy show *The Grimleys* set in the Black Country,

HP Sauce
253 Tower Road, Aston

Originally the Midland Vinegar Co., founded in 1897 by Edwin Samson Moore. In 1905, HP Sauce came into production (HP stands for Houses of Parliament). A 'must-have' with the traditional English breakfast or a bacon or sausage sandwich.

Washington Irving
(1783 - 1859)

Born in New York City he became recognized as a great satirist, historian, biographer and essayist in both the US and Europe. He lived in Birmingham in Icknield Street West, and then moved to what is now called Newhall Hill before moving onto Calthorpe Street. He wrote *Rip Van Winkle* overnight whilst staying at Newhall Hill. To this day Birmingham still has an Irving Street in his memory.

Sir Alexander Issigonis
(1906 - 1988)

Born in Turkey he was evacuated in the First World War with his family to England. He moved to the drawing office of

Humber Cars in Coventry in 1928. In the early 1940s he began work on the Morris Minor. When William Morris first saw the Minor running in 1947 he was unimpressed describing it as a "poached egg". However, within eleven years one million Morris Minors had been sold, a record for a British car. He designed the revolutionary Mini and by his death in 1988 five million had been sold. He was knighted in 1969.

Sir Barry Jackson
(1897 - 1960)

His life was devoted to the theatre and he is the founder and patron of the Birmingham Repertory Theatre. Originally in Station Street it became the training ground for famous actors including Sir Laurence Olivier, Paul Schofield and Dame Peggy Ashcroft. Between 1929 and 1937 he ran the Malvern Festival for which George Bernard Shaw wrote some of his most famous plays. He was given the honorary Freedom of the City of Birmingham in 1956. The new Repertory Theatre in Centenary Square includes a bust of Sir Barry in the foyer.

Ann Jones
(1938 -)

One of Britain's most successful tennis players. She was born in Birmingham and won the Wimbledon Ladies Championship in 1969, the mixed doubles in the same year with Fred Stolle and the French Open in 1961 and 1966. Ann was a Table Tennis International player for the country between 1953 and 1959. She is now a commentator with the BBC.

Digby Jones
(1955 -)

Director General of the employers' organisation, the CBI, he was born in Birmingham and educated at Bromsgrove School, starting his career with corporate law firm Edge & Ellison in 1978, becoming a partner in 1984. It was in corporate finance and client development that he made his name, joining KPMG as Vice-Chairman of Corporate Finance. He became Director General of the CBI in January 2000. A keen supporter of local charities, he has also done what many business leaders have advocated, and got on his bike – not looking for work but in order to raise funds for charity.

Nigel Kennedy
(1956 -)

Passionate football fan & devotee of Aston Villa FC, with a home in Malvern. He was tutored by Yehudi Mennuin as a child, studied at Julliard School in New York and came to fame with his version of Vivaldi's Four Seasons (1998). (in the Guiness Book of Records as the best selling classical work of all time). He took a 5 year sabbatical between 1992-97 and is one of Britain's most talented violinists, he has performed at 2 Royal Command performances .

Albert William Ketelby
(1875 – 1959)

This vastly under-appreciated musician, composer, pianist and organist was born in Alma Street, Aston. A child prodigy, his piano sonata performed at Worcester Town Hall when he was 11 received high praise from Elgar.

Robert Kilroy-Silk

Educated at Sparkhill Commercial School in Birmingham, elected a Labour MP in 1974 he became a daytime TV talk show host and presenter.

Frederick William Lanchester
(1868 - 1946)

Best known for designing and building the first British petrol-driven four wheel motor car in 1895 and for his work on the theory of flight and design. He lived in a house he designed himself at 128, Oxford Road, Moseley from 1924-1946.

Ian Lavender
(1946 -)

Famous for his appearance as Private Pike in *Dad's Army*, his films include *Carry on Behind* in 1975 and he has appeared in *Eastenders*, *Casualty*, *Goodnight Sweetheart*, *Peak Practice*, *The Glums*, *Keeping Up Appearances* and *The Harry Hill Show*. On the stage he has appeared in classics including Dustin Hoffman's *The Merchant of Venice* with Sir Peter Hall's company.

Sue Lawley OBE
(1946 -)

Born in Dudley, Sue is a TV and radio presenter currently presenting *Desert Island Discs* on Radio 4. She has interviewed Prime Ministers Margaret Thatcher and Tony Blair and *Harry Potter* author JK Rowling. She joined the BBC in 1970 and became one of their main presenters on the early evening current affairs programme.

Denise Lewis
(1972 -)

Born in West Bromwich she joined Birchfield Harriers and became a natural for the Seven Event Heptathlon. She won an Olympic Bronze in 1996 and Gold in 2000, she won Gold Medals in the World Championships in 1997 and 1999, and she won a European Gold in 1998 and Commonwealth Golds in 1994 and 1998.

David Lodge CBE
(1935 -)

Critic and novelist. He held a post at the School of English, the University of Birmingham from 1960 subsequently becoming a Professor in 1976 until his retirement in 1987. He has published eleven novels and he wrote several critical studies on modern literary trends and on specific literary figures including Graham Greene and Evelyn Waugh. His first full play *The Writing Game* was performed at the Birmingham Repertory Theatre in 1990 and his second play *Home Truths* was also produced there in 1998. In 1980, *How Far Can You Go* was proclaimed Whitbread Book of the Year, *Small World* was listed for the Booker Prize in 1984 and *Nice Work* in 1988.

Lunar Society
(circa 1765)

An exclusive scientific club, never having more than fourteen members with each member noted for their special area of expertise. Matthew Boulton was key to the society, having invited his most learned friends and generally hosting the meetings at his residence in Soho House. The society was formed around 1765 and its members included geologists, chemists, scientists engineers and theorists, brought together to discuss new inventions and new ideas. Frequent attendees included Boulton, Watt, Murdoch, Small and Priestley, Erasmus Darwin and Wedgewood all contributed to the ideas and visions that were shared at the Lunar Society.

Mark Lewis-Francis

(1982 -)

One of the famous Birchfield Harrier athletes who specializes in 60 metre indoor and 100 metre outdoor events. Considerable success as a Junior and is now in the GB Senior Team. He won the AAA Indoor 60 metre title in 2003 and took part in the World Indoors and went on to win a relay Silver Medal in Zurich.

Nigel Mansell

(1953 -)

The F1 Grand Prix World Champion (1992) driving a Williams and Indy Car champion the following year. He has 31 Formula One wins and 187 starts. He grew up in Hall Green.

Sir Josiah Mason

(1795 - 1881)

Son of a Kidderminster carpet weaver, he had little education and his business career began by selling cakes, copper bagging and odd-jobbing. In 1824 he joined Samuel Harrison acquiring his business in the following year and he invented a plan for making split rings by machinery that proved to be profitable. In 1829 he turned his hand to pen making. He spent a lot of his wealth on charitable objects. His most important work was the foundation of the Scientific College at Birmingham (on the site of the present Central Library) which cost him £180,000 and was opened in October, 1880. Mason College as it became known was subsequently absorbed into the University of Birmingham.

Kenneth Matthews

(1934 -)

One of Birmingham's few Olympic gold medal winners having completed the 20km walk in the 1964 Tokyo Olympics in 1:29:34. He was also a 1963 World Championship medalist in the same event.

Susan Maughan

(1942 -)

Was born in the North-East but she grew up in Birmingham, living in Greenway Street, Small Heath and attending Tilton Street School. In 1962 she was seen as the main UK challenger to chart dominance of the young Helen Shapiro following her release of 'Bobby's Girl'. She sang in numerous movies including the British Rock and Roll film *What a Crazy World*, starring alongside Joe Browne and Marty Wilde.

William Murdoch

(1754 – 1839)

The inventor of gas lighting (1792) is one of Birmingham's adopted sons and a Scotsman by birth. He worked, at one time, for Matthew Boulton.

Another adopted son is Erasmus Darwin. He was born in Nottinghamshire but became a member of the illustrious Lunar Society.

Watt, Murdoch and Boulton are all buried at St. Mary's Church in Handsworth.

The Mini

Production of Sir Alec Issigonis' iconic car began at Longbridge in 1959.

The Moody Blues

Several members of the band including Ray Thomas, John Lodge and Mike Pinder were all born in Birmingham. They started out as an R n' B band and had their first number one hit with Go Now. The band attempted to get sponsorship from local brewers Mitchells and Butlers and the band name M & B 5 was chosen.

Unfortunately the deal never materialized and the M & B 5 was transformed into the Moody Blues. Following supporting Chuck Berry at a concert they found that fame and fortune quickly spiralled and they toured with the Beatles and were then joined by Justin Hayward.

Move and Electric Light Orchestra

Formed after an impromptu after hours session at Birmingham's legendary Cedar Club in 1966, members included Bev Bevan, Carl Wayne, Roy Wood,

Trevor Burton and Chris (Ace) Kefford.

Janice Nichols

Born in Wednesbury and became famous for saying "Oi'll give it foive" on the TV show recorded in the Aston studios in the 1960s.

Ocean Colour Scene

The band was formed in Moseley in the early 90s in Birmingham. Toured with Oasis, Alison Moyet and PP Arnold. Now well established in the music scene.

William Edgar (Bill) Oddie. OBE
(1941 -)

Bill attended King Edward's School in Birmingham before going on to Cambridge to read English. He is known as a British comedian, singer, television presenter and ornithologist. He was a member of the 1970s' BBC TV trio *The Goodies* and his first published work was an article about Birmingham's Bartley Reservoir in the West Midlands Bird Club 1962 Annual Report. He has subsequently written a number of books about birds and bird watching.

Ozzy (John Michael) Osbourne

Born at 14, Lodge Road, Aston, Birmingham, he was vocalist and founding member of Black Sabbath together with fellow Brummies, Geezer Butler, Bill Ward and Tony Iommi in 1969. He left the band ten years later to pursue a solo career, returning in 1997. He has now branched out with his own TV show, *Life with the Osbournes*.

Robert Plant
(1948 -)

Born in West Bromwich, his voice helped establish Led Zeppelin, one of rocks legendary bands. He began in the 1960s with bands like The Crawling King Snakes and The Band of Joy. Led Zeppelin broke up in the 1980s but Plant rejoined Jimmy Page in 1994 to perform and record new albums and tunes. In 1999 he formed the folk rock quintet Priory of Bryon.

Enoch Powell
(1912 - 1998)

Born in Birmingham, he read Classics at Cambridge and became Professor of Greek at Sydney University, Australia in 1937 aged just 25. He returned to England during the Second World War and enlisted in the Royal Warwickshire Regiment where he became a brigadier. He then worked as a political researcher for the Conservative Party before being elected MP for Wolverhampton South West in 1950. He held the seat for 24 years. His opinionated views on immigration policies led to his sacking from the shadow cabinet following his infamous "Rivers of Blood" speech in Birmingham in April 1968. He left the Conservative Party re-entering Parliament as Unionist MP for the constituency of County Down until he lost his seat in 1992. During his life he wrote four books of verse – *First Poems* (1927), *Casting Off* (1939) and *Dancers End* and the *Wedding Gift* in 1951.

Joseph Priestley
(1733 - 1804)

He discovered that graphite was an electrical conductor and he isolated and described the properties of carbon dioxide, nitrous oxide and oxygen. He invented the 'fizzy'-drink "pop", identified the gasses involved in plant respiration and observed photosynthesis for the first time. He also isolated and described the properties of ammonia, sulphur dioxide, hydrogen sulphide and carbon monoxide. In 1770 he discovered that India gum would rub out pencil marks and he invented the eraser and gave it the common name 'the rubber'. He moved to Birmingham to become Minister of the New Meeting Society that was reputedly the most liberal congregation in England. He was a prominent member of the Lunar Society and in 1791 when a mob destroyed his chapel, house and library together with his Science Laboratory he fled for his life to London. He moved to the USA in 1794.

Sir Simon Rattle
(1955 -)

Born in Liverpool he came to Birmingham in 1980 to take up the post of Principal Conductor and Artistic advisor of the City of Birmingham Symphony Orchestra and became its Musical Director in 1990. In 1991 the Symphony Hall opened in Birmingham, one of the world's finest concert and recording halls and Sir Simon went on to lead the CBSO on many successful tours around Europe, Scandinavia, the Far East and North America. He remained with the CBSO until 1998. He is now with the Berlin Philharmonic Orchestra.

Mandy Rice-Davies

(1944 -)

She lived in Shirley before acquiring her notoriety in the Profumo scandal of 1963. A friend of Christine Keeler who had an affair with the British Secretary of State for War, John Profumo, she gave evidence in court. She has famously been quoted as saying "My life has been one long descent into respectability".

Pat Roach

(1943 -)

Nicknamed "Bomber" he was born in Birmingham, is 6ft 5in (1.97m) tall and has appeared in all three Indiana Jones films, playing four different rolls. As a former professional wrestler (British and European Heavyweight Champion) competing under the name of Pat "Bomber" Roach he has also starred in the James Bond film *Never Say Never Again*. He has had numerous television apearances including starring roles in *Auf Wiedersehen Pet* (1983). In addition to his role of acting he also runs a gymnasium and fitness centre in Erdington.

Louisa Ann Ryland

(1814 – 1889)

A true philanthropist, Miss Ryland was born in Edgbaston. When she was 29, she inherited estates in Sparkhill, Small Heath, Northfield and Moseley worth in excess of £1 million. Although she was a shy and unassuming woman, her generosity was on a grand scale. She provided the land and £3000 to build St. Barnabas' Church in Ladywood. She also gave the land and money to create Cannon Hill Park and was a major contribu-

tor to the Birmingham Government School of Ornamental Art in Margaret Street – now known as the Birmingham Institute of Art & Design.

Victor Saville

(1897 - 1979)

Born in Birmingham and in partnership with Sir Michael Balcon he set up a production company in 1923 and later became an important British director of films.

Clare Short, MP

(1946 -)

Born to Irish parents in Birmingham, she gained a degree in Political Science from Keele University, and then joined the Home Office. Working initially as Private Secretary to the Conservative Secretary, she decided that she should stand in her own right and in the 1983 General Election became Labour MP for Ladywood. She became the first Cabinet level Secretary of State for International Development in 1997-2003.

Frank Skinner

(1957 -)

Born Chris Collins, he played his first gig in December 1987 at the Birmingham Anglers' Association. As there was already a Chris Collins in equity he used the name of one of his dad's dominoes team – Frank Skinner. He won the 1991 Perrier Award at the Edinburgh Comedy Festival and he has now gone on to become a household name as a stand up comedian and a talk show host and he co-wrote the football song *Three Lions* that became a favourite on the terraces in the European Championship in 1996.

The Spitfire

The first of the Spitfire fighters was produced in Castle Bromwich in 1940. The airfield saw 33,198 test flights. Production reached 30 planes a week and in May 1942 an order for 2,990 Spitfires was placed, the largest single order for any British military aircraft. By 1945, it had built 15,634 Spitfires. The factory closed in 1958. Where it once stood is now Castle Vale housing estate.

John Benjamin Stone

(1836 - 1940)

Son of Benjamin Stone of Aston Manor he was born in Birmingham and educated at Birmingham's Grammar School. He lived at The Grange in Erdington and photographed an enormous variety of subjects. He travelled widely and in the process wrote several books. He left over 30,000 negatives which are stored in the British Museum and the Birmingham Public Library. Some of his pictures including state and private apartments, the Royal Chapel and the library at Windsor Castle proved of considerable value recently when fire damaged part of the Castle.

Joseph Sturge

(1793-1859)

He was one of Birmingham's greatest radicals, A Quaker, he campaigned continuously for peace. He was an important member of the movement to obtain universal suffrage at a time when the vote was limited to only a few male citizens. He is perhaps best known as a campaigner against slavery. His statue stands in front of the Marriott Hotel at Five Ways.

Meera Syall MBE
(1962 -)

Writer, comic playwright and actress she was born in Wolverhampton. She wrote and starred in *Goodness Gracious Me* and *The Kumars at Number 42* for TV and also wrote the screenplay, co-produced and appeared in the film *Anita and Me*. She penned the script for Andrew Lloyd-Webber's hit musical *Bombay Dreams*.

Chris Tarrant OBE
(1946 -)

Although not a native of Britain's second city he spent several years in Birmingham, first as a student at University and following his graduation, he worked as a security guard and lorry driver before teaching English in London. He returned in 1972 to work for ATV in Birmingham as presenter for the children's show *TISWAS*. He has gone on to present London's Capital Radio breakfast show and more latterly is the host of *Who Wants to be a Millionaire?*.

Thomas Telford
(1757 - 1834)

He designed and built public buildings and roads and bridges for the county of Shropshire in the 1780s. In 1820 he was asked to survey the Birmingham canals

and to suggest ways to improve them. The modifications took longer than expected and before they were complete in 1827, he became involved in the construction of the Birmingham and Liverpool junction (just outside Wolverhampton). This canal used an almost straight route, cuttings and embankments to cope with minor hills and valleys. Locks were only used where there was a permanent rise or fall in ground level. Telford unfortunately did not live to see the completion of the works in 1835.

John Ronald Reuel Tolkein
(1892 - 1973)

Most famous for writing *Lord of the Rings*, his parents were from Birmingham but he was born in South Africa. At three years old he returned to Birmingham with his mother and brother to visit grandparents and it was at that time that his father died and they stayed in England, initially at 9, Ashfield Road in King's Heath. They then moved to Sarehole in 1896 and the tiny village is said to be the model for "The Shire" - the home of The Hobbits and Sarehole Mill – Birmingham's only surviving water mill. He attended King Edward's School in New Street. Further inspiration came from the

Moseley Bog which would feature as The 'old forest' the home of Tom Bombadil and the miller at Sarehole, George Andrew covered in white dust became known to them as the White Ogre. When his mother died in 1904 together with his brother he was sent to stay with an aunt, Beatrice Suffield at Stirling Road, where he remained for four years. Just around the corner was Waterworks Road where Perrott's Folly and another Victorian tower, part of the waterworks was said to have formed the idea of the *Two Towers* for which the second volume of the Lord of the Rings was named. In 1911 he went to Oxford University where he spent the majority of the rest of his life.

Sir John Turton-Randle
(1905 - 1984)

He was awarded the Royal Society Fellowship to study electron processes in luminous solids in the Physics Department of Birmingham University between 1937 and 1943. He then became associated with Dr Henry Albert Howard Boot also at Birmingham University and together with Professor James Sayers they invented the cavity magnetron, an essential element of radar and the microwave's most important component. He became a Fellow of the Royal Society in 1942 and was knighted in 1962.

Typhoo Tea

In 1903, John Sumner – a relative of the eminent local historian, William Hutton – produced tea for his sister Mary Augusta as a cure for her chronic indigestion. The family business began at Hutton

House on High Street but soon a shop was opened in Corporation Street in order to supply demand. Sumner called his tea Typhoo Tipps as it was alliterative and sounded vaguely oriental.

UB40

A "cross-over reggae" band with their recording studio in Digbeth. The band members consist of Birmingham born and bred lads James Brown, Robin Campbell, Ali Campbell, Michael Virtue, Norman Hassan, Earl Falconer, Astro and Brian Travers. Other band members include Martin Meredith and Lawrence Parry. The band began its life in the late 1970s taking its name from the Unemployment Benefit form. Hits include 'Food for Thought', 'King, Signing Off', 'One In Ten', 'Red Red Wine' and 'Homely Girl'.

Murray Walker
(1923 -)

TV sports commentator, the voice of Formula 1 was born 214 Reddings Lane, Hall Green.

Julie Walters OBE
(1950 -)

Born in Birmingham and living in Bearwood, she attended Holly Lodge Girls' School. She was encouraged to study nursing but instead pursued her love of acting and made her London stage debut in *Funny Peculiar*. In 1980 she was cast in the title role of the Royal Shakespeare Company production of Willy Russell's play *Educating Rita*. Her many films include *She'll Be Wearing Pink Pyjamas*, *Buster*, *Stepping Out*, *Billy Elliott*, the Harry Potter films to date and *Calendar Girls*. She has three BAFTAs, one Golden

Globe and two Oscar nominations.

James Watt
(1736 - 1819)

His name appears on every light bulb as a unit of power. Watt was also the inventor of the prototype photocopier. His personal possessions were sold for £1.9million at auction in 2003.

Toyah Wilcox
(1958 -)

Jungle survivor, Shakespearean actress, TV presenter and punk diva went to school in Edgbaston.

Steve Winwood
(1948 -)

The family lived at Atlantic Road in Kingstanding in Birmingham and he attended Cranbourne Road Primary School later known as Great Barr Comprehensive. With his brother he got his first performing experience sitting in with his father's band at weddings and they started their own jazz band in 1962. Later that year he met guitarist Spencer Davies and drummer Pete York and the Rhythm and Blues Quartet were formed. The group was renamed The Spencer Davies Group and two years later he left and formed Traffic with Jim Capaldi and others whom he had met at the Elbow Room Club in Aston. He formed Blind Faith with Eric Clapton and Ginger Baker.

Roy Wood
(1946 –)

As a teenager he joined Birmingham band Mike Sheridan and the Night Riders. He later formed The Move who became one of the most legendary bands of the '60s. He had ten Top Twenty hits in the next five years. Roy joined

Jeff Lynne and The Electric Light Orchestra was born. He experimented with his image and Wizzard appered. By 1975 he had almost single-handedly created a total of eleven band and solo hit singles and two Wizzard albums.

John Wright

In the 1840s Birmingham doctor, John Wright demonstrated that items could be electroplated by immersing them in a tank of silver held in solution through which an electric current was passed.

John Wyatt
(1700 - 1766)

A notable Birmingham resident who long before Arkwright invented the "Spinning Jenny" made a spinning engine which in 1733 spun the first thread of cotton yarn ever produced by machinery.

John Wyndham
(1906-1969)

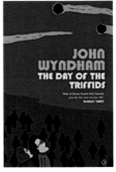

Born in Knowle, the son of a barrister; his mother was the writer Vivienne Beynon Harris. He lived in Edgbaston until 1911 and, inspired by H.G. Wells science fiction novels, began writing short science fiction stories, first he wrote *The Day of the Triffids* in 1951 (published by Penguin Books). and *The Kraken wakes*, *The Chrysalids*, *The Midwich Cuckoos* and *Chocky*.

Tourism services

Services for conference, meeting and convention planners

Birmingham Convention Bureau (BCB) assists organisers of large and small meetings, conventions and conferences with a range of services that include venue finding, booking, social programme planning and registration.

BCB - which for the past seven years has been voted Best UK Convention Bureau by readers of *Meetings and Incentive Travel* magazine - is part of Marketing Birmingham.

It provides professional, practical advice and assistance to enable organisers to find the ideal venue for any type of event in Birmingham.

Its range of services include:

- Venue finding: a free facility using BCB's contacts and members both in Birmingham and the surrounding area.

- Accommodation booking: whether in economy or luxury accommodation, in Birmingham city-centre, outer city or in the surrounding region. There is no charge for this service.

- Social programme planning: a free service for the planning of evenings out, day-trips, private lunches and dinners, activity events and partners' programmes.

- Conference registration: multi-lingual staff to assist in the registration of delegates.

Useful contacts:

Birmingham Convention Bureau

Millennium Point, Level L2
Curzon Street, Birmingham B4 7XG
www.birminghamconvention.com

Conference sales

Tel: (0121) 202 5100
Fax: (0121) 202 5123
E-mail: bcb.conferencesales@
marketingbirmingham.com

Accommodation services

Tel: (0121) 202 5005
Fax: (0121) 202 5123
E-mail: bcb.accommodation@
marketingbirmingham.com

Marketing Birmingham

Millennium Point, Level L2
Curzon Street , Birmingham B4 7XG

Tel: (0121) 202 5115
Fax: (0121) 202 5116

Meet in Birmingham

The useful *Meet in Birmingham* venues and services directory is aimed at event organisers. The user-friendly, comprehensive directory for Birmingham and the surrounding region, complements the conference and tourism support provided by Birmingham Convention Bureau.

The directory has been compiled to help business and leisure visitors take further advantage of Birmingham's facilities and make the most of their stay.

Meet in Birmingham provides invaluable advice and information for event organisers, meeting planners and group travel arrangers. The guide includes useful tables of up-to-date reference material on hotels and conference venues in Birmingham and the surrounding region. The directory's 'Future Developments' section provides information on new and planned facilities.

For a free copy contact BCB on Tel: (0121) 202 5100;
e-mail: bcb.conferencesales@marketingbirmingham.com or write to Birmingham Convention Bureau, Millennium Point, Level L2, Curzon Street, Birmingham B4 7XG.

Services for Visitors

Marketing Birmingham operate five Tourism Centres, three in the city centre and two at the National Exhibition Centre:

City Centre:

1 Tourism Centre and Ticket Shop
The Rotunda, 150 New Street,
Birmingham B2 4PA (Ref 4, map, page 16)

Opening times:
Monday – Saturday 9.30am –5.30pm
Sunday and Bank Holidays 10.30am-4.30pm

Telephone / Email:
Information: (0121) 202 5099
ticketshop@marketingbirmingham.com

Ticket Hotline: (0121) 202 5000
ticketshop@marketingbirmingham.com

Short Break Hotline (0121) 202 5050
callcentre@marketingbirmingham.com

Fax: (0121) 616 1038

Services available:

- advice on all that Birmingham has to offer
- publications including maps and guide books
- sale of National Express coach tickets
- sale of day excursion and discounted tickets to many local attractions
- free accommodation booking service
- sale of wide range of souvenirs and merchandise
- sale of tickets for The NEC Group venues, CBSO Centre, Alexandra Theatre, Birmingham Hippodrome, Wolverhampton Grand Theatre, Birmingham Repertory Theatre, Royal Shakespeare Theatre, as well as for a wide range of local events
- Ticketmaster agent, offering tickets for over 27,000 events nationwide

2 Welcome Centre
New Street, Birmingham
(Midway between Ref 1 and Ref 4, map, page 16)

Opening times:
Monday – Saturday 9am – 6pm
Sunday and Bank Holidays 10am – 4pm

Services available:

- A meet and greet Centre at the heart of New Street, staffed by multi-lingual assistants, ready to help Birmingham residents and visitors

3 The ICC Tourism Centre
The Mall, The ICC, Broad Street
Birmingham B1 2EA (Ref 20, map, page 36)

Opening times (extended for selected events):
Monday – Friday 9.30am – 5.30pm

Telephone (0121) 202 5099

Services available:

- advice on all that Birmingham has to offer
- free accommodation booking service
- sale of souvenirs and merchandise

National Exhibition Centre (NEC)

4 Visitor Information Centre
The Piazza (next to Hall 5), The NEC
Birmingham B40 1NT (See plan, page 125)

Opening times (extended for selected events):
Monday – Friday 9am – 5pm

Telephone (0121) 202 5099

Services available:

- advice on all that Birmingham has to offer
- free accommodation booking service
- sale of souvenirs and merchandise

5 Visitor Information Centre
The Atrium (next to Hall 9), The NEC
Birmingham B40 1NT (See plan, page 125)

Opening times (extended for selected events)
Monday – Friday 9am – 5pm

Telephone (0121) 202 5099

Services available:

- advice on all that Birmingham has to offer
- free accommodation booking service
- sale of souvenirs and merchandise

Where to Stay

There are over 7,000 beds in Birmingham city centre and another 47,000 out in the surrounding area. However, availability can be dramatically reduced during a busy exhibition at the NEC or a major sporting event at the NIA.

The city's only five star hotel is the Birmingham Marriott at Five Ways – once the site of the original Edgbaston High School for Girls.

The city has most international hotel chains and a host of individually owned bed and breakfast hotels (or B & Bs) primarily in the suburbs.

There are travel accommodation-style places, some with and some without restaurants, prices reflect the facilities and very often the location. The closer to the city centre, the more expensive the accommodation.

Check out deals – particularly if you are staying over a weekend as there is a lot of business accommodation, particularly around the NEC and airport offering cheaper rates over Friday – Sunday nights.

There are discounts available for children when sharing a room with their parents and the age limit varies greatly – don't assume all hotels operate the same policy. (see page 136)

When confirming rates check whether you have breakfast included and whether it's English or Continental.

The rates that are included should be used as a guideline. Some hotels offer internet booking. Star ratings etc (English Tourism Council) or AA are indicated at the end of each entry. (However, more recent hotels will not yet have been rated whilst others may not be assessed on that basis).

Central Quarter

The Burlington Hotel
Burlington Arcade, 126 New Street
Tel: (0121) 643 9191
www.burlingtonhotel.com

The Burlington is a four star Victorian hotel in the middle of the city centre. Each of the 112 bedrooms has been individually designed and facilities include fax/modem points and electronic voice - mail box. The award-winning restaurant has à la carte and table d' hôte menus. There is a gym, sauna and solarium.

Cost: ££££ ★★★★

Hotel Du Vin & Bistro
25 Church Street
Tel: (0121) 200 0600
www.hotelduvin.com

Off Colmore Row between the city centre and the Jewellery Quarter, the stylish Hotel Du Vin is in the city's

former eye hospital building. A 66 room, 4 star hotel with bar, fitness room, restaurant.

Cost: ££££ ★★★★

The Copthorne Hotel
Paradise Circus
Tel: (0121) 200 2727
www.mill.cop.com

A 4 star hotel with 212 rooms. Swimming pool, fitness centre, bar, restaurant and parking. Close to the city centre and the ICC. Does a very reasonable 3 course, traditional Sunday roast lunch from 12.30pm – 2.30pm.

Cost: £££ ★★★★

Thistle Birmingham City
St Chad's Queensway
Tel: (0121) 606 4500.
www.thistlehotels.com

133 bedroom modern hotel overlooking St Chad's Cathedral, close to Snow Hill Station. Bar, parking, restaurant, room service.

Cost: £££

Briar Rose
25 Bennett's Hill
Tel: (0121) 634 8100.
www.jdwetherspoons.co.uk

Unpretentious 41 rooms (4 family), internet connections in rooms. Bar, restaurant.

Cost: ££

Britannia Hotel
Union Passage, New Street
Tel: (0121) 631 3331
www.britanniahotels.com

In the heart of the city centre, the Britannia has 195 en-suite bedrooms, each with radio, colour TV, alarm/morning call system, direct dial telephone, trouser press, hair dryer and tea & coffee making facilities. There is a restaurant, a bar and room service.

Cost: £££

Comfort Inn Birmingham
Station Street
Tel: (0121) 643 1134

Traditional. 40 rooms. Bar, restaurant, centre of Birmingham close to the Hippodrome.

Cost: £££

Convention

Hyatt Regency Birmingham

2 Bridge Street

Tel: (0121) 643 1234.
www.birmingham.hyatt.com

319 room hotel on 23 floors with lift that looks out over the city. Private, covered walkway into the ICC. Close to Broad Street and Brindleyplace. The hotel has a bar, restaurant, fitness room, swimming pool, on site parking and internet points in rooms.

Cost: ££££

Novotel Birmingham Centre

70 Broad Street

Tel: (0121) 643 2000.
www.novotel.com

One of Birmingham's bright, new 3 star hotels right on Broad Street. There are 148 double rooms (no singles) along with a fitness centre, restaurant and bar. Rooms have modem points and room service is available.

Cost: £££ ★★★

City Inn

1 Brunswick Square, Brindleyplace

Tel: (0121) 643 1003
www.cityinn.com

All rooms have air conditioning, CD player, satellite TV, ISDN line and 24 hour service. Also restaurant, bar, terrace and fitness room.

Cost: ££££

Jurys Inn

245 Broad Street

Tel: (0121) 606 9000.
www.jurydoyle.com

Contemporary hotel. All 445 bedrooms in this 3 star hotel are en suite and include direct dial telephone, colour TV and tea/coffee making facilities. There is a restaurant with menus that change daily, a bar and secure parking is available. Some rooms have internet points.

Cost: ££ ★★★

Days Inn Birmingham Central

160 Wharfside Street, The Mailbox

Tel: (0121) 643 9344.
www. daysinn.com

In one of the choicest buildings in town, there are 90 rooms, bar, restaurant and rooms have internet connection.

Cost: £££

Crowne Plaza

Central Square

Tel: (0121) 631 2000
www.crowneplaza.com

With 284 luxury bedrooms, a well-appointed leisure club with indoor swimming pool, large restaurant and bar, Crowne Plaza provides luxury accommodation. Two minutes walk from the International Convention Centre and close to Central Quarter.

Cost: ££££ ★★★★

Malmaison Hotel

The Mailbox, Royal Mail Street

Tel: (0121) 246 5000.
www.malmaison.com

Chic 189 room hotel amidst the smartest shops in town. Bar, fitness studio, room service and smart restaurant.

Cost: ££££

Birmingham Marriott Hotel

12 Hagley Road, Edgbaston, Five Ways

Tel: 0870 400 7280.
www.marriotthotels.com/bhxbh

An elegant, beautifully furnished, 102 bedroom, 5 star hotel, close to the ICC and Broad Street. 'West Restaurant', an Egyptian themed leisure club with swimming pool, beauty salon, valet service, 24 hour room service, free parking.

Cost: ££££ ★★★★★

Ibis Birmingham Holloway Circus

55 Irving Street

Tel: (0121) 622 4925.
www.accor.com

Just outside the quarter all 51 rooms are en suite with satellite TV and tea/coffee making facilities. Own car park, bar and restaurant.

Cost: £

Chinese Quarter

Holiday Inn, Birmingham City

Smallbrook Queensway

Tel: 0870 400 9008

The Holiday Inn is a modern, 3 star hotel near to New Street station, theatres, the ICC/NIA and the nightlife of the Arcadian. There are 280 bedrooms with 24 hour room service, hairdryer, trouser press, satellite TV. Facilities include a restaurant and bar.

Cost: ££ ★★★

Ibis Centre Hotel
Ladywell Walk
Tel: (0121) 622 6010

A modern hotel with 159 rooms overlooking the Arcadian, the functional Ibis offers competitive rates for a city-centre location.

Cost: ££

Eastside

Paragon Hotel
145 Alcester Street, Digbeth
Tel: (0121) 627 0627.
www.paragonhotel.net

Formerly the Chamberlain Park Hotel, the Paragon is an impressive, character hotel about a mile from the city centre. A magnificent, grade II listed building, which has been carefully restored. There are 250 en suite rooms with TV, direct dial telephone and tea/coffee making facilities, bar, restaurant, indoor car park.

Cost: ££

Campanile Hotel
Chester Street, Aston
Tel: (0121) 359 3330

Modern canalside hotel, situated off the Aston Expressway and with easy access to the motorway network. Close to Aston Business Park and Millennium Point; 10 minute walk to city centre.

Cost: £££

Birmingham South-West

Plough & Harrow Hotel
135 Hagley Road, Edgbaston
Tel: (0121) 454 4111.
www.corushotels.com

Less than one mile from the city centre, the Plough & Harrow is a charming 3 star

hotel with lots of history and character. There has been an inn on the site since 1612 and an hotel since 1704. There are 44 en suite bedrooms, including 2 suites. Colour TV, radio, direct-dial telephone, trouser-press, hairdryer, tea and coffee making facilities. 24 hour room service. Restaurant, bar and parking.

Cost: £££ ★★★

Thistle Birmingham Edgbaston
225 Hagley Road, Edgbaston
Tel: (0121) 455 9777.
www.thistlehotels.com

2 miles from city centre. 151 rooms, bar, room service, parking, restaurant.

Cost: £££

Apollo Hotel
243-247 Hagley Road, Edgbaston
Tel: (0121) 455 0271.
www.choicehotelseurope.com

3 star, 126 rooms, bar, restaurant, 2 miles from the city centre, free parking.

Cost: ££ ★★★

Quality Hotel
166/174 Hagley Road, Edgbaston
Tel: (0121) 454 6621 www.quality-hotelsbirmingham.com

About 2 miles from the city centre, this 3 star, 213 bedroom hotel has a bar, fitness studio, swimming pool, restaurant and parking.

Cost: £££ ★★★

Portland Hotel
313 Hagley Road, Edgbaston
Tel: (0121) 455 0535.
www.portlandbirmingham.co.uk

This 3 star hotel, 2 miles from the city centre has 63 rooms (35 singles). Bar, parking, restaurant, room service.

Cost: from ££ ★★★

Comfort Inn Norfolk Hotel
257/267 Hagley Road, Edgbaston
Tel: (0121) 454 8071.
www.choicehotelseurope.co.uk

3 star, 169 rooms, bar, free on site parking, restaurant,

Cost: £££ ★★★

Hagley Court Hotel
229 Hagley Road, Edgbaston
Tel: (0121) 454 6514.
www.hagleycourt.com

26 rooms, 2 miles from city centre. Bar, parking, restaurant, room service, internet points in rooms.

Cost: ££

Premier Lodge
Ashbrook Drive, Parkway, Rubery
Tel: (0121) 460 1998.
www.premierlodge.com

Ideal travel accommodation. This Premier Lodge is off the A38 Bristol Road into Birmingham and close to the M5. There are 62 rooms and the Outside Inn is next door.

Cost: ££

Birmingham South-East

Ibis Birmingham Bordesley
1 Bordesley Park Road, Bordesley
Tel: (0121) 506 2600.
www.ibishotels.com

Bar, restaurant, on site parking and internet points in the rooms, this 87 room hotel is 2 miles from city centre, 8 miles from NEC. Travel accommodation.

Cost: ££

Formule 1
33 Bordesley Park Road, Bordesley
Tel: (0121) 773 9583

Travel accommodation with easy access to motorway network. 2 miles from city-centre, eight miles from NEC. 62 rooms. No restaurant or bar but you can use Ibis next door.

Cost: ££

Express by Holiday Inn, Hall Green
Stratford Road, Hall Green
Tel: (0121) 744 4414.
www.hiexpress.com

Travel accommodation, 51 rooms with internet connection. Parking. 6 miles to the NEC, 6 miles to city centre. Next to Robin Hood pub/restaurant.

Cost: ££

Hotels at the NEC and Airport

Novotel
Birmingham International Airport
Tel: (0121) 782 7000.
www.accor-hotels.com

Right outside the terminal entrance. 195 rooms, 3* with bar, restaurant and room service.

Cost: £££ ★★★

The Arden Hotel
Coventry Road, Bickenhill, Solihull
Tel: (01675) 445 604.
www.ardenhotel.co.uk

216 bedrooms, (mostly twin) 3* hotel with swimming pool, fitness room, bar, room service, restaurant and private parking.

Cost: £££ ★★★

Crowne Plaza
Pendigo Way, NEC
Tel: (0121) 781 4000. www.birminghamnec.crowneplaza.com

Overlooking the lake at the NEC, the 242 bedroom Crowne Plaza has a bar, fitness room, room service and 'Turners' restaurant, Onsite parking and internet connections in rooms.

Cost: ££££

Hilton Birmingham Metropole
NEC
Tel: (0121) 780 4242.
www.hilton.com

794 rooms. Bar, fitness room, three restaurants, swimming pool.

Cost: ££££

Holiday Inn Birmingham Airport
Coventry Road
Tel: (0870) 400 9007
www.forte-hotels.com

Restaurant, NEC 1 mile, Birmingham 8 miles. 3 star.

Cost: ££££ ★★★

Express by Holiday Inn
Bickenhill Parkway, NEC
Tel: (0121) 782 3222.
www.hiexpress-nec.co.uk

Travel accommodation. 179 rooms, Birmingham 13 miles away.

Cost: £££

Premier Lodge, NEC
Parkway, The NEC
Tel: 0870 700 1328.
www.premierlodge.com

Ideal travel accommodation, 199 rooms with modem point, bar, restaurant, parking.

Cost: ££

Quality Hotel
Stonebridge Manor/NEC
Tel: (024) 7640 3835
www.stonebridgemanorhotel.com

80 room, 3* hotel with gym, sauna, steam room and restaurant.

Cost: £££ ★★★

Arden Hotel & Leisure Club
Coventry Road, Bickenhill, Solihull
Tel: (01675) 443221.
www.ardenhotel.co.uk

The Arden Hotel is 1 mile from the NEC and 9 miles from Birmingham city centre. It is a 216 room, 3* hotel ideally situated for exhibitors as there are few distractions in terms of restaurants and sights to see within close proximity.   There's a bar, restaurant, swimming pool and fitness room.

Cost: ££££ ★★★

Further Afield South-West Birmingham

Abbey Hotel Golf & Country Club
Hither Green Lane, Dagnell End, Redditch
Tel: (01527) 406 600.
www.theabbeyhotel.co.uk

4* hotel with an 18 hole golf course on the outskirts of Redditch. 72 rooms, bar, restaurant, room service, pool and fitness studio.

Cost: ££££ ★★★★

Premier Lodge, Redditch
Birchfield Road, Redditch
Tel: (0870) 700 1320
www.premierlodge.com

Close to J1/M42 and next to the Foxlydiate Arms. Travel accommodation with desk and modem point in all 33 rooms.

Cost: ££

Hanover International, Bromsgrove
Kidderminster Road, Bromsgrove
Tel: (01527) 576 600.
www.hanover-international.com

Hacienda-style hotel, 3 miles from J4/M5 with 114 rooms. Fitness room, pool, two restaurants and a bar. 13 miles from Birmingham, 10 miles to the NEC.

Cost: ££££ ★★★★

Hilton Birmingham Bromsgrove
Birmingham Road, Bromsgrove
Tel: (0121) 447 7888.
www.hilton.com.

Modern, 148 bedroom hotel in its own grounds close to M42 and M5. 12 miles from Birmingham, 20 miles from the NEC. Bar, restaurant, room service and parking. Livingwell Health Club including pool.

Cost: £££ ★★★★

Perry Hall Ramada Jarvis

Kidderminster Road, Bromsgrove
Tel: (01527) 579 976.
www.ramadajarvis.co.uk

This ivy covered country house was once the home of the poet, A. E. Housman. There are 58 en suite rooms, a bar and restaurant. Use of local leisure facilities.

Cost: £££

Brockencote Hall Country House Hotel

Chaddesley Corbett, Nr Kidderminster
Tel: (01562) 777 876
www.brockencotehall.com

In a delightful setting, Brockencote (3* with 17 bedrooms) is approached via a long, regal driveway. Its restaurant is nationally acclaimed. Dinner menu starts from £27.50.

Cost: ££££ ★★★

Ramada Hotel (Kidderminster)

Habberley Road, Bewdley
Tel: (01299) 406 400.
www.ramadajarvis.co.uk

This 44 bedroom 3* hotel is set within 20 acres of glorious countryside. There's a fitness suite, pool, room service and parking. Some rooms have modem points.

Cost: ££££ ★★★

Westmead Hotel

Redditch Road, Hopwood
Tel: (0121) 445 1202 www. westmeadhotel@corushotels.com

A 3* hotel, 8 miles from Birmingham and 14 miles from the NEC. Bar, restaurant and rooms with modem points.

Cost: ££ ★★★

South-East of Birmingham

Flemings Hotel

141 Warwick Road, Olton, Solihull
Tel: (0121) 706 0371
www.flemingshotel.co.uk.

A family-run 2* hotel with 70 en suite rooms on the Warwick Road to Solihull. Restaurant, bar. NEC 3 miles, Birmingham 5 miles.

Cost: ££ ★★

Richmond House Hotel

47 Richmond Road, Olton, Solihull
Tel: (0121) 707 9746.

A guest house with 10 rooms (2 single). Parking, bar, restaurant and room service.

Cost: ££

Ramada Jarvis

The Square, Solihull
Tel: (0121) 711 2121.
www.ramadajarvis.co.uk

Located in the centre of Solihull, opposite St. Alphege church, the Ramada Jarvis has 145 rooms – including 14 suites. It's built around one of the oldest bowling greens in the country. The original 16th century building is now the Club Bar. 4 miles to the NEC, 8 miles to Birmingham.

Cost: ££

Solihull Moat House

61 Homer Road, Solihull
Tel: (0121) 623 9988.
wwwmoathouse hotels.com

Recently built 115 bedroom hotel close to the new Touchwood centre, the Moat House has a pool, sauna and steam room, fitness studio, bar, restaurant and parking.

Cost: ££££ ★★★★

Renaissance Solihull Hotel

Warwick Road, Solihull
Tel: (0121) 711 3000.
www.renaissancehotels.com/bhxsl

179 rooms, 4* hotel with indoor pool, fitness studio, bar and restaurant.

Cost: ££££ ★★★★

Moat Manor Hotel

Four Ashes Road, Dorridge, Solihull
Tel: (01564) 779988

Down a long drive, this stylish hotel is set in woodland but close to the M42 motorway. Highly commended restaurant and bar with rooms all individually decorated, each according to a month of the year.

Cost: ££££ ★★★

Nuthurst Grange

Nuthurst Grange Lane, Hockley Heath
Tel: (01564) 783 972.
www.nuthurst-grange.com

An elegant 15 bedroom, 3* country house hotel and restaurant.

Cost: ££££ ★★★

Aylesbury House Hotel

Aylesbury Road, Hockley Heath, Solihull
Tel: (01564) 779 207.
www.aylesburyhousehotel.co.uk

In 12 acres (4.85ha) of grounds, this small, country house hotel is eight miles from both the NEC and Birmingham. The 30 rooms have private facilities and there is a bar, a restaurant and room service plus parking.

Cost: ££

Ardencote Manor Hotel, Country Club & Spa

Lye Green Road, Claverdon, Warwick
Tel: (01926) 843 111.
www.ardencote.com

AA 3* hotel with 75 rooms (1 single), 15 miles from Birmingham and 14 from the NEC. there's a bar, restaurant, room service, swimming pool, fitness room, parking, an 18 hole golf course and most rooms have internet connections.

Cost: ££££ ★★★

Haigs Hotel

273 Kenilworth Road, Balsall Common
Tel: (01676) 533 004.
www.haigshotel.co.uk

23 rooms, bar, parking, restaurant. Birmingham 11 miles, NEC 6 miles.

Cost: £££ ★★

Honiley Court Hotel
**Meer End Road, Honiley,
Nr Warwick**
Tel: (01926) 859 331.

3* with 62 rooms (all twin or double). 15 miles from Birmingham and 7 from the NEC. Bar, restaurant and parking onsite.

Cost: ££££ ★★★

Clarendon House Hotel
High Street, Kenilworth
Tel: (01926) 857 668.

2* hotel. The 24 rooms have modem points, there's a bar, restaurant and parking.

Cost: ££ ★★

Le Meridien
Chesford Bridge, Kenilworth
Tel: (01926) 859 331.

218 rooms (inc. 9 single and 2 suites), 25 miles from Birmingham and 14 from the NEC. Rooms have modem points, there's a bar, restaurant, parking and fitness room including an indoor pool.

Cost: £££ ★★★

The Peacock Hotel
**149 Warwick Road,
Kenilworth**
Tel: (01926) 851 156.

Small, 22 room (7 single), 3* hotel 15 miles from Birmingham and 10 miles from the NEC. Rooms have modem points, there's a bar, restaurant, room service and parking.

Cost: £££ ★★★

Macdonald De Montfort Hotel
The Square, Kenilworth
Tel: (01926) 855 944.

A 4* hotel, 20 miles from Birmingham and 10 from the NEC, this 108 room hotel has a new fitness complex (finished Spring 2003) complete with a pool, bar, restaurant, room service and parking.

Cost: £££ ★★★★

Marriott Forest of Arden Hotel & Country Club
Maxstoke Lane, Meriden
Tel: (01676) 522 335
www.marriotthotels/cvtgs

There are two 18 hole golf courses at this 4 star hotel, including the Championship Arden Course, the British Masters 2003 and 2005 and home to the English Open 2000 – 2002. There's a swimming pool, spa, sauna, steamroom and solarium. For fitness there are 3 gymnasia, an exercise studio, 2 tennis courts and a croquet lawn. Bars and restaurant. NEC 4 miles and Birmingham 14 miles. 214 rooms.

Cost: ££££ ★★★★

Nailcote Hall Hotel
**Nailcote Lane, Berkswell,
Coventry**
Tel: (024) 7646 6174.
www.nailcotehall.co.uk

Exclusive, 40 bedroom, 4* hotel in the heart of the countryside. 4 poster beds available. Bar, fitness room, golf, swimming, restaurant. 15 miles from Birmingham, 7 miles from NEC.

Cost: ££££ ★★★★

Coventry Menzies Leofric
Broadgate, Coventry
Tel: (024) 7622 1371.

A 94 room, 3* hotel with brasserie and restaurant, just 200m from the cathedral. It was the first hotel built in Britain following the 2nd World War.

Cost: £££ ★★★

Britannia Hotel Coventry
Cathedral Square
Tel: (024) 7663 3733
www.britaniahotels.com

211 rooms (all doubles and twins), bar, terrace and restaurant. Rooms have internet access facility.

Cost: ££

Formule 1 Hotel
Mile Lane, Coventry
Tel: (024) 7623 4560.
www.formule1hotels.com

There are 86 bedrooms in this basic travel accommodation at a price that reflects the no frills facilities.

Cost: ££

Hilton Coventry
**Paradise Way, Walsgrave
Triangle**
Tel: (024) 7660 3000.
www.hilton.com

Close to the M6/M69. 172 rooms, the Hilton has a bar, restaurant, pool and fitness suite with some rooms having modem points.

Cost: £££

Chace Hotel
London Road, Toll Bar End
Tel: (024) 7630 3398.
www.corushotel.co.uk/thechace

An AA 3* hotel with 66 rooms (9 single) – some have internet connection facility. There's a bar, restaurant and parking plus room service.

Cost: £££ ★★★

Best Western Hylands Hotel
153 Warwick Road
Tel: (024) 7650 1600.

A recently refurbished 3* hotel with bar and restaurant, room service, parking and rooms with modem points. 19 miles from Birmingham, 15 miles from the NEC.

Cost: £££ ★★★

Allesley Hotel
**Birmingham Road, Allesley
Village**
Tel: (024) 7640 3272.

Just off the A45 Coventry to Birmingham road, the Allesley is a 3* hotel with 90 rooms. There's a bar, restaurant and parking.

Cost: £££ ★★★

Brooklands Grange Hotel, Coventry

Holyhead Road
Tel: (024) 7660 1601.
www.brooklands-grange.co.uk

Once a Jacobean farmhouse, now equipped for the 21st century with modern connections, TV, trouser press, hairdryer in each room. Restaurant. 8 miles from the NEC/Airport and under 2 miles to Coventry centre.

Cost: ££

Coventry Hill Hotel

Rye Hill, Allesley
Tel: (024) 7640 2151.
www.britaniahotels.com

Modern 190 bedroom hotel with a restaurant and bar, 2 miles from city centre and 5 miles from the NEC, Birmingham International Airport & Station.

Cost: £££

Britannia Royal Court Hotel

Tamworth Road, Keresley
Tel: (024) 7633 4171.
www.britaniahotels.com

Set in 11 acres (14.45ha), 20 miles from Birmingham and 9 from the NEC, the Royal Court has a bar, restaurant, room service, fitness suite and pool.

Cost: £££

Brandon Hall Hotel

Brandon
Tel: (0870) 400 8105.
www.macdonaldshotel.co.uk

A 3* hotel out of Coventry city centre, 30 miles from Birmingham and 20 from the NEC. Bar, restaurant, parking and all rooms have modem points.

Cost: £££ ★★★

Courtyard by Marriott Hotel, Coventry

**London Road,
Ryton-on-Dunsmore**
Tel: (024) 7630 1585.

A 3* hotel with 51 rooms, restaurant and fitness studio.

Cost: £££ ★★★

Tulip Inn – Stoneleigh Park

Stoneleigh Park
Tel: (024) 7669 0123.

Close to the Royal Showground, 25 miles from Birmingham, 15 from the NEC. There's a bar, restaurant, room service and internet points in bedrooms.

Cost: £££

The Glebe Hotel

Church Street, Barford
Tel: (01926) 624218.

39 room, 3* hotel in lovely village with friendly pubs. Fitness suite with pool, bar and restaurant and parking.

Cost: £££ ★★★

Hilton Warwick

Warwick By-Pass (J15/M40), Stratford Road
Tel: (01926) 499 555.
www.hilton.com

Adjacent to the motorway, the Hilton is a 4*, 181 room hotel (rooms have modem points). There's a fitness suite including a pool and a bar and restaurant.

Cost: £££ ★★★★

Days Inn Warwick North

**M40 Motorway
(Northbound), Banbury Road, Ashome**
Tel: (01926) 651 681.

Cost: ££

and the

Welcome Lodge Warwick

**M40 Motorway
(Southbound), Banbury Road, Ashome,**
Tel: (01926) 650 168

Good value, travel accommodation. Days Inn has 54 rooms and Welcome Lodge 42.

Cost: ££

The Quality Hotel, Warwick

Chesford Bridge, Kenilworth
Tel: (01926) 858 331.

48 rooms with modem points, bar, restaurant, room service and parking.

Cost: ££

Manor House Hotel

Avenue Road, Royal Leamington Spa
Tel: (01926) 423 251.

3* hotel with 53 rooms, 20 miles from both Birmingham and the NEC.. Parking, bar and restaurant.

Cost: £££ ★★★

Guest Houses:

Fairfield House

Birmingham Road, Allesley
Tel: (024) 7640 5051.

This family run Edwardian guest house is on the A45. It has recently been refurbished. En suite rooms with TV, video, hairdryer.

Cost: £

Bubbenhall House

Paget's Lane, Bubbenhall
Tel: (024) 7630 2409

A restored hunting lodge in a lovely woodland setting.

Cost: ££

Camp Farm

Hob Lane, Balsall Common
Tel (01676) 533 804

A 3* farmhouse with single, double and family rooms. Pets welcome.

Cost: ££

Croft on the Green

23 Stoke Green, Coventry
Tel: (024) 7645 7846

Family-run Victorian guest house in a conservation area. Most rooms with en suite.

Cost: ££

North-West of Birmingham

Birmingham Great Barr Hotel and Conference Centre

J7/M6, Pear Tree Drive, Newton Road, Great Barr
Tel: (0121) 357 1141.
www.thegreatbarrhotel.co.uk

105 rooms, 3* hotel. Rooms have internet connection. Bar, restaurant, room service and parking.

Cost: £££ ★★★

Birmingham/ West Bromwich Moat House

Birmingham Road, West Bromwich
Tel: (0121) 609 9988.
www.moathousehotels.com

This 168 room hotel has a fitness room and swimming pool along with bar and restaurant. 5 miles from Birmingham and 18 from the NEC.

Cost: ££££

The County Hotel
Birmingham Road, Walsall
Tel: (01922) 632 323.
www.countywalsall.co.uk

A small hotel with 45 rooms, 9 miles from Birmingham and 17 from the NEC. Bar, restaurant, room service and on site parking.

Cost: ££

Fairlawns at Aldridge
Little Aston Road, Aldridge, Walsall
Tel: (01922) 455 122.
www.fairlawns.co.uk

50 bedroom, 3* Best Western hotel. Gym, swimming pool, bar, restaurant, room service, parking and modem connections in the bedrooms. 9 miles from Birmingham and 12 from the NEC.

Cost: £££ ★★★

Holiday Inn Birmingham
J7/M6, Chapel Lane, Great Barr
Tel: (0870) 400 9009. www.reservations-birminghamgreatbarratichotelsgroup.com

3* hotel, 192 rooms, close to motorway – Birmingham 7 miles, NEC 16 miles. Usual facilities including bar, restaurant, pool and fitness room. Parking on site.

Cost: £££ ★★★

Menzies Barons Court Hotel
Walsall Road, Walsall Wood
Tel: (01543) 452 020.
www.bookmenzies.com

Recently refurbished 94 room 4* with gym, pool, solarium, sauna and steam rooms. Restaurant and bar.

Cost: ££ ★★★★

Howard Johnson Hotel, West Bromwich
144 High Street, West Bromwich
Tel: (0121) 525 8333
www.hojo.com

All 133 rooms have modem points. 7 rooms have wheelchair access. Parking. Off J1/M5.

Cost: ££

Quality Hotels Birmingham North
Birmingham Road, Walsall
Tel: (01922) 633 609.
www.choicehotels.com

Close to the M6 motorway, 17 miles from the city and 18 from NEC. 3* hotel with 94 rooms, some have modem points. Bar, restaurant, room service, parking.

Cost: £££ ★★★

Britannia Hotel
Lichfield Street, Wolverhampton
Tel: (01902) 429 922.

117 rooms (33 single), 12 miles from Birmingham. Bar, restaurant and parking on site.

Cost: £££

Copthorne Merry Hill
The Waterfront, Level Street, Brierley Hill, Dudley
Tel: (01384) 482 882.
www.mill-cop.com

4* star hotel on the newly developed Waterfront. 138 rooms, leisure facilities including pool, parking, bar and restaurant.

Cost: £££ ★★★★

Himley Country Hotel
School Road, Himley, Dudley
Tel: (01902) 896 716.

This 3* hotel has 73 rooms, bar, restaurant and onsite parking.

Cost: £££ ★★★

Holiday Inn Garden Court
Dunstall Park Centre, Gorsebrook Road, Dunstall Park, Wolverhampton
Tel: (0870) 220 0102. www.holiday-inn.com/wolverhampton

A 54 bedroom hotel within Dunstall Park Centre – ideal for Britain's only floodlit horse racecourse. Fitness room, bar and bistro. Rooms have modem points.

Cost: £££

The Mount
Mount Road, Tettenhall Wood, Wolverhampton
Tel: (01902) 752 055.

3* hotel with 56 rooms, 25 miles from Birmingham. Modem points, bar, restaurant and room service.

Cost: £££ ★★★

Park Hall Hotel and Conference Centre
Park Drive, Goldthorn Park, Wolverhampton
Tel: (01902) 331 121

A member of the Best Western group, Park Hall is a 57 room, 3* hotel around 18 miles from Birmingham. Rooms have modem points, there's a bar, restaurant and room service plus on site parking.

Cost: £££ ★★★

Village Leisure Hotel
Castlegate Park, Birmingham Road, Dudley
Tel: (01384) 216 600.

One of the De Vere group hotels, the Village Leisure has 98 en suite rooms, a bar, leisure centre with pool and parking.

Cost: ££££

Ward Arms Hotel
Birmingham Road, Dudley
Tel: (01384) 458 070.

A 3* hotel, 10 miles from Birmingham; the 72 rooms have modem points, there's a bar, restaurant, room service and on site parking.

Cost: £££ ★★★

North-East of Birmingham

The De Vere Belfry
Wishaw, North Warwickshire
Tel: 08709 000 066.
www.DeVereOnline.co.uk

Surrounded by 550 acres (222ha) of beautiful countryside including 3 golf courses, the Belfry is a large, 4* hotel with 324 rooms, restaurants, bars and fitness suite including a pool.

Cost: £££ ★★★★

Lea Marston Hotel
Haunch Lane, Lea Marston, Sutton Coldfield
Tel: (01675) 470 468.
www.leamarstonhotel.co.uk

A member of the Best Western group, Lea Marston is a hotel with 83 rooms, a health club, two 9 hole golf courses and a choice of bars and restaurants.

Cost: ££££ ★★★

Marston Farm Hotel
Dog Lane, Bodymoor Heath, Nr Sutton Coldfield
Tel: (01827) 872 133.
www.brook-hotels.co.uk

A 37 room, 3* hotel, 15 miles from Birmingham and 9 from the NEC with restaurant and bar.

Cost: ££££ ★★★

Moor Hall Hotel
Moor Hall Drive, Four Oaks, Sutton Coldfield
Tel: (0121) 308 3751.
www.moorhallhotel.co.uk

A 4* country house hotel set in parkland and overlooking a golf course. 82 rooms with modem points, fitness complex including a pool, sauna, spa and beauty treatment rooms (new in April 2003), bar and restaurants.

Cost: £££ ★★★★

New Hall Country House Hotel
Walmley Road, Sutton Coldfield
Tel: (0121) 378 2442
www.thistlehotels.com

A small (60 room), 4* country house hotel, 7 miles from Birmingham and 8 from the NEC. It has a leisure complex including a pool, an 18 hole golf course, bar and restaurant.

Cost: ££££ ★★★★

Quality Sutton Court Hotel
60/66 Lichfield Road, Sutton Coldfield
Tel: (0121) 354 4991.
www.schotel.co.uk

A 3* hotel with 52 rooms, 7 miles from Birmingham. Bar, restaurant, on site parking and room service.

Cost: £££ ★★★

Ramada Hotel and Resort Birmingham
Penns Lane, Walmley, Sutton Coldfield
Tel: (0121) 351 3111 www. ramadabirmingham.co.uk

The excellent leisure facilities at this 170 bedroom, 4 star hotel includes an indoor pool, sauna, spa, gym, aerobics studio. Modem points in bedrooms. Bar, restaurant, parking and room service.

Cost: £££ ★★★★

Coleshill Hotel
152 High Street, Coleshill
Tel: (01675) 465 527.
www.greenking.co.uk

A 3 * hotel with 23 rooms. Bar, room service, parking and restaurant. The NEC is 3 miles away and Birmingham 8 miles.

Cost: £££ ★★★

Express by Holiday Inn, Birmingham
1200 Chester Road, Castle Bromwich
Tel: (0121) 747 6633.
www.hiexpress.com

Travel accommodation, bar and parking. 110 rooms all with internet connections. Birmingham 5 miles and NEC 9 miles away.

Cost: £

Grimstock Country House Hotel
Gilson Road, Coleshill
Tel: (01675) 462 121
www.grimstockhotel.co.uk

3* hotel with 44 rooms, bar, fitness room and restaurant. 11 miles to Birmingham, 3 miles to the NEC.

Cost: £££ ★★★

Bed and Breakfast

B & Bs provide visitors with not only a bed and breakfast but also the opportunity to meet local people - normally by staying in their homes. Most are in urban areas away from the city-centre.
(For a wider selection, visit www.theaa.com).

Westbourne Lodge
25-31 Fountain Road, Edgbaston, (Birmingham south west)
Tel: (0121) 429 1003

Located on a quiet residential avenue close to the Hagley Road; range of non-smoking, thoughtfully furnished bedrooms.

Central Guest House
1637 Coventry Road, South Yardley (Birmingham south east)
Tel: (0121) 706 7757

Located between the airport and city centre, this comfortable house is run by friendly and attentive proprietors.

Ashdale House Hotel
39 Broad Road, Acock's Green, (Birmingham south east)
Tel: (0121) 706 3598
Fax: (0121) 707 2324

Located opposite a park; renovated Victorian house with a range of bedrooms.

Olton Cottage Guest House
School Lane, Old Yardley Village, Yardley, (Birmingham south east)
Tel: (0121) 783 9249

Renovated early Victorian house located in a peaceful residential area.

Windrush
337 Birmingham Road, Wylde Green, Sutton Coldfield (Birmingham north east)
Tel: (0121) 384 7534

Elegant Victorian house located between the city centre and Sutton Coldfield.

A little unusual

Renting holiday cottages:

For visitors to the region who want more flexibility than staying in a hotel offers, renting a holiday home in the countryside surrounding Birmingham may be ideal. It's a bit cosier and more home-from-home. It's possible to find a well-equipped cottage complete with period features like beamed ceilings and an inglenook fireplace. Try the following for information:

Tel: (0870) 460 9121
www.countrycottages.co.uk

Back to Backs:
Inge Street/Hurst Street

The National Trust, West Midlands
Regional Office, Attingham Park
Shrewsbury, Shropshire
Tel: (01743) 709343

Stay in Birmingham's last remaining back to back houses. It is unlikely that you will be forced to share a bed with three others, plus bed bugs, as frequently happened when they were first occupied, but the fittings and fixtures will be genuine nonetheless – plus the odd extra that 21st century inhabitants inevitably demand.

Cost: Telephone for details
(See also page 34)

Serviced Apartments:

Convention

Livingbase, The Water's Edge, Brindleyplace
Tel: (0121) 643 8585
www.livingbase.com

Stay in the heart of the Convention Quarter by renting one of 35 serviced apartments, available by the week, at Eight Brindleyplace. Cafes, restaurants and loads of nightlife are on the doorstep.

Cost: ££ - ££££

Birmingham South-West

SACO (Serviced Apartment Company), SACO House, 78-84 Hagley Road, Edgbaston
Tel: 0117 970 6999.
www.sacoapartments.co.uk

Fully furnished apartments with fully equipped kitchen. All rooms have double beds. Minimum 3 night stay.

Cost: 3 – 6 nights **£££**

Totel Serviced Apartments
Asquith House
19 Portland Road, Edgbaston
Tel: (0121) 454 5282
www.totelservicedapartments.co.uk

One of the more interesting managed suites of accommodation in a quiet, just out-of-city centre with individual rooms based on car marques.

Leasemethod Ltd
Tel: (0121) 4478 5000
www.leasemethod.co.uk

Fully furnished and serviced apartments and houses in various city locations including:

Harborne West
326 High Street, Harborne

The Old Fire Station
Station/Rose Road, Harborne

Exeter House
Exeter Road,/Hubert Road, Selly Park

Acommodation is available on short term tenancies.

Eastside

University:
Aston Business School
Management Development Centre, Aston Triangle
Tel: (0121) 359 3011

Workmanlike and ideal if you're looking for a single room (45 of the 83 rooms are singles). Fitness centre, swimming pool and restaurant.

Cost: ££

Central

Burne Jones House
Bennetts Hill
Tel: (0121) 478 5000
www.leasemethod.com

A six-storey Art Deco building built in the 1920s on the site of the house, where artist Edward Burne Jones was born in 1833. Fully furnished apartments for the professional and business rental sector.

Each apartment can be rented on a weekly inclusive basis or a 6/12 months shorthold tenancy.

Arriving in Birmingham

Arriving by air:

The principal airport is Birmingham International, located immediately adjacent to the National Exhibition Centre, and approximately eight miles from the city centre.

Other airports within easy travelling distance include:

Nottingham East Midlands Airport (www.eastmidlandsairport.com): 40 miles by car to Birmingham city centre. Scheduled & Charter flights

Coventry Airport (www.coventry-airport.co.uk): 30 miles by car to Birmingham city centre.

Birmingham International Airport

Tel: (0870) 733 5511   www.bhx.co.uk

Compared to its big brother airports serving London, Birmingham International is a pleasure to use. Even if there is not a direct flight to Birmingham from your departure point, you may well find that obtaining a connecting flight to Birmingham International, perhaps through Amsterdam, Frankfurt or Paris, provides an easier and more pleasurable journey. The airport serves 14 of the 15 top European business cities (the only one not being served being London). It was voted best UK business airport in 2003, for the fifth time in nine years. The airport serves more than 100 destinations operated by some 50 airlines.

Terminal One is the main terminal

Terminal Two serves British Airways, BA Partners and SN Brussels Airlines.

The two terminals are connected by the Millennium Link Block which includes a range of services including car hire.

It is located off the A45 Birmingham to Coventry Road, at the M42 junction 6. There are direct links with the M1, M5, M40, M6 and M6 Toll motorways.

Flight Information

In addition to the services operated by individual airlines:

www.bhx.co.uk/livearrs.cfm

Information is also available on BBC One/Two Ceefax on Page 449, ITV Teletext on Page 192, or Tel: 08707 335511.

Car Hire operators on - site include:

Avis	Tel: (0121) 782 6183
Budget	Tel: (0800) 181 181
Europcar	Tel: (0121) 782 6507
Hertz	Tel: (0121) 782 5158
National	Tel: (0121) 782 5481

Expect to pay £65 - £70 to hire a small car for a day and £180 - £200 for a week. Drivers need to be over 25 years, have a credit card in their own name and have a clean driver's license for 1 year. Road maps are available from hire companies and shops within the airport complex.

Remember to drive on the LEFT.

Airport Parking

There are three car parks close to the terminal buildings and two long stay car parks. Short stay parking starts from approx. £1.20 for up to 30 minutes. For information on rates telephone 08707 335511.

NCP Booking Service: Tel: (0870) 6067050.

Off Airport Parking: Airpark: (0800) 747777

Getting from the Airport: By Taxi

There is a black cab rank outside the terminal buildings. Approximate costs are:

From the airport to Birmingham £16
From the airport to Solihull £9
From the airport to Coventry £21
From the airport to Warwick £30
Taxi enquiries: Tel: (0121) 782 3744

Private Taxi companies will collect from the airport if prior arrangement is made. Local companies include:

A 2 B. Tel: (0121) 733 3000
Arden Cars. Tel: (0121) 770 5333
Home James: Tel (0121) 323 4717

Getting from the Airport: By Rail

Birmingham International Airport is connected to Birmingham International Rail Station and Interchange by a free SkyRail service, operating every two minutes when the rail station is open with a journey time of less than two minutes.

There are six to seven trains per hour during the day between Birmingham International Rail Station and Birmingham New Street Station (located in the city centre Central Quarter for city centre ICC and NIA). Journey time is ten to fifteen minutes. Trains are less frequent during the evening and at weekends and there are no late night trains. Tickets to Birmingham New Street are valid on all trains. Services are provided by Central Trains (local and regional), Virgin Trains (Intercity services that also connect to London Euston with a journey time of approximately 90 minutes), and Silverlink Train Services (providing an intermediate station service en route to London Euston including Rugby, Northampton, Milton Keynes and Hemel Hempstead. Lower fares are available on these services to London Euston but the total journey time is approximately 120 minutes).

Getting from the Airport: By Bus

Local buses link the airport to surrounding districts. All buses stop outside the passenger terminals. Services 900 and 966 operate from early morning until late at night but there are no overnight services. Exact change is required (this is infuriating if you arrive from overseas with only notes; it would be nice to think that the powers that be will think a little more about the needs of visitors). Some accept Euros.

900 (every 20 min) to Digbeth Coach Station in Birmingham via Sheldon, Yardley, Small Heath and Coventry.

966 (every 30min) to Solihull town centre

37A (hourly) to Birmingham via Sheldon, Olton, Acocks Green and Sparkhill.

555 (every 2 hours) to Kenilworth and Warwick.

717 (hourly) to Coleshill and Nuneaton

777 (hourly) to Chelmsley Wood, Coleshill, Water Orton, Kingsbury and Atherstone.

Fares to Birmingham and Solihull approx. £1.35 at peak times.

For further information on local buses, call 0870 608 2 608 or phone Centro on (0121) 200 2700 www.centro.org.uk

The one day Centro card (approx £5) allows unlimited travel on buses, trains and metro. It can be purchased on buses and at train stations. (See page 164)

Getting from the Airport: By Coach

National Express operates long distance coach services linking the airport to a number of cities and also provides inter-airport Flightlink coaches. Passengers are advised to book long distance coach services in advance. Digbeth Coach Station in Birmingham city centre provides services to most parts of the UK. Local bus 900 airport link passes Digbeth Coach Station. For further information on long distance coach services call 08705 808080 or 08705 75747 (Flightlink) or www.nationalexpress.com.

Getting from the Airport to the NEC:

Take SkyRail (see left) from the airport to Birmingham International Station and then covered walkway to the NEC itself. Some hotels on the NEC site operate a courtesy coach service on request, telephone your hotel on arrival.

Getting About

Despite efforts, Birmingham is still wedded to the car. This is not surprising as Birmingham is the UK's motor city and its public transport is still not all it should be.

Getting about by car

If you are planning on staying in Birmingham, especially in the city centre, or travelling to or from the NEC, a car is not required nor indeed advisable. Although Birmingham is a great city to travel around if you know it, like many others, it can be a nightmare if you are a stranger. The Birmingham rush hour is variable. Starting at around 7.30am and running through until 9.30am, resuming at 4.00pm until 6.30pm, it can be frustrating and bewildering.

The motorway network in the region is similarly blighted – although not quite as bad as it once was, with the opening of the M6 Toll, which has provided some relief for Birmingham commuters. Nonetheless, during peak hours, traffic still moves slowly. Expect delays during rush hours and on the last Friday in July, the day the region traditionally breaks up for summer. Sunny Bank Holidays are also to be avoided when it comes to motorway travel.

City Centre Parking:

Some 25,000 car parking spaces are available in the city centre. Of these, 15,000 short stay shopping spaces are available within five minutes walk of the city centre central shopping area.

With some 76 car parks, it would be impossible to list them all here but car parks that are (comparatively) pleasant to use and convenient to visitors include:

Key:

Pay and Display (PAD): decide how long you want to stay, pay the correct amount into the machine, collect the ticket and display inside the windscreen making sure the details can be seen (fines can be issued if the ticket is the wrong way round and can't be read by wardens!). Do not exceed the time stated on your ticket.

Pay on Exit (POE): take a ticket/chip coin on arrival; place in machine (not always at departure point) on departure and pay the correct amount (some machines accept credit cards).

Central Quarter: The Pallasades Shopping Centre/New Street Station, Hill Street, off Smallbrook Queensway, 1000 spaces; open 24/7; POE.

Livery Street, off Great Charles Street Queensway, 863 spaces; open Monday – Saturday 6.00am – 11.30pm; Sunday 9.00am – 9.00pm; PAD.

Eastside: Bullring Central, Smallbrook Queensway/St Martin's Circus Queensway, 1000 spaces, open daily until 11.30pm; POE

Bullring Moor Street, Moor Street, 1100 spaces, open 24/7; POE

Millennium Point, Jennens Road, 675 spaces, open 24/7; POE.

Jewellery Quarter: Ludgate Hill, off Great Charles Street Queensway, 290 spaces surface, open 24/7; PAD.

Vyse Street, 559 spaces, open Monday – Saturday 8.00am – 6.00pm, PAD.

Convention Quarter: National Indoor Arena, King Edward's Road and St Vincent Street, 2526 spaces, open 24/7; PAD.

Brindleyplace, off Sheepcote Street, off Broad Street, 909 spaces, open 24/7; POE.

Chinese Quarter: Arcadian, Bromsgrove Street, 415 spaces, open 24/7; POE.

On Street Car Parking: parking meters (pay and display) are available in designated areas, most for up to two hours. Tickets are required 8am – 6.00pm Monday – Saturday. (But do check in each parking area for specific information). As with all pay and display parking, do not exceed the specified time on your ticket as car park wardens are both prolific and rigorous.

Getting about by Bus/Train

Centro is responsible for promoting and developing public transport across the Birmingham area including trains, buses and Metro.

Tel: (0121) 200 2787
Centro Hotline: Tel: (0121) 200 2700
www.centro.org.uk

Buses:

All buses are pay on entry. Exact change is required so carry with you plenty of loose coins.

Travel West Midlands (www.travelwm.co.uk) is the largest bus operator in the West Midlands Region with nearly 600 bus routes and 1800 buses. Nearly one million passengers are carried every working day.

For information on bus services, call Travel Line Public Transport Info on 0870 608 2608 (7.00am – 10.30pm every day except Christmas Day); www.traveline.org.uk.

Travel West Midlands operates a number of "days out" services including: Birmingham Balti Triangle: including a 15% discount on a meal on production of a voucher at six Balti Restaurants; Birmingham Parks by Bus and The Tolkien Trail by Bus. (See central bus routes, page 169)

For information
www.travelwm.co.uk/events/daysout.asp.

The one day Centro card (approx £5) allows unlimited travel on buses, trains and metro. It can be purchased on buses and at train stations.

Trains:

The three city centre stations are Birmingham New Street, Moor Street and Snow Hill.

Birmingham New Street is the main intercity rail station with routes throughout the UK and with local services including University (for the University of Birmingham); Bournville (for Cadbury World); Sutton Coldfield (for Sutton Park); Cradley Heath (for Merry Hill Shopping Centre) and Birmingham International (for National Exhibition Centre and Birmingham International Airport).

Moor Street Station provides services to London (operated by Chiltern Railways and providing a slightly longer but, more scenic and cheaper alternative to the Virgin service operated from Birmingham New Street), and also to Tyseley (for the Rail Museum); Solihull (for Touchwood Shopping Centre); Stratford-upon-Avon, Warwick and the Jewellery Quarter.

Snow Hill, is on the same line as Moor Street Station.

A word of warning ....you must buy your ticket before getting on the train or, if the ticket office is closed, buy a permit to travel from the machine on the platform. If requested by a ticket inspector, and you have paid too little for your travel, you will be asked to pay the difference. The minimum fine for travelling without a valid ticket is £10.

There are standard day single tickets, standard day returns and cheap day returns. Fares are cheaper if you travel after 9.30am Monday to Fridays with a cheap day return ticket. There are also tickets that will allow you to travel anywhere in the West Midlands during one day together with weekly and monthly travel passes. Information from: www.centro.org.uk.

Midland Metro:

This new state of the art light rail system provides a fast link between Snow Hill Station, Birmingham city centre and Wolverhampton, calling at St Paul's Square and the Jewellery Quarter. The service operates between 6.30am and 11.30pm Monday to Saturday and 8.00am – 11.00pm on Sunday. There is an eight minute service between 7.00am and 7.00pm Monday – Saturday.

Getting about by Taxi

Only Black cabs are authorised to pick up street fares. Private taxi companies can only operate collecting pre-arranged fares.

Black cab services:

TOA: Tel: (0121)427 8888
Your Taxi: Tel (0121) 566 9000

Private Taxi Companies:

A2B: Tel: (0121) 733 3000
Arden Cars: Tel: (0121) 770 5333

Chauffeur Services

For that special night out or business travel:

Chauffeurs of Birmingham: Tel: (01675) 475 999
Network Chauffeur Drive Limited:
Tel: 0870 242 2442
Home James: Tel: (0121) 323 4717
Swanky limousines are also available.

Disability Access

Information on venues, facilities and services suitable for disabled people can be found on www.disabilitycharter.pwp.blueyonder.co.uk. For more information and advice contact: The Mobility Advice Line, West Midlands Rehabilitation Centre, Oak Tree Lane, Selly Oak, Birmngham B29 6JA. Tel; (0121) 414 1415. Open Mon - Thurs 10am - 4pm.

Personal Safety

Birmingham is, on the whole, as safe as any other city in the UK. In fact, the fear of crime is far greater than the incident of crime. One or two inner city areas have a higher incidence of crime but these are not normally frequented by the majority of visitors.

Much of the city centre is monitored by closed circuit television. Some are located in Birmingham Citywatch beacons – stainless steel pods that incorporate cameras, act as base stations for mobile phones, direction indicators and provide information to the public.

A few straightforward precautions are recommended:

Look confident and be aware of what is going on around you; keep to well lit areas; carry with you only what you need (keep keys in your pocket and not in bags); when on public transport, try to find a seat where there are other people.

Don't walk round wearing personal hi-fi headsets or using mobile phones; move away from cashpoint machines; don't leave purses and wallets on view in the top of an open shopping bag and, for business visitors in particular, make sure that laptop computers are not in obvious bags.

For further information: www.citywatch.org.uk.

City Centre Wardens

In the city centre shopping area, markets and Broad Street, Birmingham City Centre Partnership wardens, wear distinctive royal blue coats bearing the Birmingham 'b' logo with the words 'Street Warden' surrounded by five stars.

Each warden has a radio linked to the Police control centre and provides high visibility patrolling and a friendly presence on the streets. They'll be happy to help direct you.

What's On and When

Note: Events and activities are shown in the most likely and/or first month of the activity. You are advised to check with the organisers before making special journeys. See also festivals on page 117 and the calendar of a multi-ethnic community on page 131

January	1 – New Year's Day (Bank Holiday)
February	Chinese New Year (Chinese Quarter)
	Spring Fair (NEC – trade only)
March	Crufts (NEC)
	17 – St Patrick's Day, Ireland (Chinese and Central Quarters): third largest St. Patrick's Day parade in the world after Dublin and New York, nearest Sunday
	Birmingham Screen Festival (City centre)
April	23 – St.George's Day, England (City centre)
May	Gay Pride (Chinese/Central Quarters)
	Lord Mayor's Parade (City centre)
	Young Readers Festival (City centre)
	British International Motor Show/Motor Show Live (NEC)
	BRMB Walkathon (various)
	Birmingham Show (Cannon Hill Park)
June	Birmingham Eid Mela (Cannon Hill Park)
	International Women's Tennis Tournament (Edgbaston)
	BBC Gardeners' World Live (NEC)
July	Birmingham International Jazz Festival (City centre)
	Birmingham Canal Festival (Gas Street Basin)
August	Birmingham Carnival (Handsworth)
	Rathayatra Chariot Festival (City centre)
	Birmingham Discovery Day (City centre)
	Gallery 37 (Centenary Square)
September	ArtsFest (City centre). Heritage Open Days (City-wide)
October	Black History Month (City-wide)
	Birmingham Comedy Festival (City-wide)
	Birmingham Book Festival (City-wide)
	Diesel Gala (Severn Valley Railway)
	Star City Run (Star City)
	University of Birmingham, 5k Road Race
	Autumn Orchid Show (Botanical Gardens)
	CBI Conference (ICC)
	Horse of the Year Show (NEC)
November	Fireworks Spectacular (City centre and city-wide)
	Diwali – Festival of Light (Centenary Square)
	BBC Good Food Show (NEC)
	Music Live (NEC)
	Reebok Birmingham Cross Country Challenge (Senneleys Park)
	11 – Remembrance Day (commemoration on nearest Sunday, Centenary Square)
	Birmingham Tattoo (NIA)
	Frankfurt Christmas Market (Victoria Square)
	Brilliantly Birmingham Jewellery Festival (Jewellery Quarter)
	30 – St Andrew's Day, Scotland
December	ClothesShow Live (NEC)
	Aston Hall by Candlelight
	Santa Steam Specials (Severn Valley Railway)
	31 – New Year's Eve Celebrations (City centre, venue varies)

Telephones

Public payphones are commonplace, despite the rise in popularity of mobile phones. Most are operated by BT and take coins from 10p upwards. Certain public phones only accept phonecards (available from newsagents and post offices displaying the BT logo). A number of public phones also accept credit cards. Peak rates operate between 8am and 6pm weekdays. Telephoning from hotel rooms can be expensive.

Dialling from outside the UK:

Add country code 0044; drop 0 from code. eg For the Ticket hotline of Marketing Birmingham (0121 202 5000) when dialling outside the UK, dial: 0044 121 202 5000

Dialling within the Birmingham area code (ie 0121 numbers)

Drop 0121; dial remaining digits

e.g. For the Ticket hotline of Marketing Birmingham (0121 202 5000) when dialling from within Birmingham, dial: 202 5000

Operator services:

Domestic operator: 100
International operator: 155
Domestic directory assistance: 118 500
(Recent deregulation has resulted in a proliferation of directory assistance companies. the one listed is operated by BT but may not be the cheapest.)

In an emergency

If there is an urgent need for either the police, fire or ambulance services, dial 999, the call is free, they will want to know where you are and your name.

One of the city's initiatives to make Birmingham a safe city, are emergency help points near to cctv cameras which will automatically turn to view the caller when the alarm button is pressed. Help points are monitored 24/7. There are help points in the city's retail, business and leisure sectors. in an emergency, press the red button and you will be connected to the police. There is a penalty for irresponsible use.

Health care

Vaccinations are not required for those entering Britain. Citizens of all EU countries and others with reciprocal healthcare agreements are able to obtain free medical care at NHS hospitals (see list below). Otherwise, all medical services are charged for and insurance is recommended.

Chemists/pharmacists: a doctor's prescription is required for the majority of drugs. Most pharmacists will provide limited advice. Pharmacists normally adopt standard opening hours. Most carry a list of late opening pharmacists for out-of-hours use. For medical advice, you can also telephone NHS Direct (0845 4647).

In an emergency, dial 999.

NHS: The Birmingham Children's Hospital
Tel: (0121) 333 9999

Queen Elizabeth Hospital, Edgbaston
Tel: (0121) 472 1311

The Women's Hospital, Edgbaston
Tel: (0121) 472 1377

Selly Oak Hospital (A & E)
Tel: (0121) 472 1311

Private: The Birmingham Nuffield Hospital, Edgbaston
Tel: (0121) 456 2000

BUPA Parkway Hospital, Solihull
Tel: (0121) 704 1451

The Priory Hospital, Edgbaston
Tel: (0121) 440 2323

Weather

The British love talking about the weather, perhaps because it can change so rapidly and is so unpredictable. Birmingham does not experience great extremes. Winters tend to be mild and summers are rarely very hot. Whenever you come, you can expect rain so some wet-weather gear and/or an umbrella are advisable.

Average temperatures and rainfall											
	Jan	Feb	Mar	Apr	May	June	July	Aug	Sept	Oct	Nov	Dec
(°F)	42	43	48	54	60	66	68	68	63	55	48	44
(°C)	5	6	9	12	16	19	20	20	17	13	9	7
(inches)	3	2.1	2	2.1	2.5	2	2.7	2.7	2.4	2.7	3.3	2.6
(mm)	74	54	50	53	64	50	69	69	61	69	84	67

Banking and Currency

Britain has yet to adopt the euro and the currency for the UK is the £ (Sterling). Notes are £50, £20, £10, & £5. Coins include 1p (100 make £1), 2p, 5p, 10p, 20p, 50p, £1 and £2.

Bank opening times vary from bank to bank and city to town. As a general rule, assume banks open in the city 9am–4.30pm Mon- Fri; in the suburbs 9.30am–3.30pm Mon–Fri. Some banks open 9.30am–noon on Saturdays. Banks are closed on Sundays and on public holidays (known as bank holidays - when all the country's financial institutions take a day off – often shops close too, so it's wise to have sufficient food and money to cover any eventualities).

Most banks and shops stay open over lunch except in some rural areas.

Currency Exchange

Most banks and post offfices have tourism exchange bureaux.

The following are all located in the Central quarter:

American Express, Bank House, 8 Cherry Street. Tel: (0121) 644 5533

Barclays Bank plc, 15 Colmore Row, Tel: (0121) 480 5578

Nat West Bank, 1 St. Philip,s Place, Tel: 0845 604 2604

Post Office, 1 Pinfold Street, Tel: 08457 22 33 44

Thomas Cook, HSBC Bank, 130 New Street, Tel: (0121) 643 5057

Credit Cards

Major credit cards – Visa, Access – are commonly accepted in the UK by many restaurants, shops and hotels both in the cities and the countryside. In certain circumstances, i.e. car hire, it's a positive advantage to have one as it's nigh on impossible to hire without. If concerned, check in advance.

Traveller's cheques

Rather than carry large amounts of cash, traveller's cheques (available from major banks for a small commission) can be exchanged at all banks, normally for a further commission (approx 1.5 per cent). Make sure you keep a record of cheques as they are exchanged and report losses immediately. Companies such as American Express and Thomas Cook will normally replace lost or stolen cheques in 24 hours.

Tourism Centres

A full list of centres is given on pages 150/151.

Centres are located at:

(Central) The Rotunda, 150 New Street and New Street/Corporation Street.

(Convention) The ICC Broad Street.

(NEC) The Piazza and the Atrium.

Media

Newspapers: in addition to the national titles, Birmingham has a number of its own newspapers including:

The Birmingham Post: authoritative morning broadsheet with comprehensive local, regional and international news and an award winning business section. Published Monday to Saturday.

Birmingham Evening Mail: lively tabloid newspaper with lunchtime and evening editions, predominantly local news and with excellent entertainment section. Published Monday to Saturday.

Sunday Mercury: campaigning tabloid newspaper with both regional and national news as well as extensive features. Published Sunday only.

Sports Argus: regional sports newspaper carrying all the results from both mainstream and specialist sports. Published Saturday only.

Metro: morning tabloid newspaper dominated by national news with local input. Available free at most railway stations. Published Monday to Friday.

The Voice: Birmingham City Council newspaper dominated by city council news, events and activities. Includes comprehensive city council job advertisements section.

Express and Star: published in Wolverhampton; evening tabloid with some distribution in Birmingham citycentre.

Coventry Evening Telegraph: published in Coventry; evening tabloid with some distribution in Birmingham citycentre.

Magazines: a variety of free glossy magazines are available including **City Living, Vision** and **Select.** Other titles include:

What's On: weekly magazine with reviews and previews of film, theatre, dance, music and restaurants. Available in newsagents and also free from tourist information centres.

The Big Issue: campaigning magazine highlighting social issues. Vendors are often homeless and selling the magazine is their work. They are not begging and have to abide by a code of conduct. Buy if you wish; refuse if you don't.

Radio: in addition to the national output, Birmingham has a wide range of local radio stations. These include:

BBC WM 95.6FM: predominantly speech with phone-ins, interviews and travel news.

BRMB 96.4FM: Birmingham's first commercial radio station, playing music for teens and twenties.

Galaxy 102.2 FM: dance/R&B.

Heart 100.7FM: rock and modern-day.

Saga 105.7FM: music from the 1940s, 50s and 60s to the present day; mix of music and speech; interviews and travel news.

XL: (1296Mw) music, news for the Asian Community.

Web Sites

A search on the web reveals a wealth of material.

www.rabbitguide.com: our very own site with updated news section.

www.beinbirmingham.com: the official destination website for Birmingham.

www.birminghamconventionbureau.com: web site for conference and meeting organisers.

www.shortbreaks.org.uk: choose from a host of different short break ideas in the city including Balti weekends, fashion and football.

www.icbirmingham.co.uk: news, sport and entertainment from the *Birmingham Evening Mail*, *Birmingham Post* and *Sunday Mercury*.

www.visitheartofengland.com: official tourism website for the region.

www.locatebirmingham.org.uk: site for Locate in Birmingham, the city's inward investment service.

www.westmidlandsdaysout.co.uk: Advantage West Midlands website for the entire West Midlands region.

www.bbc.co.uk/Birmingham: news, entertainment and What's On.

www.virtualbrum.co.uk: memory lane and present day filled with photographs of how the city used to be.

www.birmingham.gov.uk: official Birmingham City Council website.

www.eat-the-midlands.co.uk: Independent guide on where to eat in Birmingham and further afield.

www.balti-birmingham.co.uk: balti restaurants galore.

Books

Old Birmingham by Eric Armstrong (Stenlake Publishing)

The Birmingham Jewellery Quarter: An Architectural Survey of the Manufactories by John Cattell, Sheila Ely and John Barry

Singer's Hill Synagogue – Voices from the Past – Josephs

Top 40 Birmingham Landmarks – Edmund Bealby-Wright

The St. Andrew's Encyclopaedia – Sean Hayes

Eating Out in Birmingham – Alison Davison (Astoria Publishing Ltd)

Birmingham City Football Club by Tony Matthews (Tempus Publishing Ltd)

Golden Years of Birmingham (published by True North Books Ltd, 1999)

Brum & Brummies by Carl Chinn (Brewin Books)

The Past, Present and Future by Christopher Upton

The Story of Ty-phoo & the Birmingham Tea Industry by Kenneth Williams (Quiller Press)

In the Midst of Life by Joseph McKenna (Birmingham Library Services)

Birmingham Remembered – A Centenary Celebration by Alton Douglas & Dennis Moore (Birmingham Post & Mail Ltd 1988)

Midlanders Who Made History Vol. 1 by William Tann

Birmingham Yesterday: Its places & people by Victor J. Price (Brewin Books)

A History of Birmingham, Chris Upton (Phillimore & Co Ltd)

A Knight Out with Chamberlain in Birmingham, Sir Bernard Zissman (Polperro Heritage Press)

Positively Birmingham by Jonathan Berg (Birmingham Picture Library)

Birmingham: The Great Working City by Carl Chinn (Birmingham City Council)

Birmingham: Bibliography of a City edited by Carl Chinn (University of Birmingham Press)

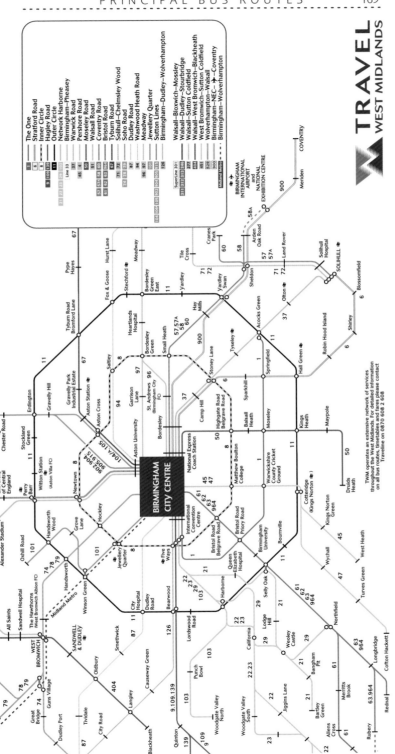

Other titles from Polperro Heritage Press

A KNIGHT OUT with CHAMBERLAIN in BIRMINGHAM by Sir Bernard Zissman

The former Lord Mayor of Birmingham and one of the driving political forces behind the city's development in the 1980s undertakes an imaginary journey back in time to meet another great civic visionary from the 19th century, Joseph Chamberlain.

Fully illustrated paperback (235x160mm) 200 pages. £12.95 (ISBN 095300127X)

THE GRAVY TRAIN by Philip Bushill-Matthews

Charts the progress of a British businessman who quits a successful career to become a West Midlands MEP. Frustrated by increasing EU regulations made by politicians with no experience in the real world, he is astonished to find himself elected and aboard the 'gravy train' to Brussels. This humorous account of what he found there lays bare many of the excesses and bureaucratic bungling of the EU, from fraud and corruption to dotty directives.

Hardback (235x157mm) 252 pages, 21 illustrations. £15 (ISBN 0954423321)

THE RELUCTANT RESTAURATEUR by Imogen Skirving

In a remarkably candid autobiography, the author recalls how she turned Langar Hall, her Nottinghamshire family home, into one of the most successful private hotels in Britain, now famed for its cuisine and feted by celebrities.

Paperback (235x157mm) 148 pages, 31 illustrations.£12.95 (ISBN 0954423305)

HUMBRIDGE - An everyday story of scriptwriting folk by Anthony Parkin

Author Anthony Parkin, agricultural story editor of the Birmingham-based BBC Radio series The Archers for 25 years, draws on his own extensive knowledge of country life and the demands of writing for a popular radio series in this, his first novel.

Paperback (190x135mm) 230 pages. £8.95 ISBN (0953001261)

MEMORIES OF A HEREFORDSHIRE FARMER by John Thacker

An evocative account of life on a Herefordshire farm during the post war years of the 20th century. Originally recorded at Poswick Farm near Bromyard for the BBC radio series The Century Speaks, this specially extended version includes anecdotes drawn from 60 years of farming.

Double audio cassette pack, 3 hours listening. £10.00

CLIFTON-upon-TEME 2000

A unique record of a Worcestershire village at the dawn of the 21st century, written and compiled by the residents themselves. Extensively illustrated in full colour throughout, this highly acclaimed publication chronicles the lives and activities of residents in 1999.

Paperback (210x268mm) 104 pages, 165 illustrations. £5.00 (ISBN 0953509915)

Polperro Heritage Press,
Clifton-upon-Teme,

Worcestershire,
WR6 6EN
www.polperropress.co.uk